After Marriage

After Marriage

RETHINKING MARITAL RELATIONSHIPS

Edited by **ELIZABETH BRAKE**

OXFORD
UNIVERSITY PRESS

OXFORD
UNIVERSITY PRESS

Oxford University Press is a department of the University of
Oxford. It furthers the University's objective of excellence in research,
scholarship, and education by publishing worldwide. Oxford is a registered
trade mark of Oxford University Press in the UK and in certain other countries

Published in the United States of America by Oxford University Press
198 Madison Avenue, New York, NY 10016, United States of America

Library of Congress Cataloging-in-Publication Data
After marriage: rethinking marital relationships / edited by Elizabeth Brake.
    pages cm
Includes bibliographical references and index.
ISBN 978–0–19–020508–9 (pbk.: alk. paper)—ISBN 978–0–19–020507–2 (cloth: alk.
paper)   1. Marriage. 2. Marriage law.   3. Marriage—Moral and ethical aspects.   I. Brake,
Elizabeth.
HQ734.B784 2016
306.81—dc23
2015009992

1 3 5 7 9 8 6 4 2
Printed in the United States of America
on acid-free paper

CONTENTS

ACKNOWLEDGMENTS

The bulk of the credit for this volume lies, of course, with the authors; many thanks for their hard work and patience.

Others contributed significantly to the existence of this book. David Chesley assisted greatly in preparing the manuscript for publication. His editorial assistance was funded with a grant from the School of Historical, Philosophical, and Religious Studies at Arizona State University. The Institute of Humanities Research at Arizona State University provided funds for professional preparation of the index. Peter Ohlin and Emily Sacharin at Oxford University Press have been wonderfully patient and helpful.

I would especially like to thank Tamara Metz and Cheshire Calhoun for discussions which prompted me, from the start, to think about what directions the collection might take and for helping me to see new angles.

LIST OF CONTRIBUTORS

Elizabeth Brake is an Associate Professor of Philosophy at Arizona State University. She previously taught at the University of Calgary, Canada. Her work is primarily in feminist ethics and political philosophy. Her book, *Minimizing Marriage* (Oxford University Press, 2012), won an Honorable Mention for the 2014 APA Book Prize. She has also written on parental rights and obligations, liberal theory, Kant and Hegel, and is currently working on a project on disaster ethics. She has held a Murphy Institute Fellowship at Tulane and a Canadian SSHRC Grant.

Samantha Brennan is Professor of Philosophy at Western University, Canada. She is also a member of the Rotman Institute of Philosophy, an affiliate member of the Department of Women's Studies and Feminist Research, and a member of the graduate faculty of the Department of Political Science. Brennan received her PhD from the University of Illinois at Chicago. Her doctoral thesis "Thresholds for Rights" was written under the supervision of Shelly Kagan. Brennan's BA in Philosophy is from Dalhousie University, Halifax, Nova Scotia. Brennan has broad ranging research interests in contemporary normative ethics, feminist ethics, applied ethics, political philosophy, children's rights and family justice, gender and sexuality, death, and fashion.

Bill Cameron holds a PhD in Philosophy from the University of Western Ontario. He works at the intersection of metaethics, feminist philosophy, and moral epistemology, with a particular focus on pluralism and intuitionism. He is also actively engaged in popular philosophy and philosophy of pop culture. He currently works in the private sector.

Clare Chambers is University Senior Lecturer in Philosophy and Fellow of Jesus College, University of Cambridge, UK. Her field is political philosophy, particularly feminist and liberal theories of justice, equality, autonomy, culture, family, and the body. Clare is the author of two books: *Sex, Culture, and Justice: The Limits of Choice* (Penn State University Press, 2008) and, with Phil Parvin, *Teach Yourself Political Philosophy: A Complete Introduction* (Hodder, 2012). She has also written numerous articles and chapters on feminist and liberal political philosophy, which recently include: "The Marriage-Free State" in Proceedings of the Aristotelian Society (2013); " 'The Family as a Basic Institution': A Feminist Analysis of the Basic Structure as Subject" in Ruth Abbey (ed.), *Feminist Interpretations of John Rawls* (Penn State University Press, 2013); "Feminism" in the *Oxford Handbook of Political Ideologies* edited by Michael Freeden et al. (Oxford University Press, 2013); "Each Outcome is Another Opportunity: Problems with the Moment of Equal Opportunity" in *Politics, Philosophy and Economics* (2009); and "Inclusivity and the constitution of the family" in *Canadian Journal of Law and Jurisprudence* (2009). Clare is currently completing a book titled *After Marriage: An Egalitarian Defence of the Marriage-Free State* for Oxford University Press.

Anca Gheaus is a Researcher in Moral and Political Philosophy at the universities of Sheffield and Umeå. She is particularly interested in the importance of caring relationships for theories of distributive justice. She has published work on parental rights and duties, the value of the family and methodological issues in political philosophy, and is currently co-editing a special issue of the *Journal of Applied Philosophy* on children and *The Routledge Handbook to Childhood*.

Peter de Marneffe is Professor of Philosophy at Arizona State University. He is the author of *Liberalism and Prostitution* (Oxford University Press, 2010) and co-author with Douglas Husak of *The Legalization of Drugs* (Cambridge University Press, 2005).

Simon Căbulea May is Assistant Professor of Philosophy at Florida State University. He has published articles on political compromise, democratic legitimacy, and moral duties in *Philosophy and Public Affairs* and *Ethics*. His current research concerns norms of democratic deliberation and negotiation in conditions of moral disagreement.

Daniel Nolan is Professor of Philosophy at the Australian National University. He is the author of *Topics in the Philosophy of Possible*

Worlds (Routledge) and *David Lewis* (Acumen/McGill-Queens), and articles in journals including *Noûs, Philosophy and Phenomenological Research, Philosophical Studies*, and the *Journal of Moral Philosophy*. He works primarily in metaphysics, though he has wide philosophical interests.

Laurie Shrage is Professor of Philosophy and Women's and Gender Studies at Florida International University, in Miami. Her books include: *Abortion and Social Responsibility: Depolarizing the Debate* (Oxford, 2003), *Moral Dilemmas of Feminism* (Routledge, 1994), an edited collection *You've Changed: Sex Reassignment and Personal Identity* (Oxford, 2009), and a co-authored textbook *Philosophizing About Sex* (Broadview, 2015). She served as co-editor of *Hypatia* from 1998 to 2003. She has contributed several pieces to "The Stone," in *The New York Times*: <http://opinionator. blogs.nytimes.com/author/laurie-shrage/>, including one on the topic of marriage reform.

Ralph Wedgwood is Professor of Philosophy at the University of Southern California; previously, he taught at the University of Oxford and at the Massachusetts Institute of Technology. He is the author of *The Nature of Normativity* (Oxford, 2007), numerous articles on ethics and epistemology, and of "The Fundamental Argument for Same-Sex Marriage" (*Journal of Political Philosophy,* 1999) and "The Meaning of Same-Sex Marriage" (*The New York Times*: <http://opinionator.blogs. nytimes.com/author/ralph-wedgwood/>, May 24, 2012). In 2000–2002, he worked as a volunteer for the Freedom to Marry Coalition of Massachusetts.

Introduction

ELIZABETH BRAKE

T HE PAST DECADE HAS WITNESSED a revolution in law and attitudes regarding same-sex marriage, in the US and internationally. In the US today, for example, a majority of Americans now favor same-sex marriage, the balance tipping only three years ago.[1] At the time of writing, seventeen countries and all fifty American states recognize (or are about to recognize) same-sex marriage; until 2001, no states or countries did. These changes are remarkable.

But deep philosophical questions implicit in these changes remain unanswered, questions which go beyond marriage itself. What role should the state should play in our intimate relationships and families? Which relationships should the state support and promote, and why? How can the state, and society, balance respect for citizens' freedom to pursue their own visions of the good life with the reality of unavoidable interdependency and vulnerability? What is the value of personal relationships, and how can individual freedom and equality be respected and secured within them? The essays in this book address these more fundamental questions while considering new possibilities for marriage reform.

As debates over same-sex marriage begin to recede, we can press on to these and other questions. While conservative opponents to same-sex marriage warned of a catastrophic slippery slope following from same-sex marriage, these essays treat the question of the next step as at least meriting debate, if not as the occasion for further positive reforms. In the public sphere, same-sex marriage has already spurred on serious debate over the status of polygamists, polyamorists, and singles. In 2011, the BC Supreme Court revisited the criminalization of polygamy in light of the recognition of same-sex marriage (the court upheld the ban). Law professors have debated whether polyamory should be understood as a protected sexual orientation in employment discrimination law, and social critics have pointed out the myriad ways in which law, society, and employers discriminate against the unmarried.[2]

The essays in this book argue, variously, for separating legal marriage from legal parenting frameworks, and for replacing marriage with some other legal framework altogether. They argue for the possibility of recognizing bigamy or polygamy, and for legal temporary marriage. They argue for modeling marriage law on friendship, not romantic love. And some essays argue, more or less, for the status quo, stopping reform at same-sex marriage.

These essays take successful philosophical arguments for same-sex marriage as their starting point, and ask what else the guiding political principles imply. Liberal arguments for same-sex marriage have typically invoked the values of liberty and equality. Through marriage, states typically provide many benefits, such as special eligibility for immigration, special tax status, and entitlement to third-party benefits such as health insurance. Not least of these benefits is that of recognition as marriage. Arguments for same-sex marriage often invoked a principle of equal treatment, arguing that the state's arbitrary exclusion of gays and lesbians from these benefits violated this principle. While opponents might argue that homosexuality was immoral, or that heterosexuality constituted an ethically superior form of relationship, liberal advocates of same-sex marriage responded that such judgments were not within the state's purview. According to theories of liberal neutrality or political liberalism, the state should not justify policy by appeal to, at least, controversial conceptions of the good.[3] But views about the morality of homosexuality or the ethical superiority of heterosexuality just are such controversial conceptions. In the absence of any other, politically relevant, justification, then, marriage cannot be restricted to different-sex couples.[4]

This reasoning has been persuasive to many. However, it prompts a further question: why marriage? The ethical value of marriage, or monogamy, is also a controversial conception of the good. The principles invoked in the argument for same-sex marriage seem to imply a further conclusion: the disestablishment of marriage itself. Recognizing marriage benefits members of some relationships (with legal perks, entitlement to third-party benefits, and recognition) and not others. But the state cannot justify this benefit by appeal to the controversial claim that such relationships are ethically valuable. And while some have tried to justify the legal benefits of marriage in terms of children's welfare, this ignores the many children outside marriage as well as the costs to children of living in high-conflict marriages.[5] In the absence of any other, politically relevant, justification, then, it seems that marriage itself cannot be justified. However, political reasons might justify new legal frameworks supporting relationships characterized by vulnerability, dependency, or care.[6]

The collection opens with responses to the disestablishmentarian position. The first two essays argue that neutrality or political liberalism do not entail abolishing marriage, as politically liberal justifications for marriage law can be found.

In the first chapter, Simon Căbulea May responds to the neutrality objection to marriage by arguing that, if certain conditions obtain, marriage can be justified neutrally. One version of the neutrality objection implies that a state which recognizes marriage must do so on the basis of a controversial "matrimonial ideal." Not so, May argues: the distinctive aspect of the marriage relationship is "presumptive permanence." If presumptive permanence—and the state's recognition of it—are beneficial to caring relationships, this may provide a neutral justification for marriage law. (In later essays, Nolan and Gheaus will challenge the claims that marriage need be presumptively permanent, and that such permanence increases the value of relationships.) Just as the state may support sports in order to promote health without endorsing a controversial ideal, so too it could support a beneficial relationship type without endorsing a controversial ideal. May's essay, more generally, thinks through how far a state may aim to promote good consequences without illegitimately imposing on citizen's free choice of ideals.

Likewise, in Chapter 2, Ralph Wedgwood argues that legal marriage can be justified within political liberalism without relying on a controversial conception of the good. This is because its legal recognition allows the fulfillment of many citizens' central "goals and aspirations," and one legitimate role of the state is to make possible the fulfillment of such goals, so long as doing so does not conflict with justice. Marriage, as it exists, has a broadly understood social meaning; were it to be disestablished, this meaning would be lost as individuals could label diverse arrangements as "marriages." Couples would no longer be able to signal the nature and value of their relationship, as many gays and lesbians have deeply desired to. Wedgwood disputes arguments that recognizing marriage harms singles by stigmatizing them or violates the rights of those excluded from its social meaning (such as polyamorists). More generally, and surprisingly, the essay shows how liberalism can accommodate what are typically thought to be communitarian concerns with the value of cultural traditions and inherited ways of life.

While Wedgwood and May defend legal marriage against arguments for its disestablishment, subsequent essays argue for radical change or abolition, exploring what legal structures, if any, should replace current marriage law. One challenge in rethinking marriage is how to protect partners, caregivers, and children. Marriage is said to serve these functions, but does it? Could other structures, less exclusive and less freighted with controversy than marriage, do so better?

Clare Chambers, who has argued elsewhere for the abolition of marriage, pursues in Chapter 3 the question of what should legally replace it.[7] Marriage "contractarians" have argued for relegating marriage to private contract; in a post-marriage state, those wishing to regulate their relationships legally could use the tools of legal contract to forge agreements. Since liberalism tends to protect individual choice, replacing marriage with contract might seem in keeping with liberal values: rather than (like marriage) foisting a ready-made set of legal obligations and entitlements on all couples, the contract model would allow partners to reach their own agreements. However, relationship contracts would be largely unenforceable and might leave the vulnerable—especially children or economically vulnerable caregivers—unprotected. Hence, Chambers argues that legal regulation of relationships in a "marriage-free state" should take the form of default, piecemeal directives. These could serve the purpose of protecting the vulnerable while adapting to the diversity of relationships. At a more general level, the essay examines how justice both limits and requires state structuring of personal relationships.

Also focusing on the vulnerable, Samantha Brennan and Bill Cameron (Chapter 4) call into question the assumption that marriage uniquely benefits children. They argue that the goods provided by marriage, such as stability and security, can be provided by alternate arrangements (and indeed, are not provided by all marriages). Given the contemporary penchant for serial monogamy, a separate parenting contract would provide a surer foundation for family than the romantic-erotic bond of marriage. As queer and radical critics of marriage have argued, the traditional nuclear family model fails to reflect the diversity of actual contemporary family structures. Because parents in a same-sex relationship require (at least) third-party gamete donation to procreate, same-sex marriage forces us to examine already dated assumptions that a child can have at most two parents; gamete donation, open adoptions, and blended families all create structures in which children can have more than two parents. Brennan and Cameron argue for replacing marriage as the foundation of the family, legally and socially, with the cluster of adults who stand in parenting relations to children—in all the diverse forms such arrangements take. Their essay suggests the possibilities of pluralism in conceptions of the family.

My own essay in Chapter 5 updates feminist criticisms of gender-structured marriage. In light of the erosion of coverture, the marital rape exemption, and the gendered legal norms which defined marriage in the past, it might be thought that contemporary marriage—especially as same-sex marriage arrives—no longer poses a problem for women's equality. Restating classic feminist criticisms, I argue that marriage must be evaluated within the wider social context: gender role socialization, economic pressures, and sexual violence can disempower women within formally equal legal structures. I then argue that power inequality, or hierarchy, within intimate relationships, different-sex or same-sex, is wrong in itself, apart from concerns about women's equality. The social and legal understanding of marriage as a union encourages the loss of individuality within it which underlies the formation of power hierarchies. I argue that we should address this by modeling our understandings of marriage on friendship, not on romantic union. In law this would take the form of "minimal marriage." More generally, the essay reflects on what is required to treat another as an equal in intimate personal relationships, and on the forces that make this difficult.

The final four essays examine what some see as definitive features of marriage: monogamy and the intention of permanence. Are group relationships or temporary marriage the next frontier in marriage equality? These essays also focus on the definition and value of marriage.

Like May and Wedgwood, Peter de Marneffe (Chapter 6) examines the implications of neutrality for marriage law, but he focuses on polygamy. Some have argued that neutrality entails that the state should recognize polygamy.[8] On this view, the special value of monogamous marriage is yet another contested ethical view which should not be the basis for policy; the polygamy bar, like the same-sex marriage bar, is another case of arbitrarily denying the benefit of marriage. According to de Marneffe, polygamy should be decriminalized. However, decriminalization is not legalization, and he argues that the state can withhold legal recognition without violating neutrality. One politically relevant difference, de Marneffe argues, concerns child-rearing. Polygamy plausibly creates a scarcity of parental resources, and empirical evidence confirms this thesis. Moreover, he argues, on at least one interpretation of neutrality, a state can recognize exclusive life partnerships as a distinctive human good without violating neutrality—so long as the recognition does not entail that other forms of life are "bad or worthless." De Marneffe's essay thinks through the grounds and interpretation of the neutrality principle.

Laurie Shrage, by contrast, makes a case in Chapter 7 for the possibility of egalitarian polygamy and bigamy. She argues that while women's equality, children's welfare, and marital privacy are commonly given as reasons against the practices, these values can be protected through the legal structures recognizing them. In assessing polygamy as patriarchal, we should keep in mind that monogamous marriage has until recently been legally gender-structured; polygamy could likewise be made formally equal in law. Indeed, as formally equal monogamy can involve the subordination of women, the value of women's equality should prompt a more general debate about measures the state might take to promote it, rather than serving as reason to exclude polygamy. A different concern is that multiple marriage will affect the quality of the romantic intimacy between partners; but, Shrage argues, polygamists or polyamorists can adopt informal rules to protect intimacy, just as monogamists must do. The problems posed by polygamy, polyamory, and bigamy are, Shrage argues, not fundamentally different than those posed by than monogamy.

While Shrage challenges the view that monogamy is definitive of marriage, Daniel Nolan (Chapter 8) challenges the requirement of intended permanence. On grounds of marriage equality, Nolan argues for legally recognizing temporary marriage—marriage intended from its inception to last for a limited time. While some might object that temporary marriages are not marriages, Nolan responds by tackling the broader question of how marriage is defined. He contrasts a positivist account of marriage (on which a practice counts as marriage if so defined by relevant institutional rules) with a functional theory of marriage (on which a practice counts as marriage if it serves certain functions). The positivist account has counterintuitive implications, such as that interracial marriages in a state which bans them are not marriages. Because temporary marriages can play similar roles as permanent marriages, they count as marriages on the functional account, Nolan argues. Moreover, as some religions and cultural groups practice temporary marriage, equal treatment for religious minorities can also be invoked for its recognition. While costs, particularly costs to children, could justify withholding recognition, Nolan argues that the benefits outweigh the costs.

Some might argue (as in fact May's arguments in Chapter 1 suggest), that the permanent commitment made in marriage increases the value of the marriage relationships. In Chapter 9, Anca Gheaus argues that permanent marriage commitments are only conditionally rational and are not valuable in themselves. Their value depends on the goods which they achieve. These goods must be weighed with the costs of commitment, in foreclosing certain options. Moreover, Gheaus argues, commitment is not a particularly suitable tool for achieving the good of romantic or sexual love. In general, such love is valued more if it is spontaneous, rather than sustained by obligation. While commitment is a useful tool for achieving goals which require sustained effort, it is less appropriate for achieving goods which are process-oriented, such as an ongoing relationship. Gheaus' essay articulates a tension between marriage and the distinctive good of sexual and romantic love which it is sometimes said to promote.

Collectively, these essays examine possibilities for reform in both legal and ethical conceptions of marital relationships. They move beyond debates over same-sex marriage to consider what kind of institution recognizing and regulating personal relationships the best reasons favor. The topics discussed here by no means exhaust questions of marriage and family law reform. For one, polyamory might require legal structures other than marriage.[9] For another, new forms of technologically assisted parenting prompt questions as to who counts as a parent.[10] And again, "the other marriage equality problem"—the class divide in marriage—suggests that marriage reform may have effects limited by socioeconomic class.[11] Once we start reimagining the law and ethics of marriage, such questions proliferate.

These questions go to the heart of the possibilities and limitations of modern liberal democracy—of how freedom and equality can be secured, how pluralism and community can be reconciled, and the vulnerable protected. They also speak to the value of relationships and of the nature of intimacy and its role in human life. Even as the law surrounding marriage continues to change, the enduring contribution of these essays lies in their attempts to address these deeper, broader questions.

Notes

1. According to PEW surveys; online at the PEW Research Center, <http://www.pewforum.org/2014/09/24/graphics-slideshow-changing-attitudes-on-gay-marriage/>, accessed February 20, 2015.

2. See British Columbia Supreme Court (2011), Reference re: Section 293 of the criminal code of Canada, 2011 BCSC 1588. See also Ann Tweedy, "Polyamory as a Sexual Orientation," *University of Cincinnati Law Review* 79 (2011): 1461–1515; and Bella DePaulo, *Singled Out: How Singles Are Stereotyped, Stigmatized, and Ignored, and Still Live Happily Ever After* (New York: St. Martin's Press, 2006).

3. This draws on a distinction between public reasons and the political realm, on the one hand, and comprehensive views of the good, which apply to all areas of life. There are many different understandings of neutrality and political liberalism; here I cite the broadest. See Chapters 1 and 2 in this volume for more on this topic.

4. See, e.g., Alex Rajczi, "A Populist Argument for Same-Sex Marriage," *The Monist* 91:3–4 (2008): 475–505; Ralph Wedgwood, "The Fundamental Argument for Same-Sex Marriage," *The Journal of Political Philosophy* 7.3 (1999): 225–242; and A. A. Wellington, "Why Liberals Should Support Same-Sex Marriage," *Journal of Social Philosophy* 25.3 (1995): 5–32.

5. On this topic, see Chapter 3 in this volume.

6. See, e.g., Elizabeth Brake, *Minimizing Marriage: Marriage, Morality, and the Law* (New York and Toronto: Oxford University Press, 2012), Part Two; Clare Chambers, "The Marriage-Free State," *Proceedings of the Aristotelian Society* 113:2 (2013): 123–143; and Tamara Metz, *Untying the Knot: Marriage, the State, and the Case for their Divorce* (Princeton, NJ: Princeton University Press, 2010).

7. Wedgwood discusses her arguments in Chapter 2. See also Chambers, "The Marriage-Free State."

8. See, for example, Cheshire Calhoun, "Who's Afraid of Polygamous Marriage? Lessons for Same-Sex Marriage Advocacy from the History of Polygamy," *San Diego Law Review* 42 (2005): 1023–1042; and Andrew F. March, "Is There a Right to Polygamy? Marriage, Equality and Subsidizing Families in Liberal Public Justification," *Journal of Moral Philosophy* 8 (2011): 246–272.

9. On this, see Elizabeth Brake, "Recognizing Care: The Case for Friendship and Polyamory," *Syracuse Law and Civic Engagement Journal* 1 (2014), <http://slace.syr. edu/>.

10. On this, see Samantha Brennan and Bill Cameron, "How Many Parents Can a Child Have? Philosophical Reflections on the 'Three Parent Case'," *Dialogue* 54:1 (2015): 45–61.

11. On this, see Linda C. McClain, "The Other Marriage Equality Problem," *Boston University Law Review* 93:3 (2013): 921–970.

1 | Liberal Neutrality and Civil Marriage

SIMON CĂBULEA MAY

MARRIAGE IS BOTH A PUBLIC institution and a cultural practice. A powerful objection to the public institution of civil marriage claims that it violates the principle of liberal neutrality. This is because the cultural practice of marriage is inseparable from a controversial philosophical conception of the good life, one that advances matrimony as an ideal type of personal relationship. In establishing an institution grounded in the cultural practice, the neutrality objection asserts, the state illicitly endorses this matrimonial ideal. In consequence, civil marriage must be replaced by a philosophically neutral array of public institutions, policies, and practices.

In this chapter, I respond to two versions of the neutrality objection. I argue that if five empirical claims are true, then the public institution of civil marriage does not imply state endorsement of the matrimonial ideal. As my thesis is strictly conditional, I do not argue that all these empirical claims are in fact true in any particular society. My present goal is not to defend civil marriage as such, but to argue that liberal neutrality does not preclude, in principle, public institutions grounded in philosophically controversial cultural practices. The neutrality objection is cogent only if certain empirical conditions fail to be met.

In §1, I set out the first version of the neutrality objection to civil marriage. In §2, I argue that marriage is distinctive in being one of very few types of presumptively permanent relationships. In §3, I claim that marriage's presumptive permanence would, in some circumstances, provide an instrumental justification for the liberal state's creation and promotion of civil marriage, a justification that does not presuppose the truth of the matrimonial ideal. In §4, I respond to the second version of the neutrality objection. I argue that the state's promotion of civil marriage does not mean that it implicitly propagates the matrimonial ideal. If the relevant conditions are met, therefore, civil marriage does not imply any state endorsement of a controversial conception of the good life. It is a separate matter whether it is at all feasible to determine if a society happens to be in the specified circumstances. It is also a separate matter whether other arguments might support the reformation, transformation, or abolition of civil marriage.[1]

1. The Neutrality Objection

The neutrality objection has two main premises. The first premise claims that the liberal state must not endorse any philosophical conception of the good life, including the matrimonial ideal. The second premise claims that civil marriage implies state endorsement of the matrimonial ideal.

A. Liberal Neutrality

The principle of liberal neutrality requires that the state not adopt a philosophical conception of the good life, that is, a view about what, if anything, gives ultimate meaning and value to life.[2] State secularism is a familiar implication of liberal neutrality insofar as different religions offer different accounts of how life is best lived. For example, some religions require that believers make a special pilgrimage to a holy site, whereas others do not. But liberal neutrality is more demanding, in one respect at least, since secularism does not itself preclude state endorsement of a non-religious conception of the good life. Whether soccer is a more excellent sport than polo is not a religious question, but it is still not a question that the liberal state should answer.

The principle of liberal neutrality does not rule out all claims about human interests, otherwise there would be no way for the state to evaluate the beneficial effects of its policies. A rough distinction can accordingly be drawn between primary goods and ultimate goods.[3] Primary goods—for example, income and wealth—are useful resources in the pursuit of a wide variety of ends whereas ultimate goods are valued as ends. Some things—for example, health and education—can be valued as both primary goods and ultimate goods. Liberal neutrality permits the state to promote these, but only as primary goods. Thus, the state's interest in the health and education of its citizens extends only so far as these goods are instrumentally valuable to individuals with different conceptions of the good life.[4]

The matrimonial ideal can be defined to encompass any belief that marriage constitutes an ultimately superior type of relationship. Because it is defined as a philosophical conception of the good life, the ideal does not just claim that marriage is instrumentally beneficial—even its critics could grant that married couples might enjoy relatively high levels of primary goods. In addition, the ideal asserts that some distinctive feature of marriage is an important part of what gives ultimate meaning and value to human existence. For instance, a religious conception might regard marriage as an integral aspect of God's desire that humans be fruitful and multiply. Alternatively, a secular conception might claim that lifelong marriages manifest the deepest kind of love between two people.

B. Civil Marriage

It follows from the principle of liberal neutrality that the state may not endorse the matrimonial ideal. The second premise of the neutrality objection claims that in creating the public institution of civil marriage, the state does precisely this. Thus, Elizabeth Brake writes that civil marriage "recognizes a single central exclusive relationship of a certain priority and duration [but] ignores alternative ideals of relationship: close dyadic friendships, small group family units, or networks of multiple, significant nonexclusive relationships that provide emotional support, caretaking, and intimacy."[5] Tamara Metz claims that civil marriage "draws the state into the most intimate corners of citizens' lives (family and sexual life, religious and cultural value systems) and effectively privileges some views of the good life while punishing others."[6] Clare Chambers argues that civil marriage violates liberal neutrality by presupposing a cultural practice with a controversial meaning and significance and by assuming that various dimensions of interpersonal relationships should be bundled together in a single union.[7] Similarly, Jeremy Garrett claims that the institution devalues "alternative ways of life, including living singly, cohabiting, and other forms of nonrecognized partnering."[8]

The neutrality objection allows that the liberal state has interests in some matters that often fall with the scope of civil marriage. Three important examples are parental rights and responsibilities, the promotion of gender equality, and the recognition of caring relationships. In each case, however, the relevant state interest fails to justify civil marriage, since some alternative policy would always be better suited to the task at hand.

The first version of the neutrality objection accordingly concludes that the justification of the institution depends on an implicit appeal to the matrimonial ideal.

First, the liberal state has a duty to protect the interests of children: they may not be physically mistreated, they must be emotionally nurtured, and they must be adequately prepared to contribute to society as democratic citizens. Although traditionalists may believe that married couples are the only proper parents for children, the state has no philosophical basis for this assumption. The state's responsibility to protect children justifies an interest in parents, not an interest in spouses as such. Since the distinction between parents and non-parents cuts across the distinction between spouses and non-spouses, the state's child welfare regulations must apply to parents whatever their marital status.

Second, the liberal state has a responsibility to safeguard gender equality in the domestic sphere insofar as this is necessary for a just and democratic society. A state that simply ignored widespread sexist family practices would fail to respect women and girls as equal members of society. Marriage has historically been a central mechanism of gender oppression, with wives legally subordinated to their husbands. This legacy can arguably be ameliorated, to some extent at least, by marriage laws designed to protect the rights of women. For instance, progressive divorce laws might ensure that both spouses receive an equitable division of assets on the dissolution of a marriage. Nevertheless, the liberal state's interest in gender equality does not explain why one particular form of intimate cohabitation should receive official recognition and approval. The gender equality argument applies to all arrangements where men and women form single households, whether or not they also participate in the cultural practice of marriage. Consequently, progressive laws should govern all cases where the dissolution of a household is likely to cause an inequitable division of assets, not just divorce as such.[9]

Third, the state can acknowledge that married couples generally take care of each other—they pool risks, resources, and labor—and that this feature of the practice has profound social benefits. A society that lacked the kind of caring relationship typical of marriage would be thoroughly dysfunctional: individuals would be much more vulnerable to economic hardships and the various ills of social isolation. In consequence, the liberal state has good reason to recognize and foster care as a primary good, as Brake argues.[10] But marriage is only one way that these important caring relationships are formed. Unmarried individuals can take care of each other just as well as married couples do. For instance, two elderly sisters could live together and look after each other. The same point holds for the members of polyamorous communes. Thus, Brake argues that the current institution of civil marriage must be fundamentally transformed to encompass these alternative, non-marital caring relationships.[11] Similarly, Metz argues that the state should recognize and protect a broad variety of "intimate caregiving unions," whatever their philosophical, cultural, or religious meaning.[12] The state must not arbitrarily privilege one form of caring relationship to the detriment of others.

In essence, marriage is a cultural practice that some people prize and others do not. A state that enshrines this specific practice in a public institution, the objection claims, unjustifiably takes sides in a philosophical, cultural, and religious dispute between its citizens. The liberal state has no more reason to distinguish between married and unmarried individuals than it has to distinguish between soccer and polo players or between religious pilgrims and secular tourists. Thus, civil marriage must be replaced by some or other configuration of neutral public institutions, policies, and practices.

2. The Presumptive Permanence of Marriage

A cogent response to the neutrality objection must demonstrate that the liberal state has a neutral way to distinguish between marital and non-marital relationships. There must be something that makes marriage special without making it special in the wrong way: it must be distinctive, but not because it is a uniquely excellent type of relationship. In this section, I claim that the concept of presumptive permanence provides a plausible solution. The first two empirical premises of the response to the neutrality objection are as follows:

(1) Marriage is a presumptively permanent relationship.
(2) Alternative caring relationships to marriage lack presumptive permanence.

These two premises can be discussed once the key concept of presumptive permanence is defined.

A. Presumptively Permanent Status

A presumptively permanent status is a social role that has a good faith entrance requirement: when a person acquires the status, she is socially expected to commit herself to its permanence. So defined, the status has four main features: First, it has distinctive normative implications: the status-holders are expected to behave in ways appropriate to their role. Second, as an empirical matter, individuals usually hold the status for a long time, quite often for the remainder of their lives. Third, individuals typically intend at the outset that they hold the status permanently. Fourth, this undertaking is itself required by a particular social norm: someone who acquired the status without intending that it be permanent would be subject to criticism as insincere or cynical. The presence of this good faith norm is the key element: the surrounding community must expect of the status-holders that they commit at the outset to the permanence of their new role.

Consider three occupations: priest, plumber, and physician. Not every novice remains or even intends to remain a priest for the rest of her life: she might be laicized or lack the required dedication. But the norms of the priesthood are such that becoming a priest should be a life-long commitment—being a priest is therefore a presumptively permanent status. In contrast, a career as a plumber involves no such commitment, even in very conservative societies—being a plumber is therefore not a presumptively permanent status. Physicians arguably provide something of a borderline case. There is no bad faith in the desire to work as a doctor for only, say, a decade or so. But the Hippocratic Oath is not a purely professional obligation: nonpracticing physicians are still expected to abide by the code and even retired doctors are never completely off duty. Thus, in some respects at least, being a physician is arguably something of a presumptively permanent status.

As the three examples show, it is a contingent sociological matter whether a particular social role is presumptively permanent. There is nothing essential to the priesthood that it be a solemn lifelong undertaking. Priests might one day become more like secular social workers, ministering to their communities for a while before exploring other career opportunities. Similarly, it is not essential to plumbing that it be regarded as just another type of job. Joining an artisans' guild could become akin to entering a sacred fraternity: once a mason, perhaps, always a mason. In addition, the social norms governing the lifelong responsibilities of physicians could evolve in any number of ways. Some societies might benefit if doctors became more like priests, and other societies might benefit if doctors became more like plumbers.

Whether a particular social role is presumptively permanent or not can be a controversial question: for example, reasonable people might disagree about whether there is a social norm requiring a commitment to permanent citizenship in the naturalization process. The existence of the social norm is one thing, however, and its justifiability is another. In many cases, the justification of a role's presumptive permanence touches on questions of ultimate meaning and value: would temporary priests, for example, be as capable of self-denial? The principle of liberal neutrality bars the state from adopting a position on the question of justification in these cases. But the principle must allow the state to recognize that the relevant social norm does exist, since this is a sociological matter rather than a philosophical question about the nature of the good life. If liberal neutrality barred the state from adopting a controversial position on the existence of a social norm, then it would be very difficult for public policies to combat informal racism, sexism, and religious bigotry. For instance, in some societies, social norms require extending greater deference to the testimony of whites than to that of blacks. The existence of such norms is often controversial, since few people like to acknowledge improper influences on their belief formation. But if the state is precluded from adopting a position on the matter, it cannot take appropriate steps to combat the influence of racism in the criminal justice system and elsewhere.[13]

B. Presumptively Permanent Relationships

A presumptively permanent relationship is a type of small-scale interpersonal relationship in which the participants are socially expected to commit in good faith at the outset of the relationship to its permanence. Each participant enters the relationship because the other does (or others do) and each thereby acquires a presumptively permanent status. A presumptively permanent relationship might not last for very long, and a participant might not intend it to last for very long. But such possibilities involve deviant cases, departures from what is expected. To illustrate, friendship is not a presumptively permanent relationship. Some friendships last from infancy until death and can be as intimate and meaningful as any other kind of relationship. Many friends intend to remain close for their whole lives: schoolchildren sometimes pledge to be best friends forever. There may also be strong social norms against ending a friendship or even allowing it to wither away. Nevertheless, there is no social expectation that people commit to a permanent bond at the outset of a friendship. Two individuals can in good faith become friends quite casually, with no thought to whether their friendship will endure into the distant future. Even the schoolchildren's pledge is just child's play—communities do not impose norms of presumptive permanence on childhood friendships any more than they impose norms of factual accuracy on children's imaginative games.

In contrast to friendship, marriage is (almost always) a presumptively permanent relationship. It is formed on the basis of a mutual commitment between (typically) two people and, aside from the unusual practice of temporary marriage, being a spouse is a presumptively permanent status.[14] When people marry, they are (almost always) expected to commit in good faith to the permanence of their new status: "till death us do part," they commonly pledge. This commitment may be defeasible: few people now marry with the understanding that their wedding vows are irrevocable. Moreover, there need not be particularly strong social norms against divorce if it should come to be desired by either spouse—indeed, some people can experience the end of a friendship as more distressing than the end of a marriage. Marriage is a presumptively permanent relationship because there is a social norm against marrying without the intention to stay married for life, not because social norms also make it difficult or undesirable to divorce.

Consider the example of marriages of convenience. Suppose that two lovers wed solely to provide the one with immigration benefits: as Agnes's husband, Bernard becomes entitled to reside and work in her home country. Their plan, however, is to divorce once he acquires citizenship in his own right. Since Agnes and Bernard intend to divorce, they do not commit in good faith to the permanence of their relationship. Their marriage is a pretense, perhaps not in the sense that it fails to be an actual marriage, but in the sense that it is not a marriage properly conceived and constituted. The two are merely mimicking the commitment of other married couples. In consequence, Agnes and Bernard are to some extent subject to social criticism as insincere. This criticism might be severe: entering a marriage of convenience may be regarded as a grave moral sin, an affront to God and nation alike. Alternatively, the criticism might be considerably muted by an awareness of the onerous legal obstacles immigrants face. Insincerity is not the worst vice, especially if the two individuals involved are honest with each other and no harm is done to others. Nevertheless, Agnes and Bernard have clearly flouted a social norm, whether or not their action is morally justifiable all things considered.

As the example of temporary marriage demonstrates, presumptive permanence is not an essential feature of marriage. It is quite possible that the cultural practice might evolve in such a way that the good faith norm dies out. Perhaps if divorce became so common that newlyweds could not reasonably expect their marriage to last a lifetime, there would cease to be any social expectation that they commit to a permanent bond. Temporary marriage might instead come to be seen as the ideal arrangement. Similarly, a culture of fashionable celebrity weddings and gaudy reality shows could conceivably degrade the solemnity of the practice to the point that it became an irredeemably kitsch diversion devoid of all norms of love, sincerity, and responsibility. Nevertheless, it is plausible that presumptive permanence is a very robust sociological feature of marriage.

C. Alternatives to Marriage

Marriage is not the only type of presumptively permanent caring relationship. Consider the example of co-parenting. Suppose that two unmarried roommates agree to adopt a child together. In deciding to become Ella's parents, Carmen and Dominic commit themselves to a lifelong arrangement, one that will endure even after the child reaches adulthood. This co-parenting relationship does not depend on their continued cohabitation. To be sure, it would presumably be much easier for them to raise Ella if they did remain living together. But if Dominic were to leave their shared apartment, his parental responsibilities would not end. No one can adopt a child in good faith if they intend to terminate the co-parenting relationship once it becomes inconvenient or awkward. It does not follow that the relationship is irrevocable—clearly, Carmen could exclude Dominic from any role in raising Ella if he became violent or abusive. Like marriage, co-parenting is presumptively permanent because it is meant to be a lifelong relationship, not because it is inescapable.

Although marriage and co-parenting are distinct relationship types, co-parenting is not an alternative to marriage. Social norms do not generally require individuals to make a choice between becoming either a spouse or a co-parent. Instead, it is far more common for social norms to encourage the two relationships to overlap: one version of the matrimonial ideal claims that the primary purpose of marriage is to raise children together. In contrast, social norms do generally present sibling cohabitation and polyamorous communes as alternatives to marriage. Suppose that Agnes marries Bernard but immediately decides to cohabit with her elderly sister in a different city. There is a significant *prima facie* tension between Agnes's social role as Bernard's spouse and her social role as Sibyl's cohabiting sister. Unless there is some weighty reason for the arrangement—perhaps her sister is terminally ill and Bernard's career prevents him from relocating too—the newlyweds' separation provides grounds for an observer to suspect that their marriage is a sham. Much the same point holds if Bernard decides to join a polyamorous commune.

The tension between a spouse's social role and the two alternative relationship types is a contingent sociological matter. Many married couples deliberately subvert existing marital norms, from the gendered division of labor to sexual and romantic exclusivity. Membership in a polyamorous commune might one day be seen as entirely compatible with marriage, in much the same way that friendship is now. Nevertheless, as the neutrality objection itself assumes, these relationship types happen now to be alternatives to marriage. Moreover, neither of the two is presumptively permanent. Agnes and Sibyl might promise to spend the rest of their lives together, and may always be true to this promise, but no such undertaking is socially expected of cohabiting siblings. Similarly, the incoming members of a polyamorous commune would not be expected to commit to permanent membership. Instead, new members would be expected only to renounce sexual jealousy and material possessiveness and to remain within the commune just as long as they found it fulfilling. Much the same point holds for other types of caring relationship that are usually regarded as alternatives to marriage.

It is possible for there to be alternative relationships to marriage that also require a lifelong commitment at the outset. Suppose aspirant monks were required to join the monastic order of a religion in small groups. Each member of the group becomes a monk because the others do, and each is expected to pledge permanent fidelity to his new brethren. The monks in each group spend their lives together, committed to helping one another live in accordance with the virtues of celibacy, charity, and poverty. Such a relationship would share marriage's presumptive permanence, but would be an incompatible alternative to marriage. It is arguable that some monastic orders are (or have been) quite similar to this type of relationship. If so, marriage is to that extent less distinctive as a presumptively permanent caring relationship. But it is more probable that being a monk is at most a presumptively permanent status. A monastic order as a whole is not an intimate small-scale relationship formed on the basis of a mutual commitment between particular individuals.

3. The Instrumental Value of Marriage

The first two empirical premises of the response to the neutrality objection claim that, relative to alternative relationships, marriage is distinctive in requiring a lifelong commitment at the outset. I take it that these two premises are relatively uncontroversial. The next two premises of the response are much more contentious. They assert that the presumptive permanence of marriage supports a neutral justification of civil marriage:

(3) The presumptive permanence of marriage amplifies the beneficial consequences it has as a type of caring relationship.
(4) The public institution of civil marriage further enhances the relatively beneficial consequences of marriage.

A. The Instrumental Value of Presumptively Permanent Relationships

Most types of interpersonal relationships lack presumptive permanence, so why should any have this feature at all? One interpretation of the matrimonial ideal claims that the lifelong commitment in marriage expresses the profound nature of the link between spouses. To vow to spend one's entire life with another person is, ideally at least, to dedicate one's life to that person and hence to commit to ends beyond one's own narrow interests. It is unselfish devotion of precisely this kind, the interpretation asserts, that provides the most valuable meaning to life. In contrast, critics of the matrimonial ideal claim that it is entirely possible to dedicate oneself to another person without any presumption of permanence: the depth and the duration of one's devotion are two separate matters.[15] Whatever the merits of these competing philosophical positions, neither helps in assessing the compatibility of civil marriage with the principle of liberal neutrality.

A quite different account of presumptively permanent relationships conjectures that they have a distinctive instrumental value. The third premise of the response claims that although caring relationships generally have many beneficial consequences, presumptively permanent caring relationships are, other things being equal, especially beneficial. In essence, the surrounding community's expectation of permanent commitment enhances their stability and thereby amplifies the good effects they have as caring relationships. This amplification could be detected both in marriage's effects on spouses and in its broader third-party effects.

First, married couples may prosper more than they would have if their relationship were not presumptively permanent. Compare a couple in two different social worlds. The first social world lacks the cultural practice of marriage. Suppose Fatima and Gwyneth are deeply in love and decide to spend the rest of their lives as a couple. They announce their desire to their friends and family, and flourish together for many years. In an otherwise identical second social world, marriage exists as a cultural practice. In this world, Fatima and Gwyneth can gather their loved ones at a wedding and solemnly vow to be together always and evermore. They do not just declare their affections and aspirations to one and all, but also place themselves under the community's good faith norm and stamp their commitment with the imprimatur of a powerful cultural tradition. Fatima and Gwyneth build their life together, not just on the assumption that their love will endure, but also on their mutual responsiveness to the familiar normative expectations of their community. This additional element surely affects how the two understand the nature of the relationship and hence how well they fare together.

It is quite possible that the presence of the marital good faith norm could have various negative effects on a couple—perhaps Fatima and Gwyneth are both too anxious to preserve their sense of independence or their self-conception as *avant garde* renegades for marriage to be good for them. But it is plausible that the good faith norm has, on balance, positive effects on couples: the presumptive permanence of marriage provides spouses with greater assurance of the stability of their union and reinforces their mutual trust. It becomes that much easier for Fatima to make financial sacrifices for Gwyneth and for Gwyneth to adapt her career plans to Fatima's needs. In consequence, it is not improbable that married couples achieve somewhat higher levels of primary goods, in virtue of being married, than they would have achieved without the social expectation of permanent commitment. However well Fatima and Gwyneth may have fared in a world without marriage, it is not implausible that they probably fare somewhat better in a world that allows them to marry.

Second, third parties may benefit more from presumptively permanent relationships than from other kinds of caring relationships. This is most obvious in the case of co-parenting, since a sense of insecurity can be especially damaging for children. But the presumptive permanence of marriage may also have distinctive third-party benefits. If it is true that married couples enjoy relatively high levels of primary goods, other things being equal, then it is probable that they can, in turn, contribute to society to a much greater extent. Whatever makes it easier for Fatima to support

Gwyneth during her studies also makes it easier for Gwyneth to acquire useful skills and productive employment. Moreover, marriage may have greater third-party benefits than other kinds of relationship even if spouses themselves fare no better than they would have fared unmarried. Consider once again the social world in which marriage does not exist as a cultural practice. In this world, people who fall in love may typically live together and care for one another, in many cases for the duration of their lives. But even the most longstanding of these relationships would not be presumptively permanent. In contrast, in the social world where marriage is relatively widespread, there is greater assurance to third parties that people's domestic arrangements are durable: other things being equal, the vitality of a cultural practice of presumptive permanence conveys a clearer signal of social stability and predictability. This in turn may well facilitate any number of good effects: increased financial investment in local communities, greater immigration of skilled workers from other countries, reduced incidence of crime, improved patterns of residential construction or urban transportation, higher rates of participation in school activities, and the like.

If the presumptive permanence of marriage does have comparatively beneficial third-party effects, relative to alternative relationship types, it is very likely that these effects are diffuse, general, and indirect. This means that it is very difficult to determine the extent to which marriage might amplify the ordinary benefits of caring relationships. Some indications can be drawn from comparisons of different couples and communities in the actual world, but this limited data cannot settle the issue: marriage might be relatively beneficial in the actual world only because it currently enjoys official state sanction. Moreover, it should not be assumed that there must be a determinate fact of the matter about whether marriage is, all things considered, instrumentally valuable relative to its alternatives. Nevertheless, it is unlikely that the presence or absence of a social norm governing the creation of an important interpersonal relationship would not have a profound social impact. It would be quite remarkable if it made no significant difference to a society whether the most intimate caring relationships between its adult citizens were, in general, presumptively permanent or not.

B. Presumptive Permanence and Civil Marriage

The third empirical premise of the response to the neutrality objection is that the cultural practice of marriage has, on the whole, greater social benefits than alternative practices. The fourth empirical premise asserts that the public institution of civil marriage enhances the cultural practice's good effects.

The fourth premise may be false even if the third is true. It is possible that civil marriage simply distorts the signal of social stability that marriage would otherwise send. Recall the example of Agnes and Bernard. If the state attaches various legal entitlements to marital status, then it encourages marriages of convenience. These, in turn, may damage the social expectation of permanent commitment. Perhaps a clearer and more effective message of stability would be sent if marriage remained a purely cultural or religious affair.

Nevertheless, in making it both easy and attractive to marry, the state very likely makes marriage more common than it would otherwise be. Civil marriage also very plausibly inherits the good faith norm of the cultural practice. Even if Agnes and Bernard's wedding is conducted by a magistrate rather than a religious cleric, they still flout a social norm by intending to divorce after a few years. It would be disingenuous for Agnes and Bernard to suggest that since their marriage is only civil, and not also sanctified in a religious ritual, it does not really matter how long they plan to remain together. As a matter of contingent sociological fact, civil marriage is not typically regarded as a purely bureaucratic matter of no normative significance. Being a spouse is (almost always) a presumptively permanent status, whether one is married in a religious ritual, civil ceremony, pop extravaganza, or internationally televised reality show.

If the four empirical premises of the response are true, then there is a *prima facie* neutral justification for the state to create and promote a distinct public institution based on the cultural practice of marriage. It does not follow that the state should not also extend some measure of recognition to alternative relationship types. There is no obvious reason, for instance, why someone should not inherit her sister's share of their common residence in much the same way that a spouse would. Additionally, it may well be the case that legal recognition of alternative relationship types, on par with marriage, would help to extend the social norm of presumptive permanence. If the two elderly sisters are prepared to register their household arrangement as an official caregiving union, they might find that their community expects them to make just as strong a commitment to one another as spouses are expected to make. If so, there would seem to be nothing currently special about the marital relationship that warrants an exclusively marital public institution. However, it is not improbable that legal recognition of alternative relationships would not go very far in making them presumptively permanent. Social norms can be affected by public institutions and policies, but they cannot be directly controlled. Thus, it is not implausible that the state's establishment and promotion of civil marriage, as a distinct institution, is the best way to enhance the beneficial social effects of presumptively permanent relationships.

In essence, the principle of liberal neutrality prohibits state endorsement of a philosophical conception of the good life, but it does not prohibit the state from recognizing that certain cultural practices have particularly beneficial effects. Liberal neutrality is not a principle of cultural detachment—it does not prohibit state involvement in and promotion of cultural practices as such. For instance, the state's health policies might encourage participation in sport and discourage social traditions associated with alcohol abuse. If the state has neutral grounds to identify marriage as a distinctive type of caring relationship (as I have argued), one with especially valuable consequences (as is plausible), then there is a cogent *prima facie* justification for the state to recognize and promote that type of relationship through institutional means. The inseparability of the matrimonial ideal from the cultural practice of marriage does not undermine the neutrality of this justification of civil marriage.

4. The Propagation of the Matrimonial Ideal

The first version of the neutrality objection claims that the state illicitly endorses the matrimonial ideal because it must appeal to the ideal in the justification of civil marriage. The second version allows that the presumptive permanence of marriage could provide the basis for a cogent neutral justification. It claims, instead, that in creating and promoting civil marriage, the state in effect encourages belief in the matrimonial ideal. State propagation of a philosophical conception of the good life violates the principle of liberal neutrality just as much as state dependence on the conception in the justification of a public policy. This is because the cultivation of belief is a matter of special concern. Suppose that widespread belief in some false claim would have various beneficial social effects. Ordinarily, the prospect of beneficial consequences would justify a public policy—for instance, the state may promote sport if sport promotes health. However, a state that encouraged citizens to believe a false proposition would fail to respect those citizens as intelligent agents. It would regard their convictions simply as resources to be manipulated in the pursuit of valuable ends, not as propositional attitudes governed by epistemic norms. Thus, if the state wishes its citizens to believe some proposition, the proposition must at least be one that the state itself can accept as true. Since the principle of liberal neutrality precludes state endorsement of the matrimonial ideal, it also precludes the state's propagation of that ideal.

A. Marriage, Sport, and Religion

The key claim of the second version of the neutrality objection is that civil marriage implies state propagation of the matrimonial ideal. Some support for this claim is given by a comparison of the state's promotion of different sports codes and its promotion of religious practices. Suppose that many citizens disagree about whether soccer or polo is an ultimately superior sport. The neutral state may not take a side in this dispute, but it may nevertheless be alive to any difference in the contingent sociological effects of the two activities. Suppose that there is good empirical evidence that soccer has a much more beneficial social impact than polo. Because it requires little expenditure on equipment, soccer is accessible to and popular within all economic groups—since any child can play the game with a cheap ball in an open space, the sport proves to be a unifying social force. As the exclusive preserve of the wealthy, in contrast, polo fosters class segregation and insulates elite social networks from the broader community. It is reasonable that the neutral state could, in response to this empirical evidence, take cautious steps to promote soccer over polo. For instance, it might establish a national soccer league but largely ignore the fortunes of the national polo association, or provide funding for soccer but not polo in all public schools. In this scenario, the state does not adopt any view about the intrinsic merits of the two codes—instead, it merely tinkers with the recreational activities of the public on instrumental grounds.

Suppose also that citizens disagree about whether the true religion requires a pilgrimage to a holy site. Although the state may not adopt a position on this question, it can recognize that the annual pilgrimage has a reliable economic impact that ordinary tourism does not have. But the secular state may not encourage its citizens to become pilgrims rather than tourists. To encourage them to become pilgrims would be to encourage them to adopt certain religious views. A state that adopts public policies so as to convert secular tourists into devout pilgrims is, in effect, an evangelical state. State promotion of pilgrimage above tourism is therefore quite different from state promotion of soccer above polo.

The second version of the neutrality objection assumes that civil marriage is more like the pilgrimage example than the soccer example. Few people value soccer as a manifestation of the divine, but many people adopt the matrimonial ideal as part of their religious convictions. Clerics do not, as a class, officiate at soccer matches, but they do officiate at weddings. Few religious doctrines have anything distinctive to say about the ethics of sport, but many religious doctrines have detailed instructions for the proper conduct of a marriage. Violations of the rules of soccer are simply fouls requiring social censure, but violations of the norms of marriage are often regarded as sins requiring pastoral intervention. Thus, although the neutral state might permissibly favor one sports code over another, the objection claims, it may not favor one form of caring relationship over another. This would be too similar to state propagation of a religion.

B. Presumptively Doctrinal Practices

The second version of the neutrality objection fails, I believe, because marriage is unlike pilgrimage in one key respect. Some cultural practices are presumptively doctrinal, that is, they are governed by a certain social norm: to participate in the practice in good faith, an individual must endorse a particular doctrine or, at least, some range of its tenets. Pilgrimage is generally a presumptively doctrinal practice insofar as sincere pilgrims must endorse the religion that designates the relevant site as holy. For example, Christians might visit Mecca as tourists, but only Muslims can go on the Hajj. The same point holds for many other religious activities. Atheists cannot sincerely baptize their children, they can only dunk them in water. Thus, if the state were to promote pilgrimage or baptism, even on entirely instrumental grounds, it would thereby promote either belief in the religious doctrine or bad faith participation in the activity. Since the state should not encourage its citizens to act in bad faith, the state's promotion of a presumptively doctrinal practice implies state propagation of the relevant doctrine.

I have argued that marriage is a cultural practice governed by a good faith norm: spouses are socially expected to commit to the permanence of their marriage. But there is no social norm that newlyweds must also endorse the matrimonial ideal. To endorse the matrimonial ideal is to adopt the philosophical view that marriage is an ultimately superior form of relationship, more excellent than alternative non-marital arrangements. Many people may marry only because they endorse this conception of the good life. It may also be that the cultural practice would not endure unless some significant number of spouses were motivated by their commitment to the ideal. But it is implausible that any such commitment is socially expected of spouses. Many other people marry simply because it is a convenient way to express the depth of their devotion to one another, because they wish to continue the cultural tradition of their parents, or because they do not want to be seen as unconventional. None of these reasons betrays any insincerity or cynicism, and none implies any belief that marriage is ultimately superior to other relationship types. Thus, as a matter of contingent sociological fact:

(5) Marriage is not a presumptively doctrinal cultural practice.

If social norms were to evolve so that commitment to the matrimonial ideal were expected of spouses, then civil marriage would in effect imply state propagation of the ideal. In this circumstance, the institution would violate the principle of liberal neutrality. But short of that eventuality, marriage is like soccer, and unlike pilgrimage, in being open to all people, whatever their conception of the good life happens to be.

Conclusion

The neutrality objection claims that civil marriage violates the principle of liberal neutrality because it implies state endorsement of the matrimonial ideal. The first version of the objection claims that the justification of the institution presupposes the ideal. The second version of the objection claims that the institution implies state propagation of the ideal. I have argued that liberal neutrality does not preclude, in principle, public institutions grounded in philosophically controversial practices. The neutrality objection fails if five empirical claims are true:

(1) Marriage is a presumptively permanent relationship.
(2) Alternative caring relationships to marriage lack presumptive permanence.
(3) The presumptive permanence of marriage amplifies the beneficial consequences it has as a type of caring relationship.
(4) The public institution of civil marriage further enhances the relatively beneficial consequences of marriage.
(5) Marriage is not a presumptively doctrinal cultural practice.

Since my thesis is strictly conditional, I have not argued that these empirical claims are all true. The third and fourth propositions, in particular, are not at all obvious. However, none of the claims is at all implausible. This means that the compatibility or incompatibility of civil marriage with the principle of liberal neutrality cannot be determined from the philosophical armchair.[16]

Notes

An earlier version of this chapter was presented at the Eastern Division meeting of the American Philosophical Association in December 2011. Some of the ideas were presented at the conferences of the Society for Applied Philosophy and the Virginia Philosophical Association in 2008. I am grateful to Melina Bell, Elizabeth Brake, Emanuela Ceva, and Lori Watson for their valuable comments.

1. In particular, I set aside the important argument that civil marriage is unfair to those who do not wish to participate in the tradition by conferring special privileges and status on those who do.

2. For various influential articulations of the principle of liberal neutrality, see Bruce Ackerman, *Social Justice and the Liberal State* (New Haven, CT: Yale University Press, 1980); Charles Larmore, *Patterns of Moral Complexity* (Cambridge, UK: Cambridge University Press, 1987); John Rawls, *Political Liberalism*, expanded edition (New York: Columbia University Press, 2005, originally published 1993); and George Klosko and Steven Wall, eds., *Perfectionism and Neutrality: Essays in Liberal Theory* (Lanham, MD: Rowman and Littlefield, 2003). A recent important conception of the principle is advanced in Alan Patten, "Liberal Neutrality: A Reinterpretation and Defense," *Journal of Political Philosophy* 20:3 (2012): 249–272. Although the meaning of the principle is contested, the prohibition of state endorsement of a controversial philosophical conception of the good life is its core element. I set aside whether the best understanding of the principle imposes any further restrictions on the liberal state.

3. On primary goods, see John Rawls, *A Theory of Justice*, revised edition (Cambridge, MA: Harvard University Press, 1999, originally published 1971), 54.

4. A weak principle of liberal neutrality would allow the state to promote certain very general human interests as ultimate goods. Such a principle could allow a non-instrumental approach to health and education. I ignore this possibility in the present chapter since I take it that even a weak principle of liberal neutrality would not permit state endorsement of the matrimonial ideal.

5. Elizabeth Brake, *Minimizing Marriage: Marriage, Morality, and the Law* (Oxford: Oxford University Press, 2012), 168.

6. Tamara Metz, *Untying the Knot: Marriage, the State, and the Case for Their Divorce* (Princeton: Princeton University Press, 2010), 7.

7. Clare Chambers, *Against Marriage: An Egalitarian Defence of the Marriage-Free State* (Oxford: Oxford University Press, forthcoming 2016).

8. Jeremy Garrett, "Marriage Unhitched from the State: A Defense," *Public Affairs Quarterly* 23:2 (2009): 168.

9. For an argument that the liberal state's interest in equality can support civil marriage, see Christie Hartley and Lori Watson, "Political Liberalism, Marriage and the Family," *Law and Philosophy* 31:2 (2012): 185–212.

10. Brake, *Minimizing Marriage*.

11. Brake claims that a transformed institution should still be called "marriage," but that it must nevertheless include non-marital caring relationships.

12. Metz, *Untying the Knot*.

13. For discussion of such cases of racist testimonial injustice, see Miranda Fricker, *Epistemic Injustice: Power and the Ethics of Knowing* (Oxford: Oxford University Press, 2007).

14. For discussion of temporary marriage, see Daniel Nolan, "Temporary Marriage," in this volume (Chapter 8). Although the presumptive permanence argument does not support the inclusion of temporary marriages within the public institution, it does not necessarily support their exclusion either.

15. For the claim that marital commitment has only instrumental value, see Anca Gheaus, "The (Dis)value of Commitment to One's Spouse," in this volume (Chapter 9).

16. For a similarly context-sensitive approach to civil marriage and the demands of liberal neutrality, see Hartley and Watson, "Political Liberalism, Marriage and the Family": 187: "[T]he actual implications of political liberalism for marriage law cannot be worked out in advance of information about a particular politically liberal society."

2| Is Civil Marriage Illiberal?

RALPH WEDGWOOD

1. Liberal Criticisms of Marriage

In the last few years, after decades of campaigning, the cause of same-sex marriage has finally scored a string of successes. By the middle of 2015, same-sex marriage was legal in the Netherlands, Belgium, Spain, Canada, South Africa, Norway, Sweden, Portugal, Iceland, Argentina, Denmark, Uruguay, Brazil, France, New Zealand, England and Wales, Scotland—and, finally, in all fifty states of the USA.

At the same time, the institution of civil marriage has recently come under intense scrutiny from political philosophers who work within a broadly liberal tradition. These philosophers agree with the advocates of same-sex marriage that it is unjust to make civil marriage available to opposite-sex couples while excluding same-sex couples. But many of these philosophers give only heavily qualified support to the same-sex marriage campaigners' fundamental goal—which is to give same-sex couples access to something that closely approximates the current institution of marriage. On the contrary, according to these political philosophers, civil marriage itself, in anything approximating to its current form, is incompatible with liberal principles of justice. In their view, marriage should ideally be either completely abolished or radically reformed, virtually beyond recognition; making civil marriage in anything like its current form available to same-sex couples is supportable only if these more radical reforms are unavailable.

In this essay, I shall defend the goal of the same-sex marriage campaigners against the arguments of these liberal political philosophers. I shall principally focus on the arguments of Elizabeth Brake, although

I shall also touch on some of the arguments of Cheshire Calhoun, Clare Chambers, and Tamara Metz.[1] That is, I shall argue that, while making civil marriage compatible with justice does indeed require legalizing same-sex marriage, it does not require the much more radical reforms that these political philosophers call for.

In particular, I shall focus on the central argument that Brake makes for the conclusion that unless marriage is radically reformed (by being, as she puts it, "minimized"), marriage is "incompatible with political liberalism."[2] By "political liberalism," she means the principle, which was famously defended by John Rawls, that the state's exercise of its authority must be justifiable on grounds that are acceptable to all reasonable citizens; the state must not exercise its authority in ways that can be justified only by appeal to controversial religious or philosophical doctrines or ideals that some reasonable citizens reject.[3]

To make an argument of this kind, one would have to rely on the claim that marriage, in anything like its current form, can *only* be justified by appeal to such a controversial doctrine or ideal. As Brake puts it, existing marriage law "favors one contested conception of the good and thereby fails to respect public reason and reasonable pluralism."[4] Strictly speaking, however, political liberalism does not prohibit exercises of political authority that are somehow more *favorable* to some contested conceptions of the good than to others; it prohibits exercises of political authority that can only be *justified* by appeal to such contested conceptions.[5] On the face of it, the claim that there is *no* adequate justification of marriage, in anything like its current form, which does not rely on some such controversial doctrine or ideal, seems debatable and in need of being defended. Defending this claim would involve "proving a negative": in principle, it would require surveying *all possible* justifications of marriage, and showing that every possible justification conflicts with liberalism (or else is inadequate in some other way). This would require surveying many more possible justifications of marriage than Brake actually considers.

In fact, in some of my own earlier work, I offered a justification of marriage that was intended to be compatible with liberalism.[6] Specifically, my justification was designed to be consistent with the principle of political liberalism that we have just discussed—the principle that the state should not exercise its authority in ways that can only be justified by appeal to controversial ideals or doctrines that some reasonable citizens reject. Moreover, it was also designed to be consistent with the classical liberal principle (which was most famously defended in J. S. Mill's *On Liberty*) that the state must respect individual autonomy, and so refrain from treating people paternalistically—that is, from undermining their autonomy for the sake of their own good.

It is because my justification of marriage is designed to be compatible with these two liberal principles that it may seem to some readers surprisingly *thin*—in the sense that there are many important facts about marriage that my justification, quite deliberately, takes no account of. The principle of political liberalism implies that the state should not justify its involvement in the institution of marriage by appeal to any of the contested conceptions of marriage that are held within the various religious traditions or subcultures of the society. This is why my justification of marriage ignores all the details of these contested conceptions. The principle of autonomy implies that the state should not pressurize people to get married—the choice of whether or not to marry should be left up to the individuals concerned. This is why my justification of marriage is not based on a detailed assessment of the various benefits and burdens that marriage confers on married couples—it is up to the individuals concerned to assess these benefits and burdens for themselves. In general, marriage undoubtedly plays a rich and complex role in our society; but the state, in justifying its involvement in the institution of marriage, does not need to take account of all these complex details.

In this essay, I shall restate my justification of marriage, and I shall try to show that this justification is not vulnerable to the objections that have been raised by Brake; in doing so, I shall also try to answer some of the other liberal critics of marriage. In this way, I hope to make it plausible that marriage—even in something approximating to its current form—is quite consistent with liberal principles of justice.

2. What Is Marriage?

The political philosophers who discuss marriage all agree about one thing: marriage essentially involves the *law*. More precisely, every society that has an institution of marriage must have some system of authoritative social rules, which play the role for that society that the law plays for us, and marriage is an institution that involves those social rules. Crucially, marriage is a *legal relationship*: the question "Was Chris married to Joe at such-and-such a time?" is a question that can be settled by a court of law.

Besides being a legal relationship in this sense, what other aspects of marriage law are most fundamental to the institution of marriage? Many theorists, including Brake,[7] seem to think that the most fundamental legal components of marriage are the *entitlements* that marriage confers to *third-party benefits*—that is, to benefits that a married person receives, not from their spouse, but from third parties such as the state, or from various private organizations such as their spouse's employer. These entitlements to third-party benefits include: health insurance benefits; tax breaks; hospital visitation rights; prison visitation rights; privileged immigration treatment for foreign spouses of citizens; the right not to be compelled to testify against one's spouse (and in general to claim an evidentiary privilege for spousal communications); and so on.

However, it seems doubtful to me whether these legal entitlements to third-party benefits are fundamental elements of marriage. These entitlements vary widely between different jurisdictions and different time periods: for example, the tax regimes for married couples are completely different in different jurisdictions; and in countries (like Britain and Canada) that have a national health service, any health insurance benefits that are attached to marriage are clearly a much less important element of marriage than in countries where access to health care depends on private health insurance. In general, it seems to me that these entitlements to third-party benefits could be detached from marriage, and provided on a different basis, without radically changing the nature of marriage.

Indeed, I am sympathetic to the proposal that many if not all of these entitlements *should* be detached from marriage, and made available to any demonstrable caring relationship. At all events, in what follows I shall set these entitlements to third-party benefits aside. In offering a justification for marriage, I shall not argue for the thesis that all of these entitlements should always be attached to marriage; and I shall certainly not argue that any of these entitlements should be withheld from other relationships. The question of exactly how these entitlements to third-party benefits should be distributed will have to be deferred for a later discussion.

According to the account of marriage that I gave in my earlier work, marriage has three fundamental elements: (i) as I have already noted, it is a *legal relationship*; (ii) it has a generally understood *social meaning*—that is, there is a body of common knowledge and general expectations about marriage that is shared among practically all members of society;[8] and (iii) spouses have *legal powers and obligations* towards each other, where these legal powers and obligations broadly reflect this social meaning.

The way in which these mutual legal powers and obligations "reflect" the social meaning of marriage is simply that these powers and obligations empower and oblige spouses to treat each other in some of the ways in which, according to this social meaning, it is generally *expected* that spouses will typically treat each other. Thus, since it is part of the social meaning of marriage that spouses are expected typically to cooperate in coping with the material necessities of life, many of the legal powers and obligations of marriage concern *property*. For example, in so-called "community property" jurisdictions (like California), property acquired during the marriage is presumed to belong jointly to both spouses; and spouses owe each other a fiduciary duty of care, good faith, and full disclosure in the management of this community property. In virtually all jurisdictions, spouses are obliged to agree to an equitable division of property in the event of divorce; and in the absence of a will, a spouse will inherit all of the other spouse's property on their death. Similarly, since it is part of the social meaning of marriage that spouses are expected typically to know each other well and to care for each other, if you are married, you will normally have priority in being recognized as having legal authority to make decisions on behalf on your spouse if your spouse is incapacitated.

In involving these three fundamental elements, marriage is broadly similar to the legal relationship of *parenthood*, which is also (i) a *legal relationship* that has (ii) a *generally understood social meaning*, and (iii) gives the parent certain *legal obligations* towards the child, as well as a degree of *legal authority* over the child. Again, the legal rights and obligations of parents reflect this social meaning because these rights and obligations oblige and empower parents to treat their children in some of the ways in which, according to this social meaning, parents are expected to treat their children. The key difference between marriage and parenthood lies in the profoundly different social meanings of the two relationships, and in the profoundly different legal rights and obligations associated with these two relationships, which reflect these different social meanings.

In fact, for the purposes of my present argument, it does not matter exactly what the social meaning of marriage is. All that matters is that marriage has a social meaning, which consists in a body of common knowledge and general expectations about marriage that is shared among virtually all members of society, and which is reflected in the legal powers and obligations that spouses have towards each other.

Admittedly, in my earlier work, which focused on defending same-sex marriage, I argued for the following two points about marriage's social meaning. First, even though it was—until quite recently—part of the social meaning of marriage that marriage was the union of one man and one woman (back in 1990, if anyone said "Chris is married," it would immediately be inferred that Chris was married to someone of the opposite sex), this exclusion of same-sex couples was never a *fundamental* aspect of marriage's social meaning (in the sense of being an aspect of marriage's social meaning that could not be changed without radically transforming the institution of marriage). The reason for this is that (as I shall explain below) the most important effects that the social meaning of marriage has on the lives of opposite-sex married couples do not in any way depend on this exclusion of same-sex couples. Secondly, if same-sex couples were allowed to marry, all of the important aspects of the social meaning of marriage could remain in place, as features of an institution that both same-sex couples and opposite-sex couples could have access to.

To make these two points plausible, my earlier work included some speculations about the precise *content* of the social meaning of marriage. This may have been a tactical mistake, since it has led to my argument's being misinterpreted. But at all events, in my earlier work, I speculated that the social meaning of marriage most centrally involves a body of generally shared expectations about what is *typical* of *most* (though not all) marriages. Specifically, I suggested, it is generally expected that typically, most marriages have the following three features: (a) *sexual intimacy* between the spouses, at least at some point in the history of their relationship; (b) *economic and domestic cooperation*—the spouses work together in coping with the necessities of life; and (c) a *mutual commitment* to sustaining the relationship, at least at the beginning of the marriage. By contrast, I suggested, it is not plausible that the content of this social meaning includes any specific conjugal ideal—or any specific conception of the kind of value that married life can have—since there seems not to be any such specific ideal that is generally shared throughout society today.

These speculations still seem plausible to me, although it must be conceded that it is an empirical sociological issue what exactly the social meaning of marriage is. At all events, even if my speculations are along the right lines, it is clear that the most that is generally expected within our society is that *most* marriages will *typically* have these three features. Everyone knows that some marriages involve much less in the way of economic and domestic cooperation than others (some married couples live apart and do not have shared finances); everyone knows that in a great many marriages, the mutual commitment to sustaining the relationship disappears as the couple separates or gets divorced; it is presumably widely assumed that some marriages involve no sexual intimacy between the spouses at any time. So these three features are unquestionably not in any sense "criteria" that marriages have to meet to count as marriages.[9]

Nonetheless, it seems plausible to me that it is generally expected that at least typically, most marriages have these three features.

The fact that marriage has this generally understood social meaning allows married couples to use marriage as a signal with a distinctive communicative power. In effect, the couple can say "We're married," confident that their audience—whoever their audience may be—will interpret their utterance in the light of this social meaning. The couple might have all sorts of reasons for having this communicative purpose (they might even be seeking to *deceive* their audience about certain facts), but one common reason for having this communicative purpose is that the couple wishes their audience to come to expect that the couple's relationship conforms to a greater or lesser extent to what is typical of married couples. There are many reasons why a couple might wish their audience to come to have this expectation about their relationship. But perhaps one of the reasons that move many couples particularly powerfully is that it helps to deepen the couple's mutual *commitment* to their relationship if they can so easily and effectively make it known to other members of their society that they have a mutual commitment of this kind.

If marriage lacked this sort of generally understood social meaning, then the couple could not be so confident that they could achieve such communicative purposes by informing others that they were married. Suppose that I told you, "James and I are each other's *blibble*." Even if there is a subculture in which being someone's *blibble* is understood as having a certain significance, if you are not a member of that subculture, I could not be confident that you would understand the significance of what I had said; and even if there is an obscure branch of the law in which being someone's *blibble* confers certain definite obligations and benefits, if you are not a lawyer specializing in that branch of the law, I could not be confident that you would understand the legal significance of what I had said either. So the fact that marriage has a stable and generally understood social meaning allows for marriage to play an effective communicative role in this way.

This reveals that the law plays two crucial roles in the institution of marriage. First, as we have seen, marriage gives spouses a package of legal powers and obligations towards each other. Many of these powers and obligations could also be acquired by making contracts, wills, trusts, power-of-attorney authorizations, and the like. But the law does more than just to enforce these mutual obligations (as it also does with ordinary contracts). It specifies a certain standardized package of powers and obligations, which it attaches to a special legal relationship that has a generally understood social meaning. As I have explained, this standardized package of powers and obligations reflects the social meaning of marriage; and where necessary, they are enforced. This reinforces society's expectations that, at least typically, the relationships of most married couples will have the features that are generally expected of typical marriages. In consequence, marriage law in effect stabilizes and reinforces this social meaning. The result is that this social meaning of marriage is understood throughout the whole of society. The social meaning of marriage is not just understood by members of a particular religious community or subculture. It is understood by practically everyone, regardless of the particular religious tradition or subculture that they adhere to; indeed, in our society, even quite young children have a basic understanding of the social meaning of marriage. In this way, the law protects marriage against the risk of its ceasing to have such a generally understood social meaning.

If marriage were not underpinned by the law in this way, but only by social custom, it could happen, at least in highly pluralistic societies like ours, that marriage would cease to have a generally understood social meaning of this kind. Different religious organizations and different communities might try to reinterpret marriage in different ways. For example, some communities might allow polygamy. Some communities might allow "temporary marriages" that were intended from the very beginning to last for just a single twenty-four-hour period. Some might allow "ghost marriages," in which a living person marries someone who has died. Some might allow people to marry their dogs or their cars. Some might allow an institution of *unilateral* and *asymmetric* marriage, which would allow me unilaterally to marry Ryan Gosling—even though unless Ryan Gosling reciprocates by marrying me in return, then while I will be married to Ryan Gosling, Ryan Gosling will not be married to me. (Presumably, to make this institution of asymmetric marriage consistent with the liberal principle of autonomy, it would have to be the case that Ryan Gosling does not acquire any obligations towards me just because I am asymmetrically married to him.) Finally, some communities might even allow *reflexive* marriages, in which a person would be allowed to marry himself.

If it became widely known that different communities were allowing marriages of these kinds, marriage could cease to have a generally understood social meaning. If you told someone, "I'm married," or appeared in public visibly wearing a wedding ring, it might be harder for other members of the community to interpret what if anything you were aiming to communicate. (Are you married to someone else, or just to yourself? To a person or a car? Is the person whom you're married to alive, and are they also married to you in return? The questions could be endless.) By underpinning marriage in the way in which it does, the law insulates marriage against the risk of its ceasing to have a generally understood social meaning in this way.

In general, marriage has a communicative function of the sort that I have been describing only because it is *familiar* institution—an institution that we have all grown up hearing about. Presumably, marriage can only become familiar in this way if the culture of the society has traditions surrounding marriage. Although it is crucial to marriage that it is a legal institution, it is also crucial that it is not just a legal institution, but also a social practice rooted in the society's culture.

It seems plausible that the main way in which the social meaning of marriage is important is precisely that it gives marriage this communicative power. If that is right, then we can see why the exclusion of same-sex couples was never a *fundamental* aspect of the social meaning of marriage. The reason for this is simply that it is already a public fact about virtually every person in our society whether that person is a man or a woman. So, opposite-sex couples did not need to get married to communicate the fact that they were a couple consisting of a man and a woman; that was already a publicly known fact about those two people.[10] Opening up marriage to same-sex couples does not fundamentally change the communicative power that marriage gives to opposite-sex couples. It is in this way that I propose to defend the two points that I relied on in my argument for same-sex marriage: first, the point that the exclusion of same-sex couples was never a fundamental part of marriage's social meaning; and secondly, the point that by allowing same-sex couples to marry, same-sex couples could have access to an institution that has fundamentally the same social meaning as marriage currently has.

So far, however, I have only explained what marriage is and what it does. I have not explained what *justifies* the institution of marriage. I shall turn to this question in the following section.

3. The Justification of Marriage

Why is civil marriage justified? It seems clear to me that marriage is not *required* by justice: in principle, a society could be perfectly just even if it had never had the institution of marriage. But not every way of justifying a social institution need involve showing that the institution is required by justice. In the tradition of jurisprudence that built up around the Fourteenth

Amendment of the American Constitution, "justifying" a law or public policy typically involves showing only that it is "rationally related" to some "legitimate government objective".[11] What is it for a government objective to count as "legitimate?" In some sense, it seems to me, a government objective is legitimate if it is in some uncontroversial way good for society as a whole. As Rousseau would put it, even if laws and social institutions are not necessary for justice, they can be justified by appeal to the "common good" or the "common interest."[12] As I shall argue in this section, it seems plausible that marriage is justified because in this way it promotes the common good.

Presumably, however, nothing that is *inconsistent* with justice could be justified, even if it did promote the common good. So to argue that marriage is justified because promotes the common good, I must also argue that even though marriage is not *required* by justice, it is nonetheless *consistent* with justice.

A justification of marriage could, as it seems to me, take two forms. First, it could be a *metaphysical* justification—a justification of the sort that might be developed by a theorist, like a philosopher or a theologian—that is, a justification that explains *why* marriage promotes the common good, on the basis of a deep theory about the ultimate nature of the common good. I believe that there is a true metaphysical explanation of this kind, but it will inevitably be intensely controversial what exactly this true explanation is. Secondly, a justification of marriage could be a *political* justification—that is, the sort of justification that is offered by people engaged in ordinary political debate, such as political campaigners and activists, legislators, and legal officials. This justification would not seek to give the ultimate *explanation* of *why* marriage promotes the common good; it would simply seek to persuade us that marriage *does* promote the common good.

It is a fascinating question what the correct *metaphysical* justification of marriage is. The account of the nature of marriage that I gave in the previous section suggests that it may be promising to look for a metaphysical justification of marriage in the ideas of Joseph Raz about the importance of "social forms" for valuable life-projects.[13] Perhaps more specifically, given my suggestion that marriage has a social meaning which gives it a distinctive communicative power, this metaphysical justification might invoke the ideas that one of the most ethically important elements of human life is the conversation or dialogue that human beings have with each other, and that one vital role for the law to play is in structuring and facilitating this conversation. However, I shall not focus here on the question of what the correct metaphysical justification of marriage is. I shall simply sketch a *political* justification of marriage instead.

For the purposes of such a political justification of marriage, it is sufficient, it seems to me, to argue for the following three points: (a) it is a central part of many people's *most fundamental goals and aspirations in life* to participate in the institution of marriage, and a legal institution of civil marriage is the best way for these people to satisfy these aspirations; (b) the existence of the institution of marriage does not in itself cause any serious harms; and (c) at least *prima facie*, marriage is consistent with justice (there is no obvious reason to think that the existence of marriage violates anyone's rights or the like). For the purposes of the political justification of marriage that I am sketching here, I shall assume here that an institution that has these three properties promotes the common good of society as a whole, and can in that way be justified.

Does marriage have the first property (a)? It seems undeniable that a great many people in our society aspire to participate in the institution of marriage, and that this aspiration is a central part of their most fundamental goals and aspirations in life. Moreover, the account of the nature of marriage that I gave in the previous section clarifies the precise content of these life-aspirations. The content of these life-aspirations to have a legal relationship with another person that involves mutual legal powers and obligations, and a generally understood social meaning, of the kind that I have described. It is reasonable for people who have this aspiration to wish for the social meaning of this legal relationship to be underpinned and stabilized by the law in the way that I have explained. Thus, the best way for the state to enable these people to satisfy these life-aspirations is by maintaining the legal institution of civil marriage. So we may assume that marriage does indeed have this first property (a).

What of the second property (b)? Does the existence of marriage cause any serious harms? We might wonder here about the widespread stigmatization of unmarried people as sad pathetic losers. This is a point that is stressed particularly by Chambers, who goes so far as to say that the existence of the institution of marriage perpetrates "symbolic violence" on young women, by making them think that their lives will be failures unless they get married.[14] (Chambers takes the paradoxical term "symbolic violence" from the work of Pierre Bourdieu.)

To assess this objection, we need to be clear about what exactly this "stigmatization" consists in. One possibility is that this stigmatization merely involves the *belief* that some members of society have, that single people are sad pathetic losers. In this case, it is not clear that the liberal state should try to engage in propaganda to eradicate this belief. According to the principle of political liberalism, the state should not take sides on disputed questions about what makes for a good life; and according to the liberal principle of autonomy, the state should leave it up to individuals to make up their own minds about such questions autonomously, without pressurizing them to adopt any particular view. In general, within a liberal framework, the state should stay neutral on the question of whether or not married life is preferable to single life. Thus, the state should not actively *promote* marriage: it should not produce propaganda to encourage people to get married, or to persuade people that married life is preferable to unmarried life. The most that the state may permissibly do is simply to make marriage available to those who wish to participate in it.

Alternatively, another possibility is that this stigmatization involves unjustly *discriminating* against single people, or in some other way infringing on their human or civil rights. In that case, the state should certainly aim to protect single people against such injustices. It is not clear, however, that the disestablishment of civil marriage is necessary or even particularly effective for protecting single people in this way. Even without civil marriage, some people will live together as couples, while others will be single, and the single people could still be stigmatized or discriminated against. The most effective way to protect single people would be to outlaw discrimination on the basis of marital status (as many American states—though not the US federal government—already do).

Does marriage harm other non-marital relationships between individuals? It seems plausible that on balance, marriage need not be particularly harmful to what many would regard as the most important of all human relationships—the parent-child relationship. Perhaps marriage harms non-marital caring relationships between adults? But again it is not clear that the existence of the institution of marriage itself is to blame for any harm to such adult caring relationships. Marriage could still exist even if the entitlements to third-party benefits (which we discussed at the beginning of the previous section) were detached from marriage and made available to any demonstrable caring relationship.

We might wonder about "polyamorous" relationships—that is, amorous or sexual relationships involving three or more people. Under our current institutions, every marriage involves exactly two people, neither more nor less; our current institutions do not permit "group marriages" involving more than two people. Moreover, it seems plausible that the institution of marriage could not be reformed to allow such group marriages without profoundly changing its social meaning. So, if the state refuses to allow such group marriages, does the institution of marriage somehow harm the people who are involved in such polyamorous relationships?

In the next section, I shall turn to the question of whether the arguments that I am sketching in this section provide adequate justification for an institution of monogamous marriage that is restricted to couples, and so not available to any group of people that is larger (or smaller) than two. The question in this section is simply whether the existence of marriage actively harms such polyamorous relationships.

In fact, there is, in some quarters, considerable hostility against poly-amorous relationships—and this hostility has sometimes influenced the courts, especially in child custody decisions.[15] But it is not clear whether the institution of marriage itself is to blame for this hostility. Marriage could still exist, in more or less its current form, even if all legal disadvantages on polyamorous relationships were removed. Even if they cannot enter into group marriages, the individuals involved in such polyamorous relationships could still be free to live together, to engage in whatever forms of consensual sexual intercourse they wish, to own property together, and to make wills and contracts with each other, and so on. As I have suggested, if they have a demonstrable caring relationship, they should also be entitled to all the third-party benefits that are currently attached to marriage. So, even though polyamorists are indeed disadvantaged in some ways that are unjust, it is not clear that they are harmed by the institution of marriage itself.

What about the third property (c)? Does marriage violate anyone's rights? Historically, marriage has unquestionably violated people's rights. In many jurisdictions, marriage still unjustly discriminates against same-sex couples by arbitrarily excluding them from the right to marry; but as I have argued, one perfectly good way of rectifying this injustice is simply to allow same-sex couples to marry.

More seriously, marriage historically violated the rights of women: it subjected wives to the power and authority of their husbands (while encouraging the marginalization of unmarried women as low-status "spinsters" or "old maids"). It was a highly significant change in the law and social meaning of marriage when it changed from being a radically hierarchical institution, in which the wife was subordinated to her husband's authority, to being, at least in theory, a partnership of equals. This change was clearly required if marriage was ever to become compatible with justice. In general, marriage can avoid violating the rights of women only if it is combined with aggressive efforts to promote gender equality, and with an explicit repudiation of marriage's egregiously sexist past. Still, it seems possible to combine marriage with an anti-sexist regime of this kind. It is presumably for this reason that marriage itself remains strikingly popular among women—even among women who have an unquestionable commitment to combating all forms of sex discrimination and other violations of the rights of women.

What about polygamists, who wish to have more than one marriage at the same time? Why is it not a form of arbitrary and unjust discrimination for marriage to exclude married people from having more than one marriage simultaneously? A number of same-sex marriage advocates—most notably, Calhoun (2005)—have argued that the state's refusal to allow polygamists to have more than one marriage at a time is essentially *unfair*, in the same way as it is unfair for the state to refuse to marry same-sex couples.

However, it seems to me that it is not arbitrary for the state to refuse to allow polygamy in this way. The history of polygamy creates a reasonable ground for concern that the reintroduction of polygamy is unlikely to be able to avoid recreating the serious harms that have historically accompanied polygamy in the past. As J. S. Mill memorably argued, polygamy in his day was even worse for women than the sexist form of monogamous marriage that he campaigned against.[16] Unfortunately, it seems clear that in spite of decades of efforts, sexism and discrimination against women have still not yet been completely eradicated. Given the deeply sexist character of polygamy in the past, it is reasonable to fear that reintroducing polygamy might exacerbate the forms of sexism that persist. Clearly, it is an empirical question whether polygamy could be reformed in a way that provides a safeguard against these dangers, but even in advance of a thorough investigation of these empirical questions, polygamy's troubling history makes it reasonable for us to treat these risks as a reason against allowing polygamy. So the state's refusal to allow polygamous marriages is not as arbitrary as its refusal to allow same-sex marriages.[17]

There is admittedly an important difference between polygamous marriage and group or plural marriage. Even though Abraham was married both to Sarah and to Hagar, Sarah was not married to Hagar. There was not one group marriage involving all three individuals, but two marriages—one between Abraham and Sarah, and another between Abraham and Hagar. Some theorists might conjecture that group marriages could avoid some of the historical problems with polygamous marriages. It is far from clear what evidence there is in support of this conjecture, but at all events, there is another reason for thinking that it is not unjust or arbitrary for the state to refuse to allow any group of people that has more than two members to form a marriage.

As I have argued, the exclusion of same-sex couples was never one of those aspects of the social meaning of marriage that made a big difference to what marriage meant for opposite-sex couples. By contrast, the exclusion of group marriages seems to be a significantly more important part of the social meaning of marriage. (Imagine that whenever one learnt that someone was married, one could not form any clear expectation about the number of people involved in the marriage in question; the communicative power of marriage would clearly be impaired by this change.) So it seems that it would not actually be possible for groups that have more than two members to be included in a legal or institutional relationship that had the core social meeting of marriage as we know it. Thus, the only complaint that the proponents of group marriage can make is that they would prefer if we had a *different* social institution, with a different social meaning, instead of marriage as we know it. In the next section, I shall turn to the question of what if anything could justify our society in choosing which of these two alternative social institutions to have.

As I said above, it seems to me that these three properties of marriage (a), (b), and (c), taken together, are enough to give a political justification of the institution of marriage. But some theorists might raise questions about this justification of marriage. For example, Brake has objected to my justification, suggesting that the desire to marry may not be a desire that the state has any reason to help citizens to satisfy.[18] In particular, she suggests, the desire to participate in a social institution that has the core social meaning of marriage is an *objectionable* preference (and in this respect, presumably, similar to a racist desire to maintain the supremacy of a certain ethnic group or the like). Her reason for taking such a dim view of this extremely common desire is that it involves desiring that marriage should maintain its core social meaning, and so in effect involves desiring that other relationships—such as polyamorous relationships or the like—should *not* be legally recognized as marriages. In this way, she suggests, this desire reveals a kind of animus against those other relationships.

However, it is surely not true that most people who seek to marry need be motivated by any such animus towards other non-marital relationships. (Just talk to your married friends: if they are at all like my married friends, you will find that few if any of them are motivated by any such animus.) Married couples may be entirely sympathetic towards polyamorous relationships, and keen to ensure that such polyamorous groups should be entitled to all the same third-party benefits as married couples. The mere fact that such group unions are not recognized as marriages is not enough to make it the case that the wish to marry need involve any animus or hostility towards such relationships.

Prima facie, then, the simple justification that I have given seems to be an adequate political justification of marriage. In the next section, I shall investigate whether this justification is consistent with political liberalism.

4. Is This Justification of Marriage Consistent with Political Liberalism?

As we have seen, Brake argues that the institution of civil marriage, in anything like its current form, is incompatible with political liberalism. A similar claim is defended by Tamara Metz, who argues that having a legal institution of civil marriage is equivalent to establishing a particular religion as the official religion of the state—in effect, in her view, it is establishing a particular ideal of family life as the official ideal of the state.[19]

As I shall argue in this section, once we accept that the best political justification for the institution of marriage in something like its current form is the simple justification that I sketched in the previous section, then it will become clear that this justification of marriage is quite consistent with political liberalism. In order to argue for this, I shall have to make it clearer exactly what this principle of political liberalism amounts to.

The Rawlsian conception of political liberalism, as I understand it, has its roots in Rawls's reflections on how to accommodate Rousseau's insights into the problem of reconciling political authority with individual freedom within the context of a liberal pluralistic society. Political authority inevitably involves the state's bossing people around, telling them what to do and what not to do, and threatening the use of coercive measures to ensure compliance. How can bossing people around in this way be reconciled with the respect that is due to the dignity of free and autonomous individuals? According to Rousseau, this reconciliation is possible only if the exercise of political authority is the expression of the *general will*, the will of the whole citizenry as a united body.[20] But how can such a general will exist in a liberal pluralistic society, where many mutually incompatible religions and comprehensive doctrines are held by different individuals?

The solution that Rawls's political liberalism gives to this problem is to propose that even in a highly pluralistic society, we can make sense of a standpoint of *public reason*. This is a standpoint that can be shared by all reasonable citizens, regardless of the comprehensive religious or philosophical doctrines that they accept. To make this solution fully clear and precise, we would have to say a great deal more about what it is for a citizen to count as "reasonable," and also about what it means for a social institution to be "justified" from a standpoint that all such reasonable citizens can share.

For these reasons, then, the idea of public reason clearly requires much greater clarification and investigation than I can give it here. One central issue that we would have to resolve is what exactly determines which principles can be appealed to from the standpoint of public reason. Some philosophers take the approach of attempting to work out what these principles are purely in the *abstract*, simply by considering citizens as free and equal individuals who are committed to living peaceably together, without giving any attention to the actual distribution of ethical views among the population.[21] In my own view, this abstract interpretation of the idea of public reason is highly problematic; I am attracted to a much more *empirical* interpretation of the idea of public reason, according to which the actual distribution of ethical views among the population is part of what determines which principles can be appealed to from the standpoint of public reason.

Unfortunately, however, I cannot probe these difficult questions here. I shall just have to rely on a rather rough-and-ready intuitive sense of what can be justified from the standpoint of public reason—although as we shall see, we shall have to confront at least one of these difficult questions eventually.

According to the political justification of marriage that I sketched in the previous section, marriage is not necessary for every just society; marriage is justified simply because, in societies that had a tradition of marriage, maintaining that tradition can promote the common good. According to this justification, maintaining the institution of marriage promotes the common good simply because marriage does not clearly violate any rights or cause any serious harms, and a lot of people make it a central part of their fundamental life-aspirations to participate in the institution.

On the face of it, this political justification does not appeal to any controversial comprehensive doctrine. It is clear for example that this justification does not rely on any controversial "conjugal" ideal—such as the idea that "finding true love" with one other person is the uniquely best or happiest way of life. This justification rests only on the assumption that helping members of the community to achieve such central aspects of their fundamental life-aspirations promotes the common good.

In this way, it seems to me, marriage can be justified without appealing to any controversial view about what is good or valuable in life. Moreover, marriage also need not actively promote any such view either. The state need not seek to propagate the view that marriage is more valuable or honorable than other non-marital relationships. Indeed, as I have argued, the state should not actively promote marriage; marriage should simply be made available for those who wish to participate in it.

Could any reasonable citizen simply reject the relevance of the fact that many members of the population make it a central part of their basic life-aspirations to participate in marriage? Could a reasonable citizen insist that this fact does nothing whatever to support the claim that marriage promotes the common good? This question is hard to answer conclusively without developing a detailed interpretation of the principle of political liberalism, and an interpretation of the notion of a "reasonable citizen." But intuitively, it does not sound reasonable to me for participants in political debate simply to brush aside the central components of their fellow citizens' fundamental life-aspirations, at least so long as those life-aspirations do not involve imposing any serious harms on anyone else.

Of course, people's goals and aspirations in life are, as always, molded by their society's particular history and traditions. This is always the case. I aspire to be a good philosopher and scholar, but it is only in societies that have traditions of such philosophical scholarship that this aspiration could arise.

Some proponents of political liberalism—and perhaps especially the more "abstract" versions that I mentioned above—might think that in justifying social institutions and policies from the standpoint of public reason, we should disregard all facts that depend for their explanation on the particular cultural traditions and history of the society in question, as if the point of such justifications were to remake society anew, from the ground up, like revolutionaries who are setting out to build a new Utopia. This is certainly not how most participants in political debate think of what they are concerned with; they take themselves to be concerned with practical questions that arise within the context of a particular set of social and political traditions. The proponents of this sort of liberalism seem to approach political deliberations from the perspective of a sort of "revolutionary vanguard." This "vanguardist" interpretation of the liberal principle may ground an objection to justifications that rest on historically contingent life-aspirations of this sort. But the attractions of this vanguardist version of liberalism are dubious, to say the least.

As I said, marriage is not a requirement of justice; a society could be perfectly just even if it had never had the institution of marriage at all. My justification of marriage implies only that, given that marriage has come to inform the central life-aspirations of many citizens, it is a perfectly defensible for us to maintain the institution of marriage, so long as we also ensure that it does not cause serious harms or violate any requirements of justice.

The final objection that I wish to consider focuses on the point that a significant number of people would prefer it if there were a somewhat *different* institution, instead of an institution that has the core social meaning of marriage as we know it today. In general, a great many people are not completely happy with the social meaning of marriage as it currently exists (for example, some traditionalist Christians may think that it would be better if marriages were generally understood to be *indissoluble*). Again, let us imagine the complaint that some polyamorists might raise against my justification of marriage. These polyamorists, let us suppose, would prefer an institution that is in some ways like marriage, but in some other crucial ways quite different—since they would prefer an institution that is open to polyamorous groups with more than two members. Not everyone can have the scheme of social institutions that they would most prefer. If I am right that allowing group marriages would profoundly change the social meaning of marriage, then we cannot have an institution that has *both* the social meaning that marriage currently has *and* the social meaning that these polyamorists would prefer. So how are we to choose?

One thing that no sensible version of liberalism can say is that every citizen can reasonably veto any law or social policy whenever he or she would prefer an alternative. It can often happen that the whole society unanimously agrees that they need to have a policy of kind K, but everyone has some objection to every particular policy of kind K. For example, there could be unanimous agreement that a road needs to be built between two towns, but for every possible route that the road might take, someone objects to the road's being built along that route. The only answer seems to be that in such cases we need to reach a collective decision by means of a generally agreed democratic procedure. Presumably, in a case where there are just two policies that we have to choose between, the democratic way to make the decision will involve some kind of majoritarian procedure. Indeed, it seems that no reasonable citizen could reject resorting to a majoritarian procedure in cases of this sort: to insist on having a veto power in such cases whenever the majority's preferences differ from one's own seems to me clearly unreasonable.

So it is at this point that it becomes relevant that marriage remains a highly popular institution, vastly more popular than any of the alternatives that marriage's radical critics have proposed. (If we had a referendum tomorrow about whether to abolish marriage, we could be confident of what the outcome would be.) Of course, this might change. If polyamory becomes much more common, people may lose interest in monogamous marriage. In that case, it might make sense to replace marriage with something else. But until then, if marriage continues to enjoy such widespread support, there seems nothing wrong in persisting with it. Since such an appeal to democratic procedures seems unavoidable in any plausible version of political liberalism, this justification of marriage seems to me to be quite consistent with political liberalism.

5. Conclusion

An astute reader will have noticed that my justification of marriage implicitly endorses certain *communitarian* ideas—specifically, ideas about how established institutions which become familiar, through the existence of contingent social and cultural traditions, can enable us to achieve certain goods which are not otherwise available. (Indeed, it is hard to think of a clearer illustration of this basic communitarian insight than the institution of marriage.) At least to a modest degree, this communitarian insight is a *conservative* idea, since it implies that there are often reasons to maintain established institutions, once they have become familiar in this way—even if those institutions only came into existence for contingent historical reasons, not because they were strictly necessary for the sake of justice.

Many philosophers think that such communitarian and conservative ideas are essentially inimical to the liberal tradition in political philosophy. I disagree with this: it seems to me that these communitarian insights are entirely compatible with certain central liberal ideas. In my view, it is possible, not only to reconcile a kind of communitarianism with the liberal principle of autonomy, but also to reconcile a kind of communitarianism with the more Rawlsian kind of political liberalism, which demands that the state should be in a way neutral between contested conceptions of the good.

At the same time, this happy reconciliation of communitarianism and liberalism does require rejecting the view that the goal of political philosophy is to produce what I have called "vanguardist" justifications of social institutions. According to this vanguardist approach, political philosophy should aim to justify a particular scheme of social institutions, but without paying any attention to the particular traditions and practices of any particular society; instead, political philosophy should develop a blueprint for the ideal society purely by considering human social life in the abstract. In my view, a different conception of political philosophy is preferable.[22] The role of political philosophy in my view is to articulate principles that we can use to evaluate actually existing social arrangements, in all their contingent messy detail, and to compare these actual arrangements with the realistically available alternatives, in order to see which are more just, and which would better promote the common good. When we approach the questions in this way, we will see that a familiar institution like marriage can be justified in a way that is quite compatible with all plausible forms of liberalism.

Notes

This essay started out as a series of comments delivered at a session on marriage at the 2013 meeting of the Western Political Science Association in Hollywood, and at a book symposium on Elizabeth Brake's *Minimizing Marriage: Marriage, Morality, and the Law* (New York: Oxford University Press, 2012) at the 2014 Pacific Division Meeting of the American Philosophical Association in San Diego. More recently, in February 2015, it was presented at the Legal Theory workshop at the Law School of UCLA. I am grateful to the members of all those audiences for very helpful comments.

1. See Brake, *Minimizing Marriage*; Cheshire Calhoun, "Who's Afraid of Polygamous Marriage? Lessons for Same-Sex Marriage Advocacy from the History of Polygamy," *San Diego Law Review* 42 (2005): 1023–1042; Clare Chambers, "The Marriage-Free State," *Proceedings of the Aristotelian Society* 113:2 (2013): 123–143; and Tamara Metz, *Untying the Knot: Marriage, the State, and the Case for Their Divorce* (Princeton, NJ: Princeton University Press, 2010).

2. See Brake, *Minimizing Marriage*, 167.

3. See Rawls, *Political Liberalism* (New York: Columbia University Press, 1993), and "The Idea of Public Reason Revisited," *University of Chicago Law Review* 64:3 (1997): 765–807.

4. See Brake, *Minimizing Marriage*, 170.

5. For an early statement of this point, see Joshua Cohen, "Deliberation and Democratic Legitimacy," in Alan Hamlin and Philip Pettit, eds., *The Good Polity: Normative Analysis of the State* (Oxford: Blackwell, 1989), 17–34, at 27.

6. See my essay "The Fundamental Argument for Same-Sex Marriage," *Journal of Political Philosophy* 7 (1999): 225–242.

7. See Brake, *Minimizing Marriage*, 170.

8. One might wonder whether this social meaning should be understood as involving not just *expectations* and *common knowledge*, but also *norms*—in something like the sense that has been defined by Philip Pettit, "Virtus Normativa: Rational

Choice Perspectives," *Ethics* 100:4 (1990): 725–755. However, I am not sure that it is necessary to include norms as part of the social meaning of marriage in this way. The main social norms surrounding marriage seem to be derivative from more general social norms. For example, we generally disapprove of those who break promises and cheat, and this seems to underlie our social norms against marital infidelity; and I speculate that a similar account could be given of the other social norms surrounding marriage. So it seems more plausible to me to suppose that the fundamental elements of the social meaning of marriage consist simply of expectations and common knowledge as I have suggested.

9. So it was a serious misinterpretation of my argument for Brake's *Minimizing Marriage*, 142, to represent me as having described these three features as "criteria."

10. My best statement of this point was probably in my blog post on the *New York Times* website, "The Meaning of Same-Sex Marriage," *The New York Times*, Opinionator, May 24, 2012 <http://opinionator.blogs.nytimes.com/2012/05/24/marriage-meaning-and-equality/>.

11. For a helpful discussion of the Fourteenth Amendment, see Ronald Dworkin, "Sex, Death, and the Courts," *New York Review of Books*, 43, no. 13 (August 8, 1996).

12. See Rousseau, *The Social Contract*, Book II, chap. 1, ¶1. Contemporary liberal political theory has an almost obsessive focus on *rights* and *justice*—see for example Jonathan Quong, *Liberalism without Perfection* (Oxford: Clarendon Press, 2011), 1. But it does not seem plausible to me that everything that the legal institutions of a society may permissibly do must promote justice, strictly speaking. Economic prosperity and public health are surely legitimate government objectives, but it is not clear that citizens have a *right* to the most prosperous possible society, or to the healthiest possible environment; it seems more plausible to me that economic prosperity and public health are legitimate government objectives because they promote the common good.

13. See Raz, *The Morality of Freedom* (Oxford: Clarendon Press, 1988), 307–313.

14. See Chambers, "The Marriage-Free State," 126.

15. I owe this point to the response that Elizabeth Brake made to my comments on her book at the 2014 Pacific Division Meeting of the American Philosophical Association.

16. See Mill, *On Liberty*, chap. 4, ¶21: "far from being in any way countenanced by the principle of liberty, [polygamy] is a direct infraction of that principle, being a mere riveting of the chains of one-half of the community, and an emancipation of the other from reciprocity of obligation towards them."

17. For some more pertinent comments on polygamy, see Samuel Rickless, "Same-Sex Marriage and Polygamy: A Response to Calhoun," *San Diego Law Review* 42 (2005): 1043–1048; for a full-length discussion, see John Witte, Jr., *The Western Case for Monogamy over Polygamy* (Cambridge, UK: Cambridge University Press, 2015).

18. See Brake, *Minimizing Marriage*, 173.

19. See Metz, *Untying the Knot: Marriage, the State, and the Case for Their Divorce*.

20. See Rousseau, *The Social Contract*, Book I, chap. 6, ¶9.

21. For an example of a philosopher who seems to take this approach, see Quong, *Liberalism without Perfection*, 261.

22. This point is connected with my criticisms of "ideal theory"; see my blog post "Against Ideal Theory," *PEA Soup*, May 3, 2014 <http://peasoup.typepad.com/pea-soup/2014/05/against-ideal-theory.html>.

3 | The Limitations of Contract

REGULATING PERSONAL RELATIONSHIPS
IN A MARRIAGE-FREE STATE

CLARE CHAMBERS

THERE ARE GOOD REASONS TO end the state recognition of marriage. From a feminist and egalitarian perspective the abolition of state-recognized marriage would be a decisive break from the patriarchal and discriminatory associations of the institution. From a comprehensive liberal perspective state-recognized marriage is problematically restrictive, since it involves the state defining the terms of personal relationships and holding people to those terms. From a political liberal perspective state-recognized marriage violates state neutrality, since when the state recognizes marriage it endorses a particular and deeply controversial conception of the good. As I have argued elsewhere, then, justice would be best served by the abolition of state-recognized marriage and the creation of what I call a marriage-free state.[1]

But even if marriage is abolished as a legal category, the question of how to regulate personal relationships remains. Personal relationships still have to be regulated so as to protect vulnerable parties, including but not only children; so as to regulate disputes over such matters as joint property; and so as to appropriately direct state benefits and taxes. These benefits might include immigration rights, next-of-kinship status, inheritance tax relief, and so on. One issue that arises is precisely which benefits and responsibilities are legitimate for the state to impose on people in particular sorts of relationships. For example, an advocate of open borders will not support differential immigration rights and some egalitarians will not support any inheritance tax relief. These questions are important but will not be addressed here. Instead, I consider what legal form the regulation of personal relationships should take.

Many theorists defend relationship contracts. Some argue that enforceable relationship contracts should be available alongside existing or reformed state-recognized marriage, and available to either married or unmarried couples. So married couples might wish to draw up a prenuptial contract to set out the financial arrangements in case of divorce, or unmarried couples might wish to draw up a cohabitation contract. Other theorists argue that relationship contracts are the best sort of legal regulation to *replace* marriage.[2] It is this latter question that concerns me in this essay, though many of my arguments are also relevant to the former question. I argue that relationship contracts are much more problematic than they first appear, so that it is not appropriate to use them as the regulatory framework to replace state-recognized marriage. Instead, the marriage-free state should implement a series of default directives setting out the rights and duties of parties in various forms of relationship. Some contractual deviation from these directives may be permitted, but to be permissible a deviation must not undermine the justice that the default directives are designed to secure.

By "contract" I mean that the legal duties and benefits that apply between partners are those that they have freely and formally agreed to, the content of which suits their precise circumstances and preferences.[3] The law does not specify what the content of the contract must be, so individuals have a great deal of freedom to develop a wide range of contractual agreements. The law does regulate contracts, by stipulating general requirements to which all contracts must adhere (for example, that contracting parties must be fully informed and freely consenting, and that certain egregious terms for contracts will not be allowed, such as contracts for slavery). The law also stipulates and provides the method by which contracts can be enforced. But these are general and limited restrictions, so that contract allows for significant diversity and freedom. For the purposes of this essay, the alternative to contract is what I call directive.

By "directive" I mean that the state dictates responsibilities and rights, in advance and for all relevant people. The usual contrast is between contract and status. But "status" implies precisely what I argue against: a category of approbation which one can apply to a person or relationship which sets them above and apart from those who lack that approbation. My meaning is closer to what lawyers refer to as "public ordering."[4]

The relationship between directive and choice is not straightforward. In some cases the directive approach will mean that regulations apply to people without their having any choice at all in the matter, if directive regulations apply between people who have no choice about their relationship to one another, such as siblings. However, directive regulation could also be used to stipulate duties in relationships that are entered into through choice, such as sexual partnerships. The existing legal regulation of marriage in the UK and the US is regulated by directive in this sense. When two people marry, their relationship is governed by the laws of marriage of their state. The marrying couple has no choice about which of those laws to follow, particularly if prenuptial contracts are not enforced. Although the spouses do consent to marry, they need not consent to the various regulations that apply to them on marriage. If the laws of marriage change, so do their responsibilities.

The Appeal of Contract

On this characterization of directive, contract seems straightforwardly more appealing. A contract approach to personal relationships seems to answer all the concerns about traditional marriage raised by liberals, and to counter many of the concerns of feminists as well. For liberals, contracts allow an extremely wide sphere of personal freedom, as individuals may draw up contracts in any form they wish (subject only to general limitations on contracts, which can themselves be drawn up along liberal lines). Contracts avoid violating state neutrality since the state does not stipulate what forms of contracts may be drawn up: it does not say who may contract, or stipulate what sort of relationship the contracting parties must have. Feminist concerns about the position of women may be addressed by the fact that, simply by being different, relationship contracts break from the traditional patriarchal symbolism of marriage. Contracts also allow women to negotiate their position in the relationship in advance, and this may help them to secure adequate recompense and financial independence if they take on domestic and caring labor rather than labor paid outside the home. And contracts meet concerns about discrimination against same-sex couples, since they too can make contractual arrangements. Finally, contracts have the practical benefit of reducing the need for additional legislation. Courts are already experienced in enforcing contracts, and while some new legislation may be needed to stipulate what the limits of legal contracts are (particularly in cases concerning children) there is no need to draw up exhaustive and comprehensive legal definitions of marriage.

Individual choice is inherent in the contract model, meaning that both holistic and piecemeal contracts would be available to contracting partners. *Holistic* regulation of relationships involves creating a status, analogous to marriage, which confers upon people a package of legal rights and responsibilities. So contracts could be made that confer such a package on the contracting parties: detailing the various arrangements that would govern their lives together, possibly with interlinked conditions. For example, partners could choose to contract such that any breach of sexual fidelity incurs an increase in housework. Such contracts could institute wide-ranging partnerships similar to marriage, detailing obligations on everything from sexual fidelity to property to domicile. Unlike marriage, however, each relationship contract could be unique to the partners.

Piecemeal regulation, in contrast, rejects both *bundling* and *special status*: rights and duties are kept separate from one another, and no special status is conferred by the state.[5] Piecemeal contracts would see individuals making a series of separate contracts about each area of their lives. Each contract could be with a different person, so that an individual could draw up a contract with her mother to govern their shared property, another with her co-parent to govern their child care responsibilities, and another with her brother concerning her wishes if he were to have to act as her next of kin. Alternatively, there could be multiple contracts within one partnership. A partnership with multiple piecemeal contracts would keep regulation of each area separate, so that one partner's failure to comply with the contract concerning child care, for example, would have no bearing on their contract concerning property ownership.

Contracts thus appear to bring a variety of desiderata: freedom, equality, neutrality, and diversity.[6] They allow for significant individual freedom: individuals have the freedom to contract in a holistic or a piecemeal fashion, the freedom to contract with whomever they please, and the freedom to design personalized contracts to suit their own priorities. Contracts break with traditional marriage and thus shed its inegalitarian symbolism, and allow partners to design progressive, equitable relationships. Neutrality and diversity are fostered since the state neither lauds one form of relationship above others nor dictates how relationships must be ordered.

As a result several theorists have argued that existing models of marriage should be either supplemented or replaced with private contracts. One notable advocate of relationship contracts, Marjorie Maguire Shultz, writes that private relationship contracting best fulfills the principles "woven into the fabric of today's intimate relationships: diversity, tolerance, privacy, choice, impermanence, individualism."[7] Although her argument is not explicitly founded on liberalism, the values she appeals to can be best understood in a liberal context: she claims, for example, that the "principal strength [of contracts] is precisely the accommodation of diverse relationships."[8] To this end Shultz envisages a variety of possible contracts that partners might agree to, including a "Domestic Services" contract that involves one partner paying the other a salary for housework; an "Open Marriage" contract that permits the partners to have sexual relationships outside the partnership under certain conditions; a "Domicile" contract that instigates rules to govern changes of domicile to further each partner's career; and a "Homosexual Marriage" contract that replicates traditional heterosexual marriage.[9]

Another prominent advocate of private relationship contracts is Lenore Weitzman. Weitzman argues that relationship contracts have many benefits. Weitzman points to *social* and *psychological* benefits: contracts help couples to clarify their expectations, to resolve problems and disagreements before they become insurmountable. Moreover, contracts are useful throughout the duration of the relationship as they provide a standard to refer back to. This guidance and security make it easier for couples to stick to their promises and goals, such as egalitarian goals, without falling into a routine that does not suit their normative commitments. And a contract "provides the parties with the security that stems from predictability."[10] Weitzman also argues that relationship contracts have *societal* benefits: they accommodate diversity, they are a quick method of enacting social change, and they are more likely to serve "the state's goal of supporting stability in marriage and other family relationships."[11] Finally, Weitzman highlights four benefits of contracts *to the couple as couple*. First, a contract allows a couple "to formulate an agreement that conforms to everyday reality" rather than being restricted by the model offered by marriage. Second, a contract "aids couples who wish to establish an egalitarian relationship." Third, a contract "affords couples the freedom and privacy to order their personal relationships as they wish." Fourth, a contract allows those who are unmarried, by choice or by legal prohibition, "to formalize their relationship."[12]

A third major figure in the relationship contract debate is Martha Fineman. Fineman advocates the abolition of marriage as legal category, as do I. Fineman advocates that "the interactions of female and male sexual affiliates" should instead

be governed by the same rules that regulate other interactions in our society—specifically those of contract and property, as well as tort and criminal law ... [T]his proposal is actually not very farfetched. We already encourage antenuptual agreements that are contractual deviations from state-imposed marriage consequences. ... My proposal would merely mandate that such bargaining occur *prior* to the termination of the relationship, ideally before the couple became too "serious."[13]

As will become clear later in the essay, this version of her proposal takes orthodox or classical contract law as the model for relationships, although Fineman does suggest that the assumptions of contract law may need to be rethought. Fineman's proposals retain a strong role for the state, but for her state directives should be centered around the Mother-Child Dyad, a phrase that is meant to capture the vital role of care, as exemplified by motherhood, since dependency is an inevitable and recurring part of everyone's lives. While the caring activities undertaken in the family deserve recompense and support, and vulnerable adults should be protected, Fineman argues that relationships between non-dependent adults should be left to those adults. For Fineman prohibiting relationship contracts treats women as inherently unequal, and so recognition of gender equality requires treating relationships contractually: "abolishing legal marriage and the special rules associated with it would mean that we are taking gender equality seriously. If people want their relationships to have consequences, they should bargain for them."[14]

Relationship contracts have therefore been advocated as promoting both equality and liberty. However, in what follows I argue that the contract model does not straightforwardly promote either value.

Contract and Equality

Relationship contracts appear to enhance equality since everyone is able to make a contract, including same-sex couples and those in non-sexual relationships, and since contracts can structure relationships in an egalitarian way. Consider both in turn.

First, it is an important benefit of contracts that they allow people who are excluded from marriage, or who choose not to marry, to gain legal security for their relationship. Weitzman is right to argue that contracts can be a crucial mechanism for couples to regain control over their own affairs and seek legal and social recognition for an alternative partnership *against the background of marriage as a state-recognized institution*. But in a marriage-free state there is no need for a couple to make a contract in order to escape the implications of an outmoded institution. Contracts are also not needed to secure fair treatment of those who cannot marry (such as same-sex couples): if there is no marriage then no one can be unfairly denied access to it. The model of regulation I set out at the end of this chapter does a better job of securing equality between relationships since it encompasses all relationships, whether contractual or not.[15]

Second, while contracts *allow* couples to regulate their relationships along egalitarian lines that best fit the desires of each member and facilitate diversity, they also allow couples to formulate contracts that conform to a norm, entrench hierarchy, or are not equally desired by both. Thus, many feminists have criticized the contract tradition for its links to patriarchy and its concealment of inequality.[16] The landmark feminist criticism of contract is Carole Pateman's *The Sexual Contract*, which argues that the contract approach as a whole is founded on an unequal "sexual contract" subordinating women to men. On Pateman's account intimate contracts, including marriage, become "universal prostitution,"[17] a claim that made particular sense when rape was not recognized as a crime within marriage. Indeed, the unwillingness to enforce "meretricious" contracts for sexual services still underpins some courts' reluctance to enforce private relationship contracts.

The contract model relies on equality between the contracting partners, but if the parties are unequal then individuals can face pressure to agree to unfair contracts—just as women have always faced considerable pressure to agree to the profound inequality of traditional marriage.[18] Outside traditional marriage partners could face romantic pressure ("If you really loved me you'd choose the Permanent Commitment Contract"), cultural pressure ("A good member of our religion would choose a Male Head of Household Contract"), or manipulative pressure ("If you don't sign this Unequal Property Contract I'll leave you and the children"). Amy Wax argues that women are systematically disadvantaged in marriage bargaining as a result of inequalities in the labor and marriage markets. This systematic disadvantage would be exacerbated by regulating relationships via contract.[19] As David McLellan puts it, "In a society where power is systematically distributed asymmetrically, contract is likely simply to reinforce such an asymmetry."[20] The problem of unjust contracts is exacerbated if those contracts concern third parties, most obviously children. Contracts may not bring about equality and justice then. This is not surprising: since one of the fundamental advantages of contracts is that they maximize diversity and individual liberty, they let in inequality.

In general terms, contracts can violate justice by violating freedom or equality, either (a) by the parties not being free and equal at the moment of contract or (b) by their agreeing to terms that leave them unfree or unequal (or a combination of both). The dominant political liberal response is to argue that inequality should be permitted by the state if individuals have chosen that inequality, where freedom of exit is taken as the proxy for choice.[21] Comprehensive liberals and feminists are rightly skeptical of such arguments, pointing out that there are limitations to "free" choice and that choice should not be used to excuse injustice.[22] It is beyond the scope of this essay to provide an exhaustive account of justice in contracts. It is worth noting here, however, that relationship contracts provide their own special concerns.

The first possible general injustice in contracts is that the contracting parties may not be in an equal position when they enter into the contract. Existing contract law contains provisions to guard against the most egregious instances of contracts founded on inequality but these may not be sufficient for personal relationship contracts. I have already mentioned Wax's argument that women's inequality in both the relationship and labor markets puts them at a disadvantage when bargaining about the terms of their relationship.[23]

The second potential area of injustice, that the contracts themselves might instantiate unequal or excessively freedom-limiting terms, is even more potent in the relationship case. There are a number of reasons why people might be inclined to agree to unjust relationship contracts. Entering into a relationship contract will typically be done at a time of optimism, even a time of heady romance. This romance can cloud people's views: it is hard to think of one's partner as a potential adversary at precisely the time one is about to make a binding contract with them. As Robson and Valentine put it, "the myth of equality may never be more powerful than at the inception of coupledom, the very time at which a relationship contract would be drafted. Thus, from a pragmatic perspective, the contract solution is flawed because it depends on the existence of real, perceived, continuing, and absolute parity."[24]

Even if people are cognitively able to put themselves in a self-interested, pessimistic mindset when drawing up a relationship contract there are social norms against such thinking, as well as strong social and religious norms about good husbandly and wifely behavior. These norms limit individuals' freedom of choice and make unequal contracts more likely than they would be in the business context.

Finally, it can be difficult for contracting partners to envisage how their lives will change and how they will feel after major life events. Several studies show, for example, that even committed egalitarian couples find it very difficult to sustain a non-gendered division of labor after having children, and many people find that their preferences about matters such as work-life balance change profoundly on becoming parents.[25] Traditional contract law requires presentation, spelling out every eventuality in advance, so that all disputes that arise can be referred back to the intentions of the parties at the moment of making the contract. But this process does not occur in intimate relationships in the same way as it might in a business deal, as John Wightman describes:

> Where the parties intend to share their lives, they abstain from presentation not so much because it is not practically feasible (although it isn't), but because it is not part of the relationship that they will individuate "performances" which are then done in return for each other. This difference is reflected in the fact that there may well be inhibitions on attempting to spell out a deal.[26]

Ira Ellman points out that "couples do not in fact think of their relationships in contract terms" and asks, rhetorically, "Do we want courts to think broadly about the rules that yield a fair dissolution of an unmarried couple's relationship or do we want to limit courts to searching the parties' conduct for evidence that at some point in the past they agreed upon terms that should now govern their mutual obligations?"[27] Clearly fairness and contract do not always coincide.

It is fairly well accepted, then, that the contract approach is problematic for egalitarians. Indeed, considerations of equality lead Fineman, a prominent advocate of relationship contracts, to include "ameliorating doctrines" so as to protect "the economically weaker party."[28] Nonetheless, she argues that contracts can be used to govern many aspects of relationships, including sexual aspects.[29] In part this is because Fineman holds the general view that contracts are liberty-promoting. In the remainder of the chapter I argue that even this aspect of relationship contracts must be questioned.

Contract and Liberty

Contracts are generally thought to uphold liberty since individuals can contract on their own terms. Couples are not limited to the regulatory form of marriage, and legal relationships are not limited to couples. They can structure their relationship in a wide variety of ways and can also choose to keep their relationship non-contractual. Thus contracts appear to foster liberty both by allowing diversity and by freeing couples from the strait-jacket of state-defined marriage. This goal is what Fineman has in mind when she imagines a contract-based regime in which "Women and men would operate outside of the confines of marriage, transacting and inter-acting without the fetters of legalities they did not voluntarily choose."[30]

However, the contract approach to regulating personal relationships does not mean that the state keeps out of relationships altogether. The state plays a vital role in regulating relationships, even if relationship contracts are allowed, for two main reasons. First, default directives are still needed. Second, contracts require state enforcement. In what follows I discuss both aspects of state involvement and show that the necessary role of the state in a contract regime actually undermines the appeal of such a regime.

Default Directives in a Contract Regime

As previously noted, even a marriage-free state requires legal regulation of intimate relationships since such relationships involve matters that cannot be left anarchic. This need for state regulation means that contract cannot be the only mechanism by which intimate relationships are regulated. As well as the problem of what to do if couples sign contracts that are mani-festly unfair or hierarchical, the state also faces the problem of what to do if people do not draw up a contract to regulate some area of their relation-ship in which there are high stakes. For example, a couple might buy a house, have children, or require a next of kin to make decisions without having drawn up a contract to govern those eventualities. In such cases the state must take some position if a dispute or need for action arises which, in the absence of a contract, requires directives.[31] The contract model does not, therefore, mean leaving individuals immune from state interference. It means allowing individuals to deviate in some way from the directives that the state cannot avoid putting in place.

State directives in a contract regime are of two types. First, the state needs default directives for those cases where regulation is needed but no contract has been made. Second, the state needs principles and limits of contract law, setting out what makes a valid contract and the recourse for breach.[32]

Thus the question "should personal relationships be organized according to contract?" is not equivalent to the question "should individuals have the freedom to organize their relationships as they see fit?" even though much of the appeal of a contract approach comes from this idea of personal autonomy in relationships. But as well as providing the general limits of contract already described, the state will have to provide default regulations for use in circumstances where no contract exists but where regulation or intervention is needed: for example, in disputes over child custody, child support, or joint property.

A contract regime is also in need of state directives since contract alone does not impose obligations on third parties. Relationships need support from third parties, be they businesses, employers, or the state itself. For example, a relationship contract on its own does not compel a US health insurance provider to extend coverage to a policyholder's contractual partner, nor does a contract on its own compel the state to grant immigration rights to the contractual partner of a citizen. The state must therefore put directives in place to determine which obligations those outside of a relationship have to those in a relationship.[33]

The same is true of third parties who have *rights* that are affected yet not provided for in a relationship contract. Children are the obvious example. If two parents contract with each other, or a parent contracts with a non-parent, the interests of the child are affected and must be protected. Providing this protection may mean overriding the contractual terms.

To see the role of state directives more clearly, consider the following aspects of personal relationships:

1. Those which need regulation because they involve non-consenting third parties, for example children, employers, or businesses.
2. Those which the state has a legitimate interest in regulating, because they concern matters of justice or because they are matters which need to be determinate in law. For example, property distribution is both a matter of justice and something about which the law must provide a determinate answer in cases of dispute. Next-of-kinship arrangements, to take another example, also require legal determinacy.
3. Those which the state has no interest in regulating, other than as part of the general state function of regulating agreements. For example, the state has no interest in regulating who mows my lawn *unless* I enter into a legally binding agreement attributing this

responsibility to someone, in which case the state has a legitimate interest in regulating my contract simply *qua* contract.

The first and second areas will need to be settled by state directive even if we take a contract approach to personal relationships: the need for regulation is such that there will need to be default rules for those without contracts. The state cannot refuse to rule on a question of who is responsible for looking after a child, or who owns a house in which more than one person has invested, simply because there is no contract in place. Moreover, the areas in which the state needs to provide default rules even under a contract approach are often, by that very logic, the most important areas of personal relationships. So even under a contract approach the state will inevitably make directives about fundamental, and possibly controversial, aspects of partnerships. It cannot be a benefit of contract, then, that it avoids state directives on these areas.[34]

Instead, the advocate of contract needs to show that the state ought to allow deviation from the default directives via the contract mechanism. She also needs to show that the state should allow contracts on aspects of relationships not governed by default laws. By definition, under the directive approach the state can refuse to rule on questions of type 3. If two partners dispute whose turn it is to mow the lawn they do not, under the directive approach, have recourse to a court to settle the dispute. Advocates of contract need to show that courts can legitimately be called upon to regulate such disputes if the two parties have chosen to draw up a relationship contract governing them. This highlights the second way in which contracts involve the state: enforcement.

Contract and Enforcement

The question of whether to allow personal relationships to be regulated by contract is therefore a question about legal enforcement. The case for relationship contracts is a case for allowing individuals to make *legally enforceable* agreements about their relationships, even on matters in which the state would otherwise have no interest. As Shultz asks, framing the question in terms of marriage, "would it be desirable for the state to decline to prescribe marital conduct and values, leaving those matters to private choice, while *at the same time* accepting the role of enforcer and dispute resolver regarding obligations privately chosen?"[35] On a contract approach the state appears to step away from personal relationships, leaving their structure to individuals, but at the same time it embroils itself firmly at the heart of such relationships, gaining *new* powers to intervene, enforce, and punish on any matter at all on which the parties have chosen to contract. There is no correlation, then, between a libertarian minimal state and the immunity of the private sphere.[36]

Both personal choice *and* enforcement are needed for a regime to be described as contractual. If the state enforces rules about personal relationships but allows for no private choice about how relationships are governed then it is clear that state uses a directive model. But a state that allows for great diversity in personal relationships but which refuses to enforce any agreements between partners is also using a directive not a contractual model. Such a state is simply using directives that are either few in number and/or libertarian in character. For example, a state that says "all disputes in personal relationships are to be solved by the private negotiations of the parties involved" is using a directive model, even though it is one that allows for unlimited diversity within relationships. It is a directive regime since it states an inescapable rule for all relationships (that they are entirely privately regulated), and since it refuses to allow state enforcement of private arrangements.

This example emphasizes that there is no direct link between liberty and state inaction, and between liberty and the choice of contract vs. directive. The directive regime of noninterference just envisaged is in no way equivalent to one maximizing individual liberty (at least not equal liberty), since it is compatible with traditional patriarchal views of marriage that allowed husbands to rape and attack their wives without fear of legal penalty. And we can envisage other directive regimes that actively manage personal relationships so as to secure maximum equal liberty for both parties. On the other hand, we can imagine both contracts that maximize individual liberty (by setting out very few restrictions on how the partners may act) and those that curtail it significantly (for example, a contract that imposes a great many restrictions on daily action and allows for enormously punitive punishments if the contract is breached or if one party seeks to dissolve the partnership).[37] So the choice between directive and contract is not a choice between liberty and constraint: the liberty inherent in either regime depends entirely on the content of the directives or the contracts.

The matter at stake, then, is not whether to maximize personal liberty. Instead the dispute is whether individuals should be able to devise their own forms of legal obligation. The defining feature of the contract approach is that it allows for private ordering of personal relationships via *legally enforceable* agreements.

Return to Weitzman's advantages of relationship contracts. Many of these refer to the way that the *process of drawing up a contract* can strengthen a relationship: by clarifying expectations and providing a standard against which the couple can measure their own behavior. These significant advantages could be secured without the ensuing discussion resulting in a contract, or without any formal written document that the couple might agree on being legally enforceable. They are advantages of full, frank, and formal discussion in a relationship, not advantages of a particular legal regime. Any acceptable, just state must of course permit or even encourage such discussion: there could be no freedom of personal relationships without the freedom for partners to debate the terms of their relationship and come to agreements about how it will be organized. In questioning the value of relationship contracts, then, I am in no way questioning the value of formal discussion and agreement between partners about their relationship. The question is whether the *legal regulation* of relationships should be contractual, and thus whether the agreements that may well be invaluable to a secure relationship should be *legally enforceable*.

A legally enforceable relationship contract, then, will either create legally enforceable duties where none previously existed, in cases such as the lawn-mowing example; or it will create legally enforceable duties that differ from the default directives. Different issues are raised in each case, so I consider each in turn.

Consider first whether individuals should be free to enter into contracts that deviate from the default directives. As discussed above, even under a contract regime there are aspects of personal relationships in which the law will have to provide regulation where there is no contract. These aspects are inevitably among the most important: they concern matters like shared property, caring responsibilities, and child custody.[38] Their importance means that they are crucial to the well-being of the partners and others affected by them, and so it is likely that some people will want arrangements different from any mandated by the state.

This issue is similar in structure to that of whether married couples, in a regime of state-recognized marriage, should be allowed to enter into legally enforceable contracts alongside their marriage. These contracts would impose legal duties on the marrying couple that were either over and above those imposed by marriage law (for example, if the couple contracted about responsibility for housework) or that modified the duties imposed by marriage law (for example, a prenuptial contract designed to prevent a divorce court from imposing its own financial settlement). Prenuptial contracts are now common in the USA, but until recently American courts usually refused to enforce such contracts, for several reasons.[39] Where contracts are designed to override marriage law then the public policy concerns that underpin that law naturally tell against allowing deviation, whether those concerns be liberal commitments to liberty and equality or communitarian or religious commitments to particular marital forms.

Even where contracts merely add to existing law, courts have been reluctant to enforce them. The reasons for this reluctance fall into two categories. The first set of reasons concerns the way that courts have interpreted contract law. According to orthodox, classical contract law a contract can exist only where there is a bargain, an exchange of benefits, and this model does not easily fit intimate relationships—particularly where there are also legal prohibitions to "meretricious" contractual exchange of sexual services.[40] The reasons in the second category are normative. They include "a fear of disrupting domestic harmony, sometimes with a suggestion that such enforcement should not be necessary in a successful marriage" and concerns about "the institutional competence of courts to deal with the issues that arise between spouses."[41]

Shultz argues that these reasons do not withstand scrutiny, and I agree that the public policy concerns that prevent contracts deviating from marriage law are insufficient normative grounds for forbidding private contracts in a society which recognizes marriage. For, as I outlined at the outset, there are not adequate public policy reasons for egalitarians, be they liberals or feminists, to support the existing institution of marriage. If the institution as it stands is unjust then there are good reasons for allowing partners to deviate from it via their own contracts. But when thinking about ideal theory we assume that the default regulations will themselves be just. Therefore allowing people to make contracts that deviate from the default directives means allowing them to make contracts that deviate from *just* directives.

Earlier I outlined the ways that contracts can violate egalitarian justice. A just state would not permit relationship contracts that were unjust in those ways. But the state might permit deviations from the default directives if those deviations were themselves compatible with justice.[42] If all deviations from the default must be just then the only reason to prevent contract would be that there is specific good that is attained by having universal directives that apply to everyone: a fixed set of duties that everyone shares and that no one can change. This argument is essentially communitarian rather than liberal, appealing to the value of shared understandings and traditions, and both liberals and feminists are rightly skeptical of such appeals.[43] So there is good reason to allow deviations from the default where those deviations are themselves compatible with egalitarian justice.[44] Indeed, Fineman associates US courts' increasing willingness to enforce prenuptial agreements with the increasing acceptance of gender equality.[45] Another way of describing this situation is that there should be a variety of available directives from which parties may choose. After all, if only just agreements are to be allowed then the state will have to stipulate which agreements are just. Stability and secure expectations would be best served if the state made such stipulations in advance where possible, so that partners knew from the outset whether their agreements were enforceable.

But the most distinctive aspect of the contract approach is that it allows for partners to make contracts creating new duties in areas where there are no default directives. A traditional marriage vow creates a number of duties between two people. Traditional vows stipulate that the spouses should have certain feelings for each other: they must love, honor, or cherish each other. They commit the spouses to do certain things and to refrain from others: to provide emotional and financial support, to share property, and to refrain from committing adultery. Traditional vows also include conditions for the permanence of the agreement: the marriage should last in sickness and in health, for better or worse, for richer or poorer, and until death. Under a traditional marital regime, though, these duties are enforceable only in the sense that failure to live up to them is in some cases grounds for divorce. Are these the sorts of duties that could be managed via contract? Should individuals be able to make such agreements, and to make them legally binding?

An argument in favor of relationship contracts of this sort is made by Elizabeth S. Scott and Robert J. Scott.[46] They argue that freedom entails the freedom to commit. It is a mistake, they argue, to think of such contracts as inimical to freedom; on the contrary, autonomy is enhanced if people are able to make binding commitments, because such commitments allow access to greater goods than can be achieved without them. These greater goods could be personal, such as when an individual finds personal fulfilment in committing herself to live a certain sort of valuable life. Or they could be goods that can only be achieved in partnership with another person. Commitments to relationship contracts enable the contracting partners to reap the benefits of cooperation without the risks of defection. The security of a permanent commitment allows people to make investments that they would otherwise be wary of making, since the costs of defection would be high. These could be financial investments, such as purchasing a house together; emotional investments, such as having a child together; or investments that allow for specialization and the division of labor, such as giving up paid employment in favor of domestic and caring responsibilities.[47]

Undoubtedly these are among the many benefits of being in a committed relationship. But we must ask not "are committed relationships beneficial?" but "is justice best served by *legal enforcement* of relationship contracts?" It is worth noting that the decision to enforce a relationship contract will almost always entail the choice to end the relationship, for surely few if any relationships would survive a legal case. Legal enforcement will therefore mean the end of the relationship, and this in itself will be a barrier to its use in those cases where the wronged party wants to continue the relationship.

There are two main methods for enforcing contracts: specific performance and compensation. Both are complex and problematic in the relationship context.

Specific Performance

As Shultz notes, "public enforcement of private bargains ... is partial at best,"[48] since many people do not seek redress, and since in most cases courts order compensation rather than specific performance. Specific performance is a legal term indicating that the court requires the defaulting party actually to perform that aspect of the contract on which she has defaulted. So if specific performance were required of an employment contract then a doctor who had refused to perform an operation would not be fired but would be compelled actually to perform that operation. In another context, a building company that had provided workmanship below the standard agreed in the contract with the client would be required not to waive the fee or pay compensation but to redo the job. There are various reasons why specific performance in cases such as these might be inappropriate, most obviously that such failures reduce the wronged party's faith in the work of the violating party (who would want to be operated on by an unwilling surgeon?).

These generic problems of enforcement apply particularly to relationship contracts. Specific enforcement may be possible in cases where couples have contracted on matters such as property division upon separation, and other matters on which the state must provide default directives. But specific performance looks particularly unlikely if couples move beyond these subject matters and contract on matters in which the state would otherwise be uninterested. Many aspects of the traditional marriage contract are too vague to be enforced: it is not clear what they require, and their requirements are likely to differ from couple to couple.[49] How could a court tell whether one partner had failed in her responsibility to "cherish" the other? And it is not possible to force someone to love another, and quite possibly honoring, cherishing, and even straightforward caring are also necessarily voluntary.

Even where a contract is clear and compliance can be objectively assessed it is still difficult to envisage legal enforcement. For example, Elizabeth Kingdom advocates relationship contracts and imagines one with "a clause to the effect that the partners take turns over relocating in order to take advantage of job opportunities, even if it involved financial loss."[50] Specific enforcement of this clause would be impossible. It would be a profound violation of individual liberty to coerce one partner into compliance, since that would entail coercing her to resign from her job, coercing her to leave her home (both the physical property and the geographical location), and coercing her to live somewhere where she did not want to live. This level of coercion is generally reserved for cases where people need to be punished for egregious criminality: to make such coercion simply what the relationship contract entails is a stunning violation of liberty. Moreover, the idea of such enforcement is virtually nonsensical, for a loving relationship could surely not survive if one partner were legally coerced in this way.

Contract-type negotiations about matters such as relocation are very difficult in an intimate relationship. This is partly because negotiations conflict with the strong norm that such relationships should not be conducted in a self-interested, maximizing manner. And it is partly because personal relationships and personal preferences develop and evolve and yet are supposed to remain voluntary and enjoyable for both parties, exacerbating problems of presentation referred to above. In a one-off economic contract it does not matter too much if one party comes to wish they had not agreed to a particular clause: it does not undermine my mortgage contract if I wish, one year after signing it, that I had not agreed to be tied in for five years. I simply have to grin and bear it. But significant grinning and bearing it, particularly over major issues such as location, is not compatible with the happiness and affection that a personal relationship is supposed to foster.

The defender of relationship contracts might respond that the purpose of the contract is simply for the parties to set their expectations at the beginning of the relationship, and that it is valuable for people to be able to negotiate and agree on matters such as this. It is clear that the state should permit these sorts of non-legal agreements, in the sense that it should permit people to discuss the terms of their relationships and to come to agreements about matters such as relocation and career priority; it is barely possible even to imagine a well-functioning relationship where such discussions and agreements did not take place. But what distinguishes the contract approach is the claim that these agreements should be legally enforceable.

Compensation

If specific performance is rarely plausible as a legal remedy then enforceability in a relationship contract context must mean the ability to impose a sanction in the case of objectively identifiable breach.[51] The most likely candidate for a sanction in the relationship contract context is compensatory fault-based alimony. Imagine, for example, that one party failed to meet their commitments and had an affair. An enforceable relationship contract might mean that the non-adulterous party would be entitled to compensatory payments from the adulterous one. Or, in the case suggested by Kingdom, the partner whose turn it was to relocate but who refused to do so could be compelled to compensate the other partner.[52] This approach, in the marriage context, is advocated by Brinig and Crafton, who argue that divorce *without* fault-based alimony renders the marriage contract unenforceable and encourages "opportunistic behavior" by encouraging default on the terms of the contract. Brinig and Crafton thus advocate the retention of no-fault divorce but the institution of fault-based alimony.[53]

The equivalent position for a contract-based regime in the marriage-free state would be that couples would not have to demonstrate fault in order to halt their contractual obligations, but that breach of contract would be compensable. The amount of money could be agreed in advance, but in order to be an effective sanction, as Brinig and Crafton advocate, it would need to be fairly considerable. Alternatively, if the compensatory payment were justified in corrective justice terms, and if the breach were such that divorce occurred, the payment would have to compensate the wronged individual for the investments she had made into the marriage, and these too could be considerable. They might include direct financial investment into joint property, emotional investment into the relationship, career sacrifices to enhance the career of the other party or to take on domestic and caring work, and sacrifices in future romantic prospects.[54]

Fault-based compensatory payments for breaches of the relationship contract face two main problems: problems concerning equality and distributive justice, and problems concerning third parties, particularly children. The problem with children is easy to see. Many partnerships include dependent children. Arrangements made for dissolving those partnerships will have to be in the interests of the children, possibly even their best interests. These considerations could easily conflict with any fault-based alimony claims. If the partner who has breached the relationship contract and is therefore liable to pay compensation will also have even partial custody of the children then any loss she suffers through having to pay compensation is also an unjust loss to her children.

The second problem relates to issues of distributive justice: need, equality, and dependence. If alimony is awarded according to fault, then the partner who has to pay compensation could be left considerably worse off than the wronged partner, and possibly even in a condition of need. This might particularly harm women, since they are more likely to take on caring responsibilities rather than paid employment within a relationship, and so if they are left having to pay compensation to their partners for breach of relationship contract (for example by having an affair) they could easily be left with little or no financial support. So fault-based alimony could result in a woman who has sacrificed her career and devoted many years to her family, leaving her with no independent source of income and a severely compromised position in both the labor and the relationship markets, having to pay compensation to a wealthy professional man who has undamaged career and relationship prospects because she has had an affair or does not wish to relocate, away from friends and family, to follow his career. This is not a position that feminists or egalitarians should support.[55]

Moreover, the two problems (children and inequality) are not independent. A partner who has been the primary caretaker of children is likely to be best placed to retain custody of them on separation, so a partner who is left in need as a result of fault-based alimony is more likely to be responsible for the care of children. Fault-based alimony will thus have extremely deleterious consequences for stay-at-home parents and their children.

One response to this problem is to say that the state should be responsible for those in financial need, not their ex-partners. Just because two people used to be in a relationship it does not follow that they should have permanent responsibility for each other's ongoing financial support. On this response a stay-at-home partner who is left in a position of need as a result of having to pay fault-based alimony should still have to pay that alimony, but should be eligible for support from the state.

This solution has some appeal when couched in theoretical terms since it reflects the idea that a relationship should not permanently define a person's financial status. However, the solution actually satisfies neither the advocate nor the critic of fault-based alimony. It does not satisfy the advocate of fault-based alimony since it lessens the motivation to comply with the contract in the first place: if the state bails out a partner who is made needy because she has to pay compensation for having breached a contract, then the contract is not a workable sanction. It does not satisfy the critic of fault-based alimony, someone who finds the idea of financial penalty for relationship failings distasteful, since it merely shifts the financial burden to the state. If it offends egalitarian sensibilities that a stay-at-home mother should have to pay her wealthy professional partner compensation for an affair it surely offends still further to think that taxpayers in general should have to provide that compensation.[56]

Finally, note that it will be very difficult for courts to identify fault in a sufficiently precise manner to allocate compensation. As Ellman and Lohr point out, allegations of fault are likely to be made by both sides. Interpreting and ruling on them require a detailed and nuanced understanding of the relationship as a whole—an understanding that is impossible to acquire without yet more investigation into the most intimate aspects of a relationship. And experience of judges' behavior, and of human behavior in general, suggests that rulings on such cases may reflect judges' explicit or implicit bias as much as they reflect an accurate interpretation of fact and contract.[57]

There are various problems, then, with allowing individuals to regulate their relationships via enforceable contracts. Some sorts of contracts cannot realistically be legally enforced at all, since it is nonsensical to think of a legal obligation to love or to care for another. Other aspects of relationship contracts are more determinate but are unlikely candidates for specific performance. The question of enforcement therefore becomes one about the appropriateness of compensation in the case of breach, and it is here that contracts between those in a personal relationship may be more problematic to enforce than those between strangers.

Relational Contract Theory

Relational contract theory (RCT), developed by Ian Macneil and others, draws attention to the limits of orthodox contract law in dealing with arrangements that are ongoing and trust-based, rather than discrete and purely based on wealth maximization. Christensen, citing Macneil, highlights the

> "massive erosion of discreteness" that occurs "when projection of exchange into the future occurs within structures such as the family." In this situation, the "mutual relation into which the transaction is integrated" may displace in importance the agreed details of the particular transaction. Hence the "relational contract," an economic reality with which traditional contract law is ill-equipped to deal.[58]

Traditional contract law works best when the contracts in question are discreet and one-off. But many contracts, both commercial contracts and *a fortiori* relationship contracts, take place in the context of an ongoing relationship and recurring transactions.[59] In these contexts the parties have an interest in maintaining the relationship, not just in enforcing the particular terms of the contract; and the parties' obligations and legitimate expectations are laid out in informal and context-sensitive norms as well as in explicit contractual terms.[60]

RCT has gained significant support in the jurisprudence of contract law, and several scholars have argued for its particular applicability to family law.[61] Some courts have also employed an RCT approach in deciding cases in which unmarried couples separate and assets must be divided. The landmark case in the USA is *Marvin v. Marvin*, in which the California Supreme Court found that non-marital relationship contracts could be enforced, whether written or not, as long as their existence could be demonstrated to the court.[62] What this approach means is that courts must look not only for explicit, formal, written contracts between parties, but also for "relational" contracts: implicit, evolving, unwritten agreements based on the realities and everyday functioning of a particular relationship. So, in deciding how to divide the equity in a house, a court might look not only at the name on the deeds but also at who has actually been paying the bills, or whether one of the parties provides unpaid domestic services to the household as a whole. To take another example, in deciding whether to grant custody of a child to a person who is not a legally recognized parent (for example, the nonbiological parent in a homosexual couple who has not legally adopted the child), a court using an RCT approach would look not just at the legal facts of biological parenthood or adoptive status, but also at who actually engages in the everyday activity of parenting.[63]

The example of parenting demonstrates one of the strengths of this approach: it is able to deal with families as they really are, not as the state imagines they should be. So relational contract theory can be a truly inclusive approach to personal relationships. The particular issue of parenthood, be it biological, legal, or functional, raises issues too complex to deal with here. But the functional approach has the potential to work well in adult relationships. One of the benefits of such an approach is that it helps to remove the vulnerability that is suffered by partners who, whether by their own volition or by the reluctance of their more powerful partners, have neither a marriage nor a relationship contract.

However, a relational contract theory approach is not without problems. Christensen points out that, since it does not rely on simply enforcing a formal, written contract, RCT requires a court to delve into the realities, actual assumptions, and everyday actions of the partners. This inquiry is possibly a violation of privacy and certainly takes contract away from its libertarian roots, roots which appeal to many of its advocates.[64]

Moreover, Robson and Valentine point out that an attempt to discern an implied contract can lead to results that are surprising to the parties:

> Because of a judge's power to find an implied contract—even if the couple has not expressly documented their promises and agreements—contract principles may enter a … relationship unexpectedly. In jurisdictions that follow *Marvin v. Marvin* and effectuate the "intent" of the parties, "conduct may give rise to an implied contract completely at odds with the intent of one or more of the parties; or unanticipated equitable relief may be granted contrary to expectation. Thus, both parties may be surprised by the consequences of verbal statements and nonverbal acts."[65]

So relational contract theory lacks the determinacy of both traditional contracts, where determinacy is provided by the explicit terms of the contract to which both parties have formally agreed, and state directives, where determinacy is provided by explicit laws that are defined in advance and which apply to all couples in functionally similar relationships.

An RCT approach attempts to capture the advantages of both contract and directive. It attempts to mirror the beneficial aspects of the directive approach by involving the courts in making judgments about fairness in relationships. And it attempts to mirror the advantages of the contract approach by tailoring judgments to individual couples and their circumstances, rather than imposing a one-size-fits-all model. But this hybrid also replicates the disadvantages of both forms of relationship regulation. RCT replicates traditional contract's potential for inequality since it requires courts to make judgments with reference not to universal principles of justice but to an implied contract between the parties—a contract which might itself be unjust. And RCT replicates the potential that the directive approach has for state rulings that are heavy-handed and unwanted by either party.

Proposal: Piecemeal Directives with Limited Contractual Deviation

The shortcomings of the RCT model indicate a similar but preferable alternative: a system of piecemeal directives with the possibility for deviation along traditional contractual lines. Advocates and critics of relationship contracts alike often imply that contracts are the only alternative to marriage or a similar state-recognized status. But there is an alternative: piecemeal directives with the possibility for limited contractual deviation.

As I outlined earlier, *piecemeal* regulation rejects both *bundling* and *special status*. Each of these features replicates some of the advantages of the contract approach. Firstly, unlike holistic forms of directive, such as traditional marriage or the alternative statuses endorsed by several contemporary theorists, piecemeal regulation does not bundle together a set of regulations concerning diverse matters such as child care, property ownership, immigration, and next-of-kinship. Instead it regulates each of these matters separately. There is no necessary connection between co-parenting with someone and being their next of kin, or between sharing property with someone and having the right to immigrate to be with them. This rejection of bundling replicates the diversity of contracts: a contract can be made with one other person or with many, and the contract can regulate just one aspect of life or many. So too piecemeal regulation allows for relationships that are specific in their scope, as well as for relationships such as traditional marriage that combine many functions.

Secondly, the rights and duties of piecemeal directives are attained not by adopting some special status such as marriage, but rather simply by standing in the relevant functional relationship to someone. This idea of functionality echoes the insight of RCT that what matters is not so much whether an explicit contract or status has been attained, but how everyday life is patterned and whether legitimate expectations have arisen. Unlike RCT, however, the piecemeal directive approach does not leave a couple in the dark about how the courts might interpret their relationship.

Instead the directives state clearly which relationship functions give rise to which rights and duties. For example, a piecemeal directive might be of the following form:

> A person acquires full or partial ownership of a residential property by: being named on the lease; or residing in the property and contributing financially to that property for a year or more without a formal tenancy or lodger's agreement; or by residing in the property and providing unpaid domestic services to the household for a year or more. Ownership is assessed according to the proportion that each has contributed to maintaining the property. Unpaid domestic services are assessed as an hourly contribution equivalent to the hourly wage of the other owner's paid work.

The point of this example directive is not the justice or otherwise of its content, but rather its form. Such a directive is responsive to the realities of each particular relationship, as with RCT or traditional contract, but is determinate in advance and is formulated with egalitarian justice in mind.

In some cases, justice might permit deviation from a given directive, since there might be areas which must be determinate in law (and thus deserving of a directive) and yet in which considerable diversity is compatible with justice. In such cases deviation should be allowed, within set parameters, but any deviation should be via the format of traditional written contract, not via imputed relational contracts. In other words, vulnerable parties should enjoy the full protection of the law as set out in the piecemeal directive, unless they have explicitly and formally agreed to a different distribution, enforcement of which is forthcoming only if compatible with justice. For example, the hypothetical directive just given might be supplanted with the following:

> Deviation from this directive is permitted by explicit contract, but any such contract must be compatible with the following requirements: any children of the contracting parties must be left no worse off than they would have been without the deviation; and neither party can be left with a share smaller than 20% of the property or that which they would have received without the deviation, whichever is the smaller.

Again, I make no claims about whether this precise regulation is correct in content. Formulating each piecemeal directive is a considerable task in itself. I aim simply to demonstrate the form that regulation might take, and to illustrate how a regime of piecemeal directives with the possibility of limited deviation by traditional contract could work.

This approach, of piecemeal directives with the possibility of limited contractual deviation, avoids the problems of (i) the contractual approach and (ii) marriage or marriage-like holistic regulation. The lack of a special status means that no one relationship format is singled out for state approbation, and no one is left without legal protection because they (or their parents) lack the relevant status. The possibility of contractual deviation protects liberty and means that people are still able to make clear and consensual statements about their relationship.

Maxine Eichner writes that "eliminating a civil route for formalizing relationships would . . . be a mistake" since

> this formalization helps to identify the intent of its members and their own understandings with respect to the intended primacy and permanency of the relationship. In entering into a marriage, participants indicate their assent to a specific formal status that comes with a set of enforceable legal rights and responsibilities. And surely such understandings should be relevant in determining the default rules that apply to that particular relationship. For example, a commitment to a permanent relationship should be pertinent to the state's determination of whether and how long income should be redistributed between parties who have separated.[66]

But what Eichner misses is that the intent and understandings of a couple can be expressed by opting *out* of default directives, not just by opting *in* to a status such as marriage which, after all, offers considerably less scope for personalization. She also misses the fact that intent and understandings can change over time, rather than being isolated in one moment of entering into a marriage. She fails to note that understandings can be expressed by actions within the relationship, such as buying a house together or having a child. And her account does not take adequate account of the fact that one person's intent and understandings might be incompatible with justice and fairness, either to the other partner within the relationship or to third parties such as children.

The default, function-based directives in my account must be formulated with equality and the protection of the vulnerable in mind. They can be constructed so as to safeguard a number of policy concerns, such as supporting caring relationships or incentivizing stability for children. They avoid the patriarchal and religious resonance of marriage, and leave no one unprotected, thus eliminating unjust inequalities between married and unmarried people and their children.

The fact that there is a limit on permissible contractual deviations is crucial for equality. But it also helps my proposal deal with some of the practical problems of the contract model. Limits on the possibility for deviation are limits on the problems of enforcement. Carefully constructed limits mean that the state will not enforce unjust contracts or penalties.[67]

Conclusion

Relationship contracts have been advocated as a means of protecting both equality and liberty. In the first part of the chapter I explored familiar egalitarian critiques of contract, and showed how these critiques are particularly applicable to relationship contracts. In the second part of the chapter I argued that contracts are not as beneficial to liberty as is often supposed. A contractual regime for regulating relationships does not keep the state out of family life, since default regulations are still needed and since a contract regime requires state enforcement.

Moreover, these aspects of the state's involvement should make even non-libertarians wary of relationship contracts. It is hard to see how the state could meaningfully enforce relationship contracts without requiring specific performance, which would be a profound violation of liberty, or compensatory fault-based alimony, which would be a profound violation of equality.

Instead, I have argued for a regime of piecemeal regulation via default directives. Contractual deviation might be permitted, but only subject to clearly defined justice-based limits. My position thus supports neither a contract-based model of relationship regulation nor an alternative holistic relationship status that people enter into. The state should put in place default directives governing personal relationships but these should be piecemeal in character, referring only to particular aspects of a relationship and with no assumption that multiple aspects should all be located in one primary relationship. It should allow contracts that deviate from these default directives only if those contracts are themselves compatible with justice, in both procedure and content, and only if those contracts are legally enforceable without violating other considerations of justice. It therefore combines the beneficial diversity, adaptability, and specificity of contract with the ability of directive to ensure equality and limit vulnerability.

Acknowledgments

I began and completed work on this essay during two periods (in 2009 and 2013) as a Visiting Scholar of the Center for the Study of Law and Society (CSLS), part of the Boalt School of Law at the University of California, Berkeley. I am grateful to all at the Center for hosting me and for their support during my time there. In between I worked on this material as an Early Career Fellow of the Centre for Research in the Arts, Social Sciences, and Humanities (CRASSH) at the University of Cambridge, for which I am also grateful. Earlier versions of this essay, or materials that ended up here, were presented at the CSLS and at CRASSH, and at the 2012 Political Thought Conference held at St Catherine's College, Oxford; the University of Cambridge Political Philosophy Workshop; the University of Essex Political Theory Seminar; and the University of Leeds Centre for Ethics and Metaethics. I have also benefited from written comments from Elizabeth Brake, Ira Ellman, and Jo Miles.

Notes

1. I make these claims in more detail in my "The Marriage-Free State," *Proceedings of the Aristotelian Society* 107:2 (2013): 123–143, and *Against Marriage: An Egalitarian Defence of the Marriage-Free State* (Oxford: Oxford University Press, forthcoming 2016).

2. See, for example, Lenore J. Weitzman, *The Marriage Contract: Spouses, Lovers and the Law* (New York: The Free Press, 1981); Marjorie Maguire Shultz, "Contractual Ordering of Marriage: A New Model for State Policy," *California Law Review* 70:2 (1982): 204–334; Elizabeth A. Kingdom, "Cohabitation Contracts: A Socialist-Feminist Issue," *Journal of Law and Society* 15:1 (1988): 77–89; Martha Albertson Fineman, *The Neutered Mother, The Sexual Family and Other Twentieth Century Tragedies* (New York: Routledge, 1995); Fineman, *The Autonomy Myth: A Theory of Dependency* (New York: New Press, 2005); Fineman, "The Meaning of Marriage," in *Marriage Proposals: Questioning a Legal Status*, ed. Anita Bernstein (New York: New York University Press, 2006), 29–69.

3. In this essay I sometimes refer to the jurisprudence of legal scholars who have considered the limitations of contract law in dealing with intimate relationships. Often such scholars point to issues that are of fundamental relevance to my argument, such as the difficulties of enforcing contracts or the undesirability of doing so. However, this essay is a work of normative political philosophy, not a work of jurisprudence. That is to say that I focus on the *normative* limitations of contract, not the legal limitations to upholding personal relationship contracts within the Anglo-American contract law tradition, as set by case law and precedent. So the use of the term "contract" in this essay is not synonymous with "contract law," classical or otherwise.

4. I discuss the sense in which status implies approbation in my book *Against Marriage*. For an example of the "public ordering" terminology see Craig W. Christensen, "Legal Ordering of Family Values: The Case of Gay and Lesbian Families," *Cardozo Law Review* 18 (1996–1997): 1299–1416.

5. Chambers, "The Marriage-Free State."

6. A detailed account of the advantages (and disadvantages) of contract is found in Jana B. Singer, "The Privatization of Family Law," *Wisconsin Law Review* (1992): 1444–1567.

7. Shultz, "Contractual Ordering of Marriage," 245.

8. Shultz, "Contractual Ordering of Marriage," 248.

9. Shultz, "Contractual Ordering of Marriage," 219–23.

10. Weitzman, *The Marriage Contract*, 232–237.

11. Weitzman, *The Marriage Contract*, 238–239.

12. Weitzman, *The Marriage Contract*, 227–228.

13. Fineman, *The Neutered Mother*, 228–229.

14. Fineman, "The Meaning of Marriage," 57–58; chapter 5 of Fineman, *The Autonomy Myth*, is similar.

15. As Jana Singer writes, "the privatization of family law is most likely to increase opportunities for individual control where the most salient barriers to that control have been barriers set up by the state. The state's traditional ordering of marriage and its refusal to recognize consensual alternatives to marriage may be one such example. Where, by contrast, the efforts of individuals to control their lives have been thwarted primarily by private concentrations of power, or by power inequalities within the family, the link between privatization and control becomes considerably more problematic. At best, a shift from public to private ordering in these areas is likely to enhance the control of some family members at the expense of others" ("The Privatization of Family Law," 1537).

16. See Carole Pateman, *The Sexual Contract* (London: Polity, 1988); K. O'Donovan, *Sexual Divisions in Law* (London: Weidenfeld and Nicholson, 1985); M. Neave, "Private Ordering in Family Law—Will Women Benefit?" in *Public and Private: Feminist Legal Debates*, ed. M. Thornton (Melbourne: Oxford University Press, 1995), 144–173; P. Goodrich, "Gender and Contracts" in *Feminist Perspectives on the Foundational Subjects of Law*, ed. A. Bottomley (London: Cavendish, 1996), 17–45; M. J. Frug, "Re-reading Contracts: A Feminist Analysis of a Contracts Casebook," *American University Law Review* 34 (1985): 1065–1140; Patricia A. Tidwell and Peter Linzer, "The Flesh-Colored Band Aid: Contracts, Feminism, Dialogue, and Norms," *Houston Law Review* 28 (1991): 791–817, p. 791; Martha Minow and Mary Lyndon Shanley, "Relational Rights and Responsibilities: Revisioning the Family in Liberal Political Theory and Law," *Hypatia* 11:1 (1996): 4–29; Mary Lyndon Shanley, *Just Marriage* (Oxford: Oxford University Press, 2004).

17. Pateman, *The Sexual Contract*, 184.

18. Notable historical critics of traditional marriage include Mary Wollstonecraft, *Vindication of the Rights of Woman* (New York: Everyman, 1992); John Stuart Mill, *The Subjection of Women* (Indianapolis: Hackett, 1988).

19. Amy Wax, "Bargaining in the Shadow of Marriage: Is There a Future for Egalitarian Marriage?" *Virginia Law Review* 84:4 (May 1998): 509–672.

20. David McLellan, "Contract Marriage—The Way Forward or Dead End?" *Journal of Law and Society* 23:2 (June 1996): 234–246. See also Singer, "The Privatization of Family Law," 1540ff.; Maxine Eichner, *The Supportive State* (Oxford: Oxford University Press, 2010), 102.

21. See, for example, Martha Nussbaum, *Sex and Social Justice* (Oxford: Oxford University Press, 1998); Brian Barry, *Culture and Equality* (Cambridge, UK: Polity Press, 2001); Chandran Kukathas, *The Liberal Archipelago* (Oxford: Oxford University Press, 2007).

22. I argue for this point more extensively in *Sex, Culture, and Justice: The Limits of Choice.* (University Park, PA: Pennsylvania State University Press, 2008).

23. Although this essay considers how personal relationships should be ideally regulated, it would be naïve and complacent to assume that such regulation would take place against a background of generic gender justice, for the realization of full gender equality is remote. As theorists such as Susan Moller Okin have shown, establishing gender justice requires policies more radical than even those required to realize more general liberal theories of justice such as those of John Rawls and Ronald Dworkin, and neither Rawlsian nor Dworkinian justice looks politically imminent. So it is essential to consider the possibility that relationship contracts will take place against a background of structural gender inequality. In *The Sexual Contract*, Carole Pateman argues that the structural inequalities between men and women undermine the use of contract not only for marriage but in general.

24. Ruthann Robson and S. E. Valentine, "Lov(h)ers: Lesbians as Intimate Partners and Lesbian Legal Theory," *Temple Law Review* 63 (1990): 511–541, p. 524.

25. See, for example, Pepper Schwartz, *Love Between Equals: How Peer Marriage Really Works* (New York: The Free Press, 1994); Ira Mark Ellman, " 'Contract Thinking' Was *Marvin*'s Fatal Flaw," *Notre Dame Law Review* 76 (2000–2001): 1365–1380, p. 1369; Melvin A. Eisenberg, "The Limits of Cognition and the Limits of Contract," *Stanford Law Review* 47 (1995): 211–259, pp. 251–258.

26. John Wightman, "Intimate Relationships, Relational Contract Theory, and the Reach of Contract," *Feminist Legal Studies* 8 (2000): 93–131, p. 108.

27. Ellman, " 'Contract Thinking'," 1367–1368.

28. Fineman, "The Meaning of Marriage," 58.

29. Fineman, "The Meaning of Marriage," 61.

30. Fineman, *The Neutered Mother*, 229.

31. In the current regime these default directives are found in forms of law that are neither marriage-specific nor contractual, such as property law and family law pertaining to children.

32. The first sort of directive, default rules for non-contractors, might seem more extensive than the second, but in practice the directives involved in regulating contracts can be extensive. As Shultz writes, "To argue that marriage ought to be governed to a greater degree by private choices about behavior and obligation is not to recommend the abandonment of public policy considerations. Important public policies already permeate contract law. If marriage contracts were legally recognized, special policies would be developed to meet the particular needs of this subject area as they have been in other areas of contract law. Thus, even while conceding greater private governance of marriage, the law might choose to retain public policy barriers that might, for example, render invalid contracts such as the Homosexual or Open Marriage examples" (Shultz, "Contractual Ordering of Marriage," 304).

33. See Christensen, "Legal Ordering of Family Values"; Mary Lyndon Shanley, "The State of Marriage and the State in Marriage," in *Marriage Proposals: Questioning a Legal Status*, ed. Anita Bernstein (New York: New York University Press, 2006), 188–216; Martha Albertson Fineman, "The Meaning of Marriage," 58.

34. As Singer notes, the need for state directives on matters such as these should not be a source of regret. There is a crucial role for state involvement in family life, since it allows not only for protection of individuals within families but also for the promotion of basic justice. See "The Privatization of Family Law," Part IV.

35. Shultz, "Contractual Ordering of Marriage," 213, emphasis added.

36. As Christensen puts it, "As a starting position, ideological proponents of private ordering are favorably disposed towards the state's legal abstention from nonmarital family affairs. ... Such libertarianism works well enough so long as family members are willing to honor their agreements or to sensibly modify terms in light of evolving circumstance. As in traditional families, it is when relationships deteriorate irreparably (or end by death), that the state's legal intervention may be required" (Christensen, "Legal Ordering of Family Values," 1326). Now of course state intervention to enforce contracts has a different flavor from state intervention to enforce directives, in that the former need not imply that the state approves of the contract which is being enforced. Yet enforce it it does.

37. Here I set to one side the complicated question of whether a contract can properly be said to restrict individual liberty if it is entered into freely. I discuss this question at length in my *Sex, Culture, and Justice*, particularly in chapter 7.

38. As noted above, the default directives on these cases may be found in other branches of law, such as property law.

39. Shultz, "Contractual Ordering of Marriage," 232ff.

40. See Christensen, "Legal Ordering of Family Values"; Wightman, "Intimate Relationships, Relational Contract Theory, and the Reach of Contract," 93–131. Alternative interpretations of contract law exist which do not have these limitations, most notably Ian Macneil's Relational Contract Theory set out in works such as his "Contracts: Adjustment of Long-Term Economic Relations Under Classical, Neoclassical, and Relational Contract Law," *Northwestern University Law Review* 72 (1977): 854–905. Relational contract theory is discussed later in this chapter.

41. Shultz, "Contractual Ordering of Marriage," 235.

42. Another reason to allow contracts as a supplement to default directives is as a mechanism for a couple to achieve greater certainty in cases where the default directive allows for the exercise of judicial discretion. I am grateful to Jo Miles for this observation.

43. See Susan Moller Okin, *Justice, Gender, and the Family* (New York: Basic Books, 1989) and "Is Multiculturalism Bad for Women?" in *Is Multiculturalism Bad for Women?*, ed. Susan Moller Okin et al. (Princeton, NJ: Princeton University Press, 1999), 7–26; Brian Barry, *Culture and Equality* (Cambridge, UK: Cambridge University Press, 2001); John Rawls, *Political Liberalism* (New York: Columbia University Press, 1993).

44. Of course, a great deal more needs to be said about what sorts of relationships are just and thus what sorts of deviations count as being compatible with justice. I am not able to say more about that here, but have done so with respect to Rawlsian justice in my " 'The Family as a Basic Institution': A Feminist Analysis of the Basic Structure as Subject," in

Feminist Interpretations of Rawls, ed. Ruth Abbey (University Park: Pennsylvania State University Press, 2013), 75–95.

45. Fineman, *The Autonomy Myth*, 125ff.

46. Elizabeth S. Scott and Robert J. Scott, "Marriage as Relational Contract," *Virginia Law Review* 84:7 (October 1998): 1225–1334, pp. 1246–1247.

47. For discussion of these issues see Antony W. Dnes and Robert Rowthorn, eds., *The Law and Economics of Marriage & Divorce* (Cambridge, UK: Cambridge University Press, 2002).

48. Marjorie Maguire Shultz, "Contractual Ordering of Marriage: A New Model for State Policy," *California Law Review* 70:2 (March 1982): 211–334, p. 216.

49. For discussion see Ira Mark Ellman and Sharon Lohr, "Marriage as Contract, Opportunistic Violence, and Other Bad Arguments for Fault Divorce," *University of Illinois Law Review* (1997): 719–772, pp. 744–746.

50. Elizabeth Kingdom, "Cohabitation Contracts and the Democratization of Personal Relations," *Feminist Legal Studies* 8:1 (2000): 5–27, p. 19.

51. This is also true for other contracts. If an employee breaches her contract of employment by refusing to perform her contracted duties the employer will not be able to use the courts to force her actually to perform those duties. Its rights are limited to the right to terminate the contract, and possibly to extract a financial penalty if it has suffered losses.

52. Note that the wronged party is unlikely to feel happy with the situation: monetary compensation is unlikely to compensate. Financial compensation seems to be the wrong sort of thing. Unlike in a commercial contract, where the ultimate objective for both parties is financial gain broadly construed, personal relationships are not pursued with that objective. The very wording of the clause imagined by Kingdom highlights this: the parties agree to take turns to relocate "even if it involve[s] financial loss." If the wronged party prefers that, in accordance with their relationship contract, the partnership persists but relocates to the new location, whereas the wronging party prefers that the partnership persists in the existing location, it is somewhat unsatisfying that the only legal recourse is that the partnership should break up, that the two parties should live in separate locations, but that one partner should pay the other some money.

53. Margaret Brinig and Steven Crafton, "Marriage and Opportunism," *Journal of Legal Studies* 23:2 (June 1994): 869–894.

54. Note that, in order to be a sufficient disincentive for breach, such payments might also be significant disincentives against contracting in the first place—a result that would displease most advocates of relationship contracts.

55. Ellman and Lohr point out that US courts do in fact award alimony on the basis of need rather than fault ("Marriage as Contract," 743). They also raise the horrifying fact that in some states a spouse cannot receive alimony *at all* if she has committed adultery, meaning that "In those states a violent husband could physically abuse his adulterous wife mercilessly, without triggering any consequences insofar as his alimony obligations were concerned" (Ellman and Lohr, "Marriage as Contract," 747–748). Now, a contract regime is preferable to a profoundly unjust directive regime such as this, since it at least allows some couples to draw up more tolerable agreements. But of course a contract regime also allows couples to draw up agreements that replicate or exacerbate such injustice, such that an abused woman could be left unable to leave her abusive partner since

some other, more minor, fault of hers would lead her destitute if the relationship were to be dissolved and its contract enforced.

56. A related but inverse consideration applies to the alternative remedy of community service considered by Elizabeth F. Emens in her "Monogamy's Law: Compulsory Monogamy and Polyamorous Existence," *New York University Review of Law and Social Change* 29 (2004): 277–376. While this may act as a deterrent or punishment of breach it does not act as compensation for the wronged party. It also implicates the state or the community, as beneficiary of the remedy, as endorsing the initial contract. Depending on the content of the contract this may fall outside the public interest, even if only as a breach of neutrality.

57. Ellman and Lohr, "Marriage as Contract," 735.

58. Christensen, "Legal Ordering of Family Values,"1335; quoting Ian R. Macneil, "Contracts: Adjustment of Long-Term Economic Relations Under Classical, Neoclassical, and Relational Contract Law," *Northwestern University Law Review* 72 (1978): 854–905, pp. 857–858.

59. Eisenberg goes further, stating boldly "Every aspect of [classical contract law] was incorrect." However, he is also critical of relational contract theory. Melvin A. Eisenberg, "Why There Is No Law of Relational Contracts," *Northwestern University Law Review* 94 (1999–2000): 805–821, p. 808.

60. Wightman, "Intimate Relationships."

61. See, for example, Christensen, "Legal Ordering of Family Values"; Kellye Y. Testy, "An Unlikely Resurrection," *Northwestern University Law Review* 90 (1995): 219–235; Scott and Scott, "Marriage as Relational Contract"; Tidwell and Linzer, "The Flesh-Colored Band Aid."

62. *Marvin v. Marvin* 18 Cal.3d 660 (1976). For a critique see Ellman, "'Contract Thinking'."

63. See Christensen, "Legal Ordering of Family Values."

64. Christensen, "Legal Ordering of Family Values," 1338.

65. Robson and Valentine, "Lov(h)ers: Lesbians as Intimate Partners," 522, quoting H. Curry and D. Clifford, *A Legal Guide for Lesbian and Gay Couples: A NOLO Press Self-Help Law Book* §8 (Berkeley, CA: Nolo Press, 1989).

66. Eichner, *The Supportive State*, 103.

67. Notice too that a directive approach does not mean that all relationships have to be ordered according to the directive. The directive approach would not forbid voluntary transfers between individuals. The directive is enforced only in situations of conflict. In other words, if one party wished to be more generous to the other than the law required there would be no legal hindrance.

4 | Is Marriage Bad for Children?

RETHINKING THE CONNECTION BETWEEN HAVING CHILDREN, ROMANTIC LOVE, AND MARRIAGE

SAMANTHA BRENNAN AND BILL CAMERON

THIS ESSAY ARGUES THAT IT is time for our legal and cultural institutions to move away from assuming that there always ought to be a connection between parenting and marriage, and to think about children, rather than romantic love, as another possible foundation for the family. The argument here is presented both as a rejoinder to those on the right who say "But what about the children?" and as a response to worries raised by queer activists and feminists about the focus on same-sex marriage as the single most important political issue facing progressive communities today. Protection of the vulnerable strikes us as the only good reason to have the state involved in marriage in the first place. While we are not going to argue here for the abolition of the state's role in marriage, or endorse something like Elizabeth Brake's "minimal marriage" proposal,[1] we mean the suggestions we make here to be consistent with the spirit of these ideas. This essay has three parts: a look at the background and the changing face of the family, a child welfare argument for putting children at the center of the institution of the family, and an argument for a child-centered family based on the diversity of families and existing *de facto* parenting arrangements as well as the ways in which parenting contracts might provide more stability and security for children than other family arrangements. We will conclude by looking at some of the more likely objections to views like ours and how they might be answered.

To begin, some background is warranted. The tight connection between marriage and children, like that argued for in some of John Finnis' work[2] and forming part of a much older tradition, has been coming undone in different ways and by different means.[3] First, there is the increasing rate of childless couples, and second, there is at the same time an increasing rate of children born outside marriage: in the United States, 40.7% of all children are now born to unmarried mothers.[4] Third, there is an increasing marriage gap between the rich and the poor across much of the developed world. While about a half of American adults are married, that rate isn't even across all income levels.[5] Nearly two-thirds of college graduates are married, compared with fewer than half of those with a high school diploma or less. Those with less education are less likely to marry and more likely to divorce if they do.[6]

As the new Canadian census data make very clear, the Canadian family is also changing. For the first time the census recorded that barely 25% of Canadians live in the traditional nuclear family made up of mom, dad, and kids at home.[7] Single-parent households, opposite-sex couples deciding not to marry, singles living alone, same-sex couples, and couples without children are some of the other forms families are taking. Around the world, and throughout time, families are often larger than the nuclear family, many taking the shape of multigenerational households. And now we see creative, intentional relationships—families of choice—in other forms too.

Daniela Cutas and Sarah Chan in *Families: Beyond the Nuclear Ideal*, for instance, look at relationships that challenge the "nuclear ideal." They begin by describing that ideal in this way:

> That children should be conceived *naturally*, born to and raised by their two young, heterosexual, married to each other, genetic parents; that this relationship between parents is also the ideal relationship between romantic or sexual partners; and that romance and sexual intimacy ought to be at the core of our closest personal relationships—all these elements converge towards the ideal of the *nuclear family*.[8]

As they go on to say, however, not only has this ideal not been realized in many modern Western families (whether by design or not), but it has not even historically stood as an ideal in the West, let alone in the rest of the world.[9]

This is an exciting time to be thinking about marriage and the family as new possibilities for marriage seem to have caught the public's attention. In October 2012, for example, the *New York Times* Fashion and Style section ran a discussion piece by Matt Richtel focused on the possibility of renewable twenty-year marriage contracts. "The rough idea: two people, two decades, enough time to have and raise children if that's your thing; a new status quo, a ceremony with a shelf life, till awhile do us part."[10] This suggestion ties marriage and child-rearing together. Our suggestion is that we separate marriage contracts from parenting and think about children as a possible basis for family building, outside the aegis of marriage or even romantic love.[11]

Next, we want to examine the argument from child welfare for parenting contracts. We want to ask that we consider breaking the notion of "parent" off from loving, romantic relationships altogether, both legally and in broader social terms. For instance, marriage would no longer include a presumption of paternity, and marital status would have little to no weight in the assignment of parental rights. After all, if children require stability, it is not at all clear that marriage (as we as a society practice it) meets this need. Nor can we easily imagine a return to marriage as a legal requirement for cohabitation or as something difficult to end, through restrictive divorce law. We believe that most of our audience are liberals when it comes to the practice of marriage. We are very alert to the harms to individuals that come from marital bonds that are more bond-like.

We assume here that very few people accept something like Finnis' conservative account of marriage according to which marriage is seen as

a distinct fundamental human good because it enables the parties to it, the wife and husband, to flourish as individuals and as a couple, both by the most far-reaching form of togetherness possible for human beings and by the most radical and creative enabling of another person to flourish, namely, the bringing of that person *into existence* as conceptus, embryo, child, and eventually adult, fully able to participate in human flourishing on his or her own responsibility.[12]

Disregarding the moral and practical merits of such a view—one which privileges traditional marriage as the unique institution best suited for raising children—the statistics about the changing face of marriage mentioned above demonstrate that it is simply not a popular view of marriage in modern Western culture, in practice if not in public pronouncements.

Further, even of those who do feel this best speaks to their own understanding of marriage, not all would be so keen to impose it on others. Practically speaking, though, many of us do think that the care of children is the best, or even the only reason, for the state to be in the marriage business at all. Writes Elizabeth Brake, "it is widely accepted that the state should protect children. If two-parent families benefit children, incentives to marry may be justified as promoting two-parent families and hence children's welfare."[13] The benefits to children of married two-parent families are often claimed to be both emotional and economic, but note that the benefits only accrue, at most, to children in intact marriages, as opposed to children of divorce. Such benefits also may accrue to children in other, less traditional family settings. Thus the link between marriage and benefits to children is tenuous at best.

That is, there does not appear to be any intrinsic link between the goods that accrue to children from marriage (granting that these are indeed goods in most if not all cases) and the kind of marriage that is supposed to anchor the nuclear family. These emotional and economic benefits at the very minimum include the following, though one could probably come up with a much longer list which would not be much more controversial: stability and security; intimate nurturing relationships with adult role models; a steady source of the resources necessary for survival; and the conditions necessary for later socioeconomic flourishing, whatever they may be. These goods, however, could be afforded to children by any number of conceivable family arrangements; indeed, we have difficulty imagining any essential good of childhood which could not be provided by a great diversity of family arrangements, suggesting that marriage is not necessary for the provision of such childhood goods.[14] Conversely, it is very easy to imagine romantic marriages which begin with the best of intentions, where two partners are committed to and love each other, but which eventually end in ways that are downright detrimental to children,[15] so marriage is not sufficient for the provision of the aforementioned benefits either. Admittedly, intact and healthy marriages are certainly capable of providing these goods, but even an ideal marriage, the kind that one imagines at the heart of the most successful and traditional of nuclear families, can still fail to provide at least some fundamental goods of childhood, for the simple reason that marriage and child-rearing have different (or at least somewhat divergent) goals, with different conditions for success.[16]

So one might ask, why place the care of children under the very fragile bond of romantic-erotic love? We ought to take seriously the concern for the welfare of children that is often voiced as part of the package of concerns about the decline of marriage and the traditional family. If marriage is no longer (or perhaps never was) playing the role of a lifelong bond dedicated to the having and raising of children, how might we seek to protect society's more vulnerable members? We are not sure that even the old-fashioned family did the best job of this, but that is not the argument we wish to have today.

One might argue that families formed around the care of children, committed to providing and nurturing them, might be more stable than modern-day marriage. In *The Atlantic*, essayist Sandra Tsing Loh explores this idea in a piece of personal reflection about her divorce called "Let's Call the Whole Thing Off."[17] Reflecting the fondness for marriage in America, Loh notes that the United States is a country with a very high rate of marriage, divorce, and remarriage. But even romantic Loh suggests it's time to be more pragmatic about families: "Clearly, research shows that what's best for children is domestic stability and not having to bond with, and to be left by, ever new stepparent figures."[18] Serial, aspirational monogamy may be the most preferred relationship style among adults, but it is not clear that it is what is best for children, particularly considering that so little attention has been given, especially in the West, to what other options there might be.

This leads into the third part of our essay: our other argument for separating parenting contracts from marriage contracts comes from the diversity of family structures which seem to be good for children but which are not modeled on traditional marriages. If our first argument acknowledged the conservative concern for the well-being of children, this argument acknowledges the radical's point about the diversity of family relationships. Recognizing the diversity of patterns of lives which support the well-being of children serves to recognize both parental rights and the best interests of the child.

We have previously explored the question of how many parents a child can have in light of the creation of alternative models of family.[19] The traditional legal answer, in Canada and the United States, has been that a child can have at most two parents. While this answer has an obvious biological underpinning, it seems inadequate to the reality of many families. We argued that we ought to recognize multi-parent families when doing so is in the best interests of the child and when not doing so would violate the parental rights of one or more of the adults who stand in a relevant relation to the child. As Deborah Wald writes, "when we look to intent and conduct—instead of only biology or marriage—to create legal parent-child relationships, it quickly becomes clear that there may be more than two people who are candidates for the legal title 'parent'."[20] We think it important to say that there is nothing special about the number two, particularly given that modern medical procedures can lead to more than two people who can legitimately be called "biological" parents,[21] and

furthermore that a child can indeed have three or more parents in a coherent, largely uncontroversial sense.

While radical queer activists might argue that the focus on marriage
is fundamentally mistaken, our own impulses are more pluralist. We like
the idea of many models of family life, many different kinds of close-knit
groupings of persons in which we thrive. When it comes to one of the families we write about in our aforementioned essay, the members describe
the family as having grown up around children, rather than children having been brought into an existing marriage. In this family Jake is the partner of Torsten, the biological father of Eli, child of Erin and Marcie. The
extended family includes also Torsten's ex, Andrea, his partner at the time
Eli was conceived. This collection of loving adults considers itself a family, and they generally play an aunt/uncle role in the lives of the children.
Jake concludes as follows: "It seems to me that families grow spontaneously around children. I never intended for Erin and Marcie to be such
important parts of me, or for Andrea and her lovers to be family. I certainly
never intended to be eyeing the 'Someone who loves me very much goes
to U of T' socks at school with such intent. We draw lines between 'family' and 'friend,' based on blood or marriage, and as a result can consider
ourselves closer to people we see every few years than to people we see
once a week. But now people I barely knew well enough to call friends,
people I still only see a few times a year—like Eli's back-up guardians and
uncles, Bear and J—are without question part of my family. With Eli at
the centre, those connections just appeared, and now I can't imagine life
without them."[22] This strikes us as a healthy, thriving example of a creative
family arrangement providing a stable and nurturing environment for children, mobilizing the multiplicity of romantic relationships to compensate
for harms which could result from the way that such relationships are more
or less in a state of flux and taking advantage of the variety of resulting
parental resources. Every member of the family counts as such because he
or she is committed to raising the children, not because he or she is in (or
at least is trying to maintain) a particular romantic relationship. Therefore,
the variable stability of romantic relationships has minimal impact on the
stability of the child-rearing environment, at least when compared to the
impact of changes to the romantic relationship within traditional marriage
at the core of the nuclear ideal.

That being said, multi-parent cases occur for a wide range of reasons,
not just through queer relationships. There are also multi-parent families
that arise from divorce, from the use of reproductive technology, and from
open adoption. It is only when we think about monogamous marriage as

the foundation of family that two seems like a natural number. Of course, whether that is right for marriage or whether there are good arguments for allowing, legally and socially, unions of more than two people is another complicated argument, one outside the scope of our work here and not obviously relevant to it. Our point is that there is no necessary tie between marriage and parenting and that the state's interest in the rights and well-being of children gives it a reason to think about parenting contracts as separate from marriage contracts.

What would parenting contracts look like for families that are of the traditional sort: two people in love, making a life together, which they want to share with children? The parenting contract would require the couple to discuss plans for parenting the children of their union in the event the marriage ended, guided solely by the children's welfare and touching on all relevant areas of family life. In this case the marriage contract and the parenting contract could both be in place and the family would have two separate though connected elements at its foundation. If we talked to our children about parenting, as separate from marriage, this would help make it clearer to children that the end of the marriage need not be the end of the family.

That being said, marriage and the ideal of the nuclear family are deeply entrenched parts of our cultural consciousness, at least in theory. Indeed, recent public debates about gay marriage have shown that people are very concerned about the erosion of these institutions and ostensibly the effect it might have on families and children in particular. As a result, we ought to examine some of the more common objections against changing the nuclear ideal.

Recall that, broadly speaking, our point here is just to suggest that we consider ways in which marriage contracts and parenting contracts might come apart and be treated separately. One obvious way this might occur is where two people who do not have an interest in a romantic relationship with one another come together to have children, simply because they have a strong and healthy interest in doing so and a respect for one another's parenting potential. For instance, while it might seem unlikely under current cultural conditions, a loosening of the bonds between having children and romantic love could allow two close heterosexual male friends, perhaps long-time roommates, to decide to adopt a child and become parents together.

We imagine that this is precisely the kind of case that advocates of the traditional link between marriage and children would find alarming. After all, friendships, even very close ones, are generally taken to be, in a sense, casual and informal in ways that the bonds of romantic love are not, to say nothing of marriage. Friendships often drift apart or decay over time, while romantic relationships have a more formal character. One-time friends sometimes come to dislike or even hate one another, and without the structure of marriage or at least romantic love, there is no system in place for dissolving the relationship (at least in our present society). This creates the potential for children to be trapped between parents, in the midst of a hateful battlefield or simmering cold war every bit as poisonous as the worst marriages, without even the eject button of traditional divorce as an escape.

To be frank, though, we think it unlikely that such scenarios would actually be worse than bad marriages, even if separating parenting from romantic love might technically allow for the possibility of hostile partnerships. First of all, there does not seem to be anything about these scenarios that makes the risk or severity of negative consequences significantly worse for children than in the case of marriage.[23] Indeed, appealing to the mechanism of divorce as a kind of "eject button" for unhealthy relationships not present in less formal relationships like friendships strikes us as putting the cart before the horse. Friendships and the like generally lack a formal method of dissolution precisely because they are easily dissolved; divorce, messy and difficult as it might sometimes be, is an institution introduced for the purpose of ending what has traditionally been among the only social relationships which could not be ended rather simply even when all parties involved recognized that they would be better off if the relationship ended.

To be fair, having children would certainly complicate the ending of a friendship, but not necessarily more than it does for a marriage. As we will discuss further below, having children tends to "level up" a relationship, whether that is a marriage or just a close friendship.

There is one type of relationship, however, which would almost certainly serve as a worse foundation for parenting than romantic love: those where the parties begin with a strong dislike or even a hatred for one another, without even the veneer of civility a marriage contract might be supposed to convey. We find it unlikely that many people would set out to have children with one or more persons that they actually hated, but if the point is just that we should fully sever the bonds between parenthood and romantic love, then perverse possibilities like this one cannot be ruled out entirely.

That being said, we still believe there is a good response to even this largely academic objection. As we have said, separating the raising of children from marriage and romantic love does not imply that there ought not be any laws, limitations, or other involvement of the state in the raising of children. On the contrary, this opens up the possibility of contracts where stable, beneficial parents constitute the specific and deliberate goal from the beginning. If children are no longer simply an extension of romantic love, legally speaking, but the singular end product of a *sui generis* legal mechanism, that mechanism should (and presumably would) be geared exclusively towards their protection and flourishing.

So uncoupling parenting relationships from romantic relationships allows the state to endorse, even sanction, only those child-rearing circumstances which meet a minimum standard for stability and material well-being, along with whatever other criteria might be appropriate. With such a system in place, even if it relies solely on fairly gentle and non-intrusive regulatory implements, it becomes hard to imagine that any child-rearing effort involving two or more parents would even be allowed to get off the ground if the prospective parents were unable to get along rather well, let alone hated one another.

The fact is that such a system would likely serve to "professionalize" parenting, for lack of a better term. Marriage contracts, in the ideal form most commonly conceived in contemporary Western society, are founded upon strong feelings of romantic love between the parties to the contract; when all is said and done, having these feelings (along with some basic level of civility, sexual exclusivity, and in some cases, economic support on dissolution) is virtually all that is needed for the contract to be fulfilled. The kinds of parenting contracts we envision, on the other hand, would require much more specific, ongoing, practical commitments to one or more children, and would have very little to say about the feelings parents would have to have towards each other,[24] so long as appropriate parenting duties are fulfilled. Such an approach would almost certainly rule out people who hated one another entering into well-constructed and properly regulated parenting contracts simply because they would not be capable of fulfilling the basic prerequisites of such a contract.[25] Indeed, if anything, the current marriage-based approach allows more opportunity for people who hate one another or otherwise cannot get along to have children, simply by virtue of not requiring any formal interest at all in the relationship between parties who have children unless severe problems actually arise.

Beyond this somewhat academic concern about the unlikely situation of people who hate each other deciding to have children, though, specific parenting contracts would help prospective parents focus on just what their obligations are. Even in the best families centered around romantic love where children are happy and well cared for, there nevertheless exists a certain ambiguity about the ultimate goals of the family, particularly regarding any attendant obligations the parents might have. In such a healthy and well-functioning family, they would presumably see themselves as having obligations to their children, but they also have an obligation to maintain their own romantic relationship. Now, in a healthy relationship these would probably not feel like obligations, or at the very least the parties would fulfill them happily and without complaint. Still, there can be tensions when one owes such significant time and emotional energy to different parties in different ways, and this is where real-world, non-ideal families might begin to show cracks.

Of course, any real family has problems. But separating parenting out from romantic love at the very least removes this one possible barrier to effective child-rearing.[26] And more than just saying that people who are parents ought to focus their family energy on their children, such a move towards a more specialized kind of parenting would open the door for people who might make extraordinary parents but are not particularly interested in a romantic relationship (whether with their co-parents or with anyone at all). This brings us back to the idea of people who are just friends, or possibly barely even acquaintances, who manage to recognize in one another a drive and talent for parenting and want to pursue that path together, whether or not they might be interested in romantic relationships outside their parent-child relationships.

We believe that such people would in many cases make excellent parents. They are limited in the legal ways in which they might become parents under the current arrangement (e.g., adoption and access to artificial reproduction technologies tend to be much more difficult under such circumstances[27]), but they would not be under our proposal; this ought therefore to count as evidence in favor of severing the bonds between parenting and marriage. Furthermore, the notion of a more specialized, child-focused view of childrearing is one beneficial result of approaching parenting, among other family concepts, with creativity and thoughtfulness.

On the other hand, there are definitely those who worry about the impact that parenting contracts might have on some of the less tangible psychological or relational aspects of parenting and the relationship between parents and children. An overly legalistic approach to parenting, on this view, would inhibit much of the unique value of the parent-child relationship, value which cannot be captured in the language of rights, duties, and obligations. Judith Suissa, for instance, has argued that "the nature of the parent-child relationship remains occluded by the language of rights, duties and entitlements,"[28] even under present circumstances, to say nothing of some of the suggestions we have made about child-based parenting contracts not centered around marriages or other romantic-erotic relationships. Suissa feels that when talk about parenting is entirely taken up with "the language of rights, duties, authority and responsibilities,"[29] we are going to be left with "difficulty in finding the space to simply be—or the language to describe what is involved in simply being—with our children."[30] According to some critics, this kind of difficulty finds its most extreme and troubling expression in parenting contracts, which fail "to take into account that peculiar kind of duty parents feel they have towards their children, a duty that is crucially connected to that peculiar kind of relationship that they have with their children—intimate, unchosen, unequal."[31] The idea is that the parent-child relationship does not fit with the standard picture of contract law and state regulation; that its rewards, demands, and other key characteristics cannot be captured by the language of duty and obligation; and that attempting to do so ignores and possibly even diminishes what is special and valuable about being a parent. On this view, "the discourse of the 'expert mom' and the 'skilful dad' has distanced parents from *being a parent* and made them *act like* good ones."[32]

Perhaps the most clear and potent strand of this objection is inspired by Annette Baier's argument that while contracts and obligations might be appropriate in some contexts, they are only suitable for laying down and enforcing "minimal moral traffic rules,"[33] ignoring the full moral spectrum where complex relationships are involved. We would not want to create a world in which, "under the spell of . . . contractual engagement, parenthood stands in danger of being conceived in terms of a minimally guaranteed service."[34] We should certainly encourage, even expect, parents to do more than the bare minimum for their children, in the sense of providing stability and economic goods but even more so in terms of actually enjoying their children and providing a source of genuine love, encouragement, and affection. If parenting contracts result in parents conceiving of their responsibilities only (or perhaps even just more often) in terms of the bare minimum of concrete standards, then perhaps they are indeed a step in the wrong direction.

We believe, however, that this objection, well-intentioned though it may be, misses the main point of our suggestion. We certainly do not want the parent-child relationship to become overly legalistic and lacking in the unique goods of intimacy and affection to be gained. At the same time, though, we believe that some minimal standards for concrete parental care can be put in place without taking away in the least from trust, affection, and other aspects of the intimate bond between parent and child.[35] These are the obligations of or expectations for parents which are, relatively speaking, easy to enforce and therefore conceivably within the purview of the state, while requirements for trust, affection, and the rest could not feasibly be regulated or enforced, and therefore ought not form part of the state's interest in parenting and children's well-being. We take it that the burden of proof lies on those who would argue to the contrary, and that reason for serious concern has not yet been given by Baier and others who take this line of criticism.

Furthermore, our primary argument has more to do with severing the link between marriage (or other relationships based on romantic-erotic love) and parenthood than with treating parenthood as a contract; we believe that such a severing would open up a place for a new kind of parenting contract, but such contracts are not necessary to our main point. Moreover, we do not think there is anything in the arguments of Baier, Suissa, Lambeir and Ramaekers, or others who argue for similar points to suggest that romantic love between parents is necessary to a healthy flourishing of the more emotional goods of the parent-child relationship. Indeed, we take it that what little empirical anthropological and sociological evidence exists on this topic supports our view. For example, the roles of parenthood and romantic love are distinct in Mosuo society, for whom "separating marriage from the raising of children ensures that the vagaries of romance do not disrupt the happiness and health of the child and its mother."[36]

If anything, we think it likely that moving away from a supposed necessary connection between marriage and child-rearing will encourage the flourishing of the more intangible goods to be gained by both parents and children, regardless of what reasonable types of parenting contracts might or might not be adopted.[37] This is because a move away from the traditional Western view of the role of marriage and parents, together with a specific refocusing on the unique character of the parent-child relationship, is likely to foster creativity, openness, and thoughtfulness. In the best scenarios, this would then lead to a plethora of new ideas about how to raise children, all guided by a concern for their well-being and unshackled from the restrictions of marriage and other romantic relationships. Such an open-minded and pluralistic environment would, it is to be hoped, produce the precise circumstances best suited to encouraging children to flourish not only in concrete, material ways but also in the more psychological yet equally important ways emphasized by Baier and others.

Even if this were not the case, if we did not through such means witness an explosion of new, interesting, and positive forms of parenthood, then we would still manage to avoid some of the worst dangers resulting from the close link between marriage and parenthood, largely resulting from the instability, tension, and even violence that too often forms a central part of romantic conflict. Coupled with a specific refocusing on the needs of children and the unique character of the parent-child relationship, we believe that this improvement would also come without having to sacrifice what value is to be had in the current form of parent-child relationships.

Our answer to the question posed by the title of this essay, whether marriage is bad for children, therefore, is no, not necessarily. What is bad for children, though, is assuming that the commitment in marriage is or at least ought to be strong enough to bear the weight of their care. One could argue that very traditional marriage in the past here (and still widely practiced elsewhere) was such an arrangement, with family rather than love as its foundation and no possibility of divorce, as well as a hefty dose of involvement from extended family. But for a variety of reasons, that version of marriage is one to which we would not want to return. It also had its own problems for children, the details of which are also somewhat outside the scope of this essay.

Here we suggest something more modest than abandoning romantic love, a proposal that is not likely to be very popular or practical, let alone enforceable. In the spirit of pluralism, we have urged readers to begin thinking about parenting contracts as separate from marriage contracts. Indeed, many of us already think of our decision to become parents as far more significant and binding that the legal ties of marriage. You might marry and then think of the decision to have children as a kind of "leveling up" which changes the rules of the game entirely. Divorce from which you can walk away and never see the other person again is no longer possible once you have kids, given the likely legal obligations of visitation rights, shared custody, and child support; at the very least, it is not consistent with the most plausible norms of good parenting. Our suggestion merely takes this realization seriously, and couples it with the observation that the norms of good parenting do not necessarily have anything to do with the norms of romantic relationships. Therefore, the two need not be joined so closely together as they have been (indeed, not at all), and bringing them apart might allow us to conceive of new means of improving both, means which might well be unavailable to us if we insist upon continuing to tie together child-rearing with romantic-erotic love and relationships.[38]

Notes

1. See Elizabeth Brake, *Minimizing Marriage* (Toronto: Oxford University Press, 2012).

2. For instance, see John Finnis, "Marriage: A Basic and Exigent Good," *The Monist* 91 (2008): 388–406. We discuss this work further below.

3. One excellent philosophical work against continuing the current tradition of marriage and legitimate romantic partnership can be found in Claudia Card, "Against Marriage and Motherhood," *Hypatia* 11 (1996): 1–23.

4. "Unmarried Childbearing," Centers for Disease Control and Prevention, January 2014, http://www.cdc.gov/nchs/fastats/unmarried-childbearing.htm.

5. See, for example, Jason DeParle, "Two Classes, Divided by 'I Do,'" *New York Times*, July 14, 2012, http://www.nytimes.com/2012/07/15/us/two-classes-in-america-divided-by-i-do.html; Derek Thompson, "How America's Marriage Crisis Makes Income Inequality So Much Worse," *The Atlantic*, October 1, 2013, http://www.theatlantic.com/business/archive/2013/10/how-americas-marriage-crisis-makes-income-inequality-so-much-worse/280056/; and Michael Greenstone and Adam Looney, "The Marriage Gap: The Impact of Economic and Technological Change on Marriage Rates," Brookings Institution, February 3, 2012, http://www.brookings.edu/blogs/jobs/posts/2012/02/03-jobs-greenstone-looney.

6. Much of the empirical data behind this position can be found at "Survey of Income and Program Participation Data on Marriage and Divorce," United States Census Bureau, November 2014, http://www.census.gov/hhes/socdemo/marriage/data/sipp/index.html.

7. See, for example, the Canadian Press, "Census Shows New Face of the Canadian Family," *CBC News*, September 19, 2012, http://www.cbc.ca/news/canada/census-shows-new-face-of-the-canadian-family-1.1137083; Philip Cross and Peter Jon Mitchell, "The Marriage Gap Between Rich and Poor Canadians," Institute of Marriage and Family Canada, February 2014, http://www.imfcanada.org/sites/default/files/Canadian_Marriage_Gap_FINAL_0.pdf; and Peter Jon Mitchell, "The Rich-Poor Marriage Gap in Canada," Family Studies: The Blog of the Institute for Family Studies, March 11, 2014, http://family-studies.org/the-rich-poor-marriage-gap-in-canada/.

8. Daniela Cutas and Sarah Chan, "Introduction: Perspectives on Private and Family Life," in *Families: Beyond the Nuclear Ideal*, eds. Daniela Cutas and Sarah Chan (New York: Bloomsbury Academic, 2012), 1; emphasis in original.

9. Ibid., 1–2.

10. Matt Richtel, "Till Death, or 20 Years, Do Us Part," *New York Times*, September 28, 2012, http://www.nytimes.com/2012/09/30/fashion/marriage-seen-through-a-contract-lens.html.

11. Though we will not have time to examine them in detail here, there are other interesting suggestions for reimagining marriage. In particular, see Daniel Nolan, "Temporary Marriage," Chapter 8 in this volume.

12. Finnis, 389; emphasis in original.

13. Elizabeth Brake, "Marriage and Domestic Partnership," *Stanford Encyclopedia of Philosophy*, July 11, 2009 (substantial revision August 8, 2012), http://plato.stanford.edu/entries/marriage/.

14. For additional interesting discussion and a longitudinal study of multiple polyamorous families, see Elisabeth Sheff, *The Polyamorists Next Door: Inside Multiple-Partner Relationships and Families* (Lanham, MD: Rowman & Littlefield Publishers, 2013).

15. Marsha Garrison, "Promoting Cooperative Parenting: Programs and Prospects," *Journal of Law & Family Studies* 9 (2007): 265–280, p. 266.

16. Some more strictly traditional conceptions might actually see child-rearing as an essential and inseparable part and goal of marriage; for instance, see Finnis, 388–406. Still, we take our point here to be fairly straightforward and uncontroversial: so long as one can accept that there can be both (a) childless marriages which are nevertheless successful, and (b) children who are successfully reared by some arrangement other than a monogamously married heterosexual couple, then one must accept that the goals of marriage and childrearing do not entirely overlap.

17. Sandra Tsing Loh, "Let's Call the Whole Thing Off," *The Atlantic*, July 1, 2009, http://www.theatlantic.com/magazine/archive/2009/07/lets-call-the-whole-thing-off/307488/.

18. Ibid.

19. See Samantha Brennan and Bill Cameron, "How Many Parents Can a Child Have? Philosophical Reflections on the 'Three Parent Case,'" *Dialogue* 54 (2015): 45–61.

20. Deborah H. Wald, "The Parentage Puzzle: The Interplay Between Genetics, Procreative Intent, and Parental Conduct in Determining Legal Parentage," *American University Journal of Gender, Social Policy & the Law* 15 (2007): 381.

21. See Brennan and Cameron, "How Many Parents Can a Child Have?"

22. Torsten Bernhardt, et al., "The Spawn, the Spawnlet, and the Birth of a Queer Family," in *And Baby Makes More*, eds. Susan Goldberg and Chloë Brushwood Rose (London, ON: Insomniac Press, 2009), 123–124.

23. This might not be strictly true, as we can imagine a specific case where the circumstances would be worse than marriage, at least to begin with: if children were raised by people who actually started out hating one another. Though we do not take this to be a particularly powerful or convincing objection, we nevertheless deal with it briefly below.

24. This is not to say that the state would not be able to require that parents have certain kinds of feelings towards their children (or at least behave in ways consistent with certain kinds of feelings). If there is good evidence that children require their parents to demonstrate some amount of affection and attachment, then failing to do so might well make one an unfit parent. Laying out the consequences of such a determination, however, would be beyond the scope of this essay.

25. Again, this is a case where the state need not get into the business of investigating and regulating emotions (an endeavor both undesirable and impossible), but only looking for certain relatively explicit behaviors.

26. There are also some other possible barriers to effective child-rearing that our approach might foreseeably avoid, including feelings of jealousy or neglect, and acts of infidelity.

27. For instance, in the US, some fertility clinics refuse treatment to unmarried women, or health insurance may cover fertility treatments for married, but not unmarried, women.

28. Judith Suissa, "Untangling the Mother Knot: Some Thoughts on Parents, Children and Philosophers of Education," *Ethics and Education* 1 (2006): 65–77, p. 65.

29. Ibid., 67.

30. Ibid., 75.

31. Bert Lambeir and Stefan Ramaekers, "The Terror of Explicitness: Philosophical Remarks on the Idea of a Parenting Contract," *Ethics and Education* 2 (2007): 95–107, p. 102.

32. Ibid., 105; emphasis in original.

33. Annette Baier, *Moral Prejudices: Essays on Ethics* (Cambridge, MA: Harvard University Press, 1994), 116.

34. Lambeir and Ramaekers, 103.

35. Indeed, loving marriages are themselves strong evidence that there can be effective, fulfilling, affectionate relationships which are nevertheless governed by a legal contract.

36. Jonathan Harrison, "Separating Marriage from Childrearing: The Mosuo," *Sociological Images*, September 22, 2014, http://thesocietypages.org/socimages/2014/09/22/separating-marriage-from-childrearing-the-mosuo/.

37. We say "reasonable" parenting contracts because we take the critics of such contracts to be correct in arguing that there are indeed some types of contracts which would conceivably be overly restrictive and legalistic, thereby smothering many of the intangible goods discussed above. But we think that a reasonable, liberal, and somewhat minimal approach to parenting contracts, like that which we have tentatively put forward in this essay, would be entirely capable of avoiding such pitfalls.

38. Samantha Brennan would like to thank audiences at the two conferences at which she presented a preliminary version of this chapter: the Society for Analytical Feminism and the Association for Political Theory, both at Vanderbilt University in Nashville.

5 | Equality and Non-hierarchy in Marriage
WHAT DO FEMINISTS REALLY WANT?

ELIZABETH BRAKE

F FEMINISM CALLS FOR EQUALITY within marriages or marriage-like relationships, what is the relevant sense of "equality," and what is wrong with its absence? The question of the subtitle, like that on which it plays ("What do women really want?"), incorporates the false assumption that there is a single generic answer. One feminist cannot, of course, speak for how all feminists would diagnose the relationship between marriage and inequality or propose to remedy it. Any substantive proposal is bound to be contentious. However, here I defend some widely shared feminist criticisms of inequality in marriage by showing how they have been misunderstood. Having tried to illuminate some shared feminist concerns, I then develop a feminist ideal of egalitarian relationships modeled on friendship. At the end, I turn to the law, asking whether marriage must be abolished to achieve such equality.

"Marriage equality" has come to be synonymous with the call for same-sex marriage. While I agree that equal treatment requires recognizing same-sex marriage if any marriages are legally recognized, this essay focuses on equality *within* relationships, not on the equal legal standing of different relationships.[1] In my focus on power equality *within* marriages, I also bracket "the other marriage equality problem"—marriage rates correlate with economic class, and this marriage class divide reproduces socioeconomic inequalities in the next generation.[2] In the first part, I focus on male-female relationships, which have been the subject of the feminist criticism I review. However, my subsequent discussion of hierarchy in marriage applies equally to same-sex and different-sex marriages as well as to other intimate relationships such as friendships.[3]

1. Equality and Marriage: Does It Still Matter?

Fifty years after Betty Friedan's *The Feminine Mystique* and twenty-five years after Susan Moller Okin's *Justice, Gender, and the Family*, when the majority of married women work outside the home and legal spouses have equal rights in US marriage law, how relevant are their critiques of the gendered expectations placed on married women? Very, as it turns out.[4] Women's disproportionate household labor—especially after children arrive—still costs women time and money, and it still contributes to gender discrimination in the public sphere. And even though marriage law no longer contains gendered legal responsibilities, men and women lack equal legal rights insofar as women's reproductive rights and rights against sexual harassment and assault are inadequately recognized and enforced, and these inequalities affect their relationships.

That women still earn less than men in the US is likely due to many factors, including discrimination in employment, sexual harassment, differential pay for gendered work, and the difficulties of combining work and parenthood. In this essay I focus on one strand of the complex system linking gender, marriage, and power. Ending marital hierarchy would not be sufficient to end gender inequality; this requires systemic change. While here I isolate one strand, the relationship between spouses, the other strands work systematically with marriage to affect arrangements within it. Background gender inequalities, pressures, and socialization can lead to a gendered division of labor and economic inequality between spouses even when they espouse egalitarian ideals. For example, a woman may have trouble finding equal work for equal pay due to gender discrimination, or she may earn less in a "pink-collar" job than daycare will cost, and so it may seem economically rational for her to support her husband's career through unpaid domestic labor.

Socially, marriage is often understood in terms of gender roles, and expectations surrounding marriage define social gender roles in and out of marriage. Multiplied by millions of marriages, marital gender roles have large-scale economic effects. Where marriage is legally restricted to members of different sexes, it is the most significant legal institutionalization of sex and gender (except for the public registration of sex itself, and rules regarding recognition of sex change).

A key gender division within marriage is, of course, division of household labor. "Drudge wives" work a second shift of housework after returning from work outside the home; women typically perform more caring labor for children, the ill, and the elderly than their male partners. In 2007–2011, on average, full-time working mothers with children under 18 spent three times as much time on housework daily as full-time working fathers, and such mothers spent almost 50% more time daily "caring for and helping household members" than such fathers.[5] Such unequal divisions of labor lead to further inequalities: a woman may have less time and energy for paid work, and she may invest more in a male partner's career as his earning power grows relative to hers. As the gap in earning power increases, women's exit options decrease relative to their male partners', affecting decision-making power between them.[6]

Child-care responsibilities account for a large share of such inequality, as attested by the "motherhood wage gap": "mothers earn about 70 percent of the mean wages of men, and childless women earn 80 to 90 percent."[7] In 2010, among full-time and salaried workers, women earned 81.2% of what men earned.[8] Among part-time workers, men and women had comparable weekly earnings in 2012. However, working women were twice as likely to work part-time as working men (26% vs. 13%)—and part-time workers earned much lower weekly median wages ($226–236) than full-time working women ($691) or full-time working men ($854). Women with young children are much more likely to be out of the labor force than women with older or no children, and such career interruptions have cumulative costs.[9] These differences reflect social gender roles as well as their institutional reinforcement, for example, in workplaces which fail to accommodate parents.

Assumptions about women's gendered roles as wives and mothers also affect unmarried women. They can lead to workplace discrimination. A recent study found that "employed men in traditional marriages [in which wives were not employed] tend to (a) view the presence of women in the workplace unfavorably, (b) perceive that organizations with higher numbers of female employees are operating less smoothly, (c) perceive organizations with female leaders as relatively unattractive, (d) deny qualified female employees opportunities for promotion more frequently than do other married male employees. Moreover, our final study suggests that men who are single and then marry women who are not employed may change their attitudes toward women in the workplace, becoming less positive."[10] Employers may also make decisions on the basis of women's expected life trajectories, reasoning that as women are more likely to take on more responsibilities at home, they will perform worse as employees: as hedge fund manager Paul Tudor Jones recently expressed the thought, "As soon as that baby's lips touch that girl's bosom, forget it. . . Every single investment idea, every desire to understand what's going to make this go up or go down, is going to be overwhelmed by the most beautiful experience, which a man will never share, about a mode of connection between that mother and that baby."[11] The expectation of marriage can shape unmarried women's choices (as Simone de Beauvoir pointed out), as when a young woman, expecting to marry and assuming that a wife's career will be secondary, chooses less well-paid work.[12]

The 1970s feminist slogan "the personal is political" means that political structures affect and shape our personal lives and that our personal decisions in turn reinforce those political structures. Women's choices are shaped within political and social power hierarchies, increasing power inequality within ongoing marriages. In turn, women's individual choices within marriage contribute to larger economic and social inequalities between men and women as groups.

But to any given set of spouses, such structural considerations may not seem pressing. Even to spouses with egalitarian ideals, demands of caring for children, managing domestic life, and earning enough money to keep afloat will likely overshadow political concerns about divisions of labor. To others, inequalities may not seem onerous in principle or practice. Some spouses might endorse hierarchy for religious reasons or be unreservedly willing to trade equal power for access to a spouse's salary. Some wives, seized by the new domesticity, may take over the lion's share of baking, sewing, and pickling; such retro domestic goddesses may happily pursue a small business selling baked goods or craft-blogging while their husbands earn the lion's share of income and make the major decisions.

Are power hierarchies problematic in themselves? As risky as it is to generalize about feminism, one widely shared feminist view is that men and women have unequal power, that gender-structured marriage is one locus of that inequality, and that such inequality is wrong. What exactly is wrong with power inequalities within marriage?

2. What Is the Feminist Critique of Hierarchy in Marriage?

Under a model of marriage once legally enforced, and still prevalent in some religions, the husband makes the important decisions; he leads and guides the wife under his "tutelage," as Kant put it.[13] While many liberals are likely uncomfortable with rigid gender hierarchy in marriage, why should not marriage, like other associations, be hierarchically ordered—that is, allocate greater power to one spouse—on the basis of attributes such as "beauty, attractiveness, personal charm, popularity or confidence" or "contribution, achievement, effort?"[14] In a recent essay, Iddo Landau attacks the "non-hierarchy principle" (NHP) prohibiting hierarchy within marriage. He formulates NHP thus: "marital or quasi-marital relationships of heterosexual and same-sex couples should be non-hierarchical; neither partner to the relationship may be overall more dominant than the other. Relations can be hierarchical in many dimensions, but I will focus here on only two: a difference in the power that the partners to the relationship have over jointly used assets, and a difference in their power to determine joint activities."[15] I will argue that Landau's attack on NHP, even if successful, is irrelevant to much feminist critique of marital hierarchy. I then go on to defend NHP.

NHP should be clarified, in line with Landau's intentions. It would be absurd to hold that neither party can have more decision-making power at any moment or in any domain. Power shifts in dynamic and enduring relationships in small ways from day to day and year to year. For example, on my birthday, my partner might suggest that I choose everything we do on that day, and I might later reciprocate. I might consistently choose all the movies we watch, while my partner chooses TV shows.[16] NHP implies that neither party may be *overall* dominant in decision-making over time and in areas of at least some importance (would it matter if one partner ceded the choice of toothpick color, a matter on which both were entirely indifferent?).

Moreover, hierarchy must respect background moral constraints. Hierarchy, as Landau defends it, could not include violence, humiliation, or coercion. As Landau puts it, hierarchy must be compatible with Kantian respect for autonomy.[17]

Landau rejects NHP, arguing that marital hierarchy may be just. Landau assumes that showing hierarchy in the family to be unjust would require directly applying distributive principles to its internal organization (that is, showing that hierarchy is unjust in itself). He argues that principles of distributive justice such as those of John Rawls permit hierarchy in associations, and so would allow marital hierarchy. Furthermore, he points out that few theories of distributive justice require strict equality, and yet NHP seems to require strict equality in decision-making power.

However, these arguments ignore the scope of some political theories and the content of feminist critiques of hierarchy. For one thing, macro-level distributive principles such as Rawls's simply could not apply as principles of internal organization at the micro-level. It would make no sense, for instance, to divide up household resources using Rawls's difference principle: other considerations will apply. Accordingly, while it is a hallmark of feminism that the family is not exempt from justice, this does not imply that the family must be internally organized by principles of justice.[18]

In contrast to Landau's analysis, Rawls as well as some of his feminist interpreters explicitly argue that one injustice of marital hierarchy (when it is politically unjust) lies in its *effects*, not in the failure of the internal organization of the family to conform to distributive principles.[19] That is, marital hierarchy can lead to outcomes violating distributive principles of justice. Susan Moller Okin, for instance, criticizes gender inequalities within the family in part because such inequalities undermine fair equal opportunity and political stability.[20] I have argued that family hierarchy can deprive girls of the primary good of self-respect.[21] If family hierarchy conflicts with justice *in its outcomes*, it is unjust. Feminist analyses have shown how hierarchies within marriage lead to politically significant inequalities, particularly when marriages dissolve. Hence one key feminist claim is distinct from NHP: while NHP holds that hierarchies are unjust in themselves, the feminist political analysis argues that hierarchies *cause* injustices. The attack on NHP gets wrong (part of) what feminists want—that is, what the claim that hierarchy is unjust consists in.

One widely shared aspect of the feminist critique of marital hierarchy concerns its effects. Certainly, attention to effects does not exhaust the feminist critique. Feminists disagree over whether the family should be internally organized by principles of justice, just as they disagree on what the correct principles of justice are.[22] For some, internal hierarchy is morally problematic but not itself politically unjust, so long as it is consensual, and the state should not interfere, just as it should not interfere with other moral failings such as promise-breaking. For other feminists, the state should intervene in the internal organization of the family because hierarchy is itself unjust. Despite these differences, one thing feminists tend to agree on is that the *effects* of marital hierarchy are unjust and these resulting injustices require political action.

This claim cannot be assessed in a contextual vacuum. Feminism, generally speaking, focuses on how the interaction of social, biological, legal, and institutional factors disempowers women. Thus feminist analysis of an institution like marriage could not proceed by considering hierarchy in the abstract. I'll consider three contextual aspects which suggest why marital hierarchy is often unjust.

A. Gendered Division of Labor

Inequality in gendered division of household labor leads to economic inequality and reinforces broader cultural stereotypes which disadvantage women at work. Household work is work, and doing it reduces time and energy for work outside the home, increasing economic inequality.[23] For example, a study of MBAs looked at how gendered patterns in child care affected men's and women's earnings:

> Although male and female MBAs have nearly identical (labor) incomes at the outset of their careers, their earnings soon diverge ... The presence of children is the main contributor to the lesser job experience, greater career discontinuity and shorter work hours for female MBAs. Some MBA mothers, especially those with well-off spouses, slow down in the labor market within a few years following their first birth. Disparities in the productive characteristics of male and female MBAs are small, but the pecuniary penalties from shorter hours and any job discontinuity are enormous for MBAs.[24]

Income inequalities within marriage affect distributive outcomes on divorce, leading to politically relevant inequalities between men and women as groups. Within ongoing marriages, increasing economic inequality between spouses reduces the worse-off party's exit options. This, in turn, leads to power inequality in decision-making, as the less powerful party is less able to protect her interests and consequently becomes even less powerful. Okin calls this the "cycle of vulnerability."[25]

It might be rebutted that such inequalities are not politically relevant if they reflect differences in ambition.[26] However, another feminist insight is that the gendered division of labor, with its attendant costs, is usually not freely chosen in a fair bargaining situation. Once the cycle has begun and women lose power, they have less ability to negotiate or to opt out. Moreover, the initial acquiescence to gendered roles does not always reflect ambition but is shaped by social and legal pressures which constrain choice. For example, "the U.S. has a household-based taxation system which subsidizes married families when one person stays home and taxes most people extra if they choose to marry and both work full-time. The average tax cost of marriage for a dual-income couple is $1,500 annually."[27] Such penalties constrain choice and are part of a larger system pressuring women's choices in ways which disadvantage them—a system of oppression.[28] If, by contrast, two socially similar same-sex roommates established an uncompensated inequality in domestic chores, this might be ethically problematic—exploitative, perhaps—but would lack oppressive background pressures. These pressures suggest the gendered division of labor does not reflect (only) differences in ambition, but (to some extent) factors for which the parties are not responsible.[29]

Hierarchy and the gendered division of labor are distinct. A gendered division of labor need not be hierarchical; however, it can arise from and cause hierarchy. Eliminating all marital hierarchy would not end the gendered division of labor (other pressures would persist). My point is that the gendered division of labor is one context for much existing marital hierarchy, and actual hierarchies must be evaluated in light of their related social pressures and effects. The next sections will explore other contextual features.

B. Background Constraints: Injustices and Social Norms

Domestic hierarchies may arise as a direct result of injustice. This happens when, for example, a woman leaves a hostile work environment of sexual harassment and becomes economically dependent on her husband. This also happens when a woman is discriminated against in employment, or works in a lower-paid "pink-collar" field, or is paid less because she is a woman. In these cases, the woman's loss of power in her personal life is caused by a political injustice.

Some injustices consist in the failure of social institutions to conform to principles of distributive justice. Some hierarchies which appear to arise from choice or biological necessity reflect underlying institutional injustice. For example, new mothers without maternity leave may leave their jobs, reducing their power vis-à-vis their male partners. However, child care can be shared between men and women. The design and duration of maternity and paternity leave are social and institutional. If a woman has no maternity leave, or she has maternity leave but her male partner has no paternity leave, this will affect the distribution of child care labor (and hence of earning power, and hence of decision-making power). If paid parental leave is required as a matter of fair equal opportunity, but not offered, this is another case of domestic arrangements shaped by background injustice.

Social gender norms also shape women's choices within a system of oppression. When such roles are taught in public schools, as in some abstinence-only education curricula, or when they limit a child's developing autonomy and self-respect, their transmission is unjust.[30] Learned expectations that women will be nurturing, self-sacrificing, and passive, and that men will be independent, decisive, and powerful, shape marital arrangements. For example, a recent study found that "gender identity—in particular, an aversion to the wife earning more than the husband—impacts marriage formation, the wife's labor force participation, the wife's income conditional on working, satisfaction with the marriage, divorce, and the division of home production. . . Couples where the wife earns more than the husband are less satisfied with their marriage and are more likely to divorce."[31] Women earning more than their husbands did *more* household work than other women: "One explanation . . . is that, in couples where the wife earns more than her husband, the 'threatening' wife takes on a greater share of housework so as to assuage the 'threatened' husband's unease with the situation."[32] Thus, "the prevalence of this norm [that a man should earn more than his wife] helps explain the distribution of relative income within US households, patterns of marriage, divorce and women's labor market attachment, and the division of home production activities between husbands and wives."[33] This norm plays a role in a system of oppression; it gives women incentive to earn less by penalizing those who earn more.

Another set of norms tied to marriage concerns sexuality. Expectations concerning sexual gender roles—such as male dominance and female passivity—affect power within marriage. If the male is expected to initiate sex, for instance, he will have greater decision-making power over this joint activity. Indeed, the distinction between licit and illicit sexuality, so closely tied to marriage (as in US abstinence-until-marriage education), affects the public political debate over women's reproductive rights and the rights of victims of sexual assault. (Women seeking contraception and women bringing sexual assault charges have been publicly attacked as women engaging in illicit, that is, unmarried, sex.) To the extent that policies concerning reproductive rights and sexual assault affect all women, these norms also shape the power women bring to and possess in marriage.[34]

This picture is incomplete. The point is that some marital hierarchies arise from injustices such as discrimination, and some result from state-sponsored injustice. Others are shaped by social norms. Such background injustice and social norms are further reason for the point made in the last section, that income inequality between men and women in gender-structured marriages looks less like the effect of differences in ambition and more like the effect of an arbitrary difference of birth.

C. Gendered Violence

Like inequalities in reproductive rights, the background threat of gendered violence affects the power men and women bring to marriage. Women experience street harassment and sexual assault and in many cases have no recourse for such treatment: "According to a 2013 global review of available data, 35 per cent of women worldwide have experienced either physical and/or sexual intimate partner violence or non-partner sexual violence."[35] Of course, not all male-female relationships contain violence. But the experience of harassment and the threat of violence affect women's development: according to a 2001 study, 83% of 12–16-year-old girls in the US experienced sexual harassment in school.[36] Further, many intimate relationships do contain violence: "some national violence studies show that up to 70 per cent of women have experienced physical and/or sexual violence in their lifetime from an intimate partner. In Australia, Canada, Israel, South Africa and the United States, intimate partner violence accounts for between 40 and 70 per cent of female murder victims."[37] Feminists such as Claudia Card have argued that marriage law in some jurisdictions enables violence or mitigates penalties for it.[38] Furthermore, economic inequality makes it difficult for victims of abuse to leave. A major study of rape in marriage found that "90 percent of wives who stayed with their husbands following a rape depended on the husband for money, whereas only 24 percent of those who left faced this financial constraint.…. *100 percent* of those women who were the sole providers for their households at the time of the rape left their husbands following the act."[39]

Here we see again a feminist critique of marital hierarchy in its effects and its origins. Hierarchy rendering a woman dependent can trap her in an abusive relationship. Hierarchy may arise from a background of sexual and gendered violence: members of a group known to use violence may gain power simply through their connection to that group (even if they do not use violence), while members of a group who are likely to have suffered violence may acquiesce in the hopes of avoiding violence (even if their male partner is not violent).

Feminists' shared concerns about hierarchy within marriage focus on its effects and its roots in a context of inequality. Most feminists (I venture to say) see marital hierarchy as inextricable from a larger system of oppression, such that it is impossible to consider it as freely chosen and untainted by injustice in the way that hierarchy within a chess club might be. The feminist critique is broader than NHP, and thus, attacking NHP does not rebut it.

However, by the same token, an analysis of gender-structured marriage as unjust due to its effects and etiology does not entail NHP. Were a couple freely to choose marital hierarchy, with no background injustice or oppression, and if they were to divide their property fairly on divorce and made no costly career decisions, and if they had no children whose equal opportunity or self-respect would be adversely affected by witnessing their parents' power inequality, it is more difficult to see how such a marital hierarchy would be unjust. Thus, Landau could respond that hierarchy without effect, if it is chosen from an acceptable range of options, is just. While it might seem inevitable that inequalities will arise from hierarchical marriage in a context of social inequality, it is theoretically possible and philosophically interesting to evaluate hierarchy itself. Indeed, such cases are not only theoretical: men can be subordinated in marriage,[40] and hierarchy can arise in same-sex relationships where there is no background of gender inequality. I now want to argue that hierarchy itself is objectionable in personal relationships.

3. What's Wrong with Hierarchy? Defending NHP

To investigate whether hierarchy is itself objectionable in intimate relationships I will, for the sake of argument, grant the assumption that there can be freely chosen marital hierarchies without unjust outcomes. Defending NHP requires showing that certain hierarchies are unacceptable in themselves. However, not all inequalities are problematic. All relationships contain inequalities in some respects and, at times, dependency. Spouses may have unequal power in the external world. They may be unequal in strength, intelligence, income, charm—indeed, numerous such inequalities will exist, fluctuating over time. And in most long-term relationships, one partner will at times depend on the other's care. Such inequalities in power are not in themselves problematic; the problematic hierarchy is the ongoing alienation of decision-making power from one spouse to the other.

In another context, Richard Arneson describes a society in which marriage is structured unequally but gender makes no difference to life chances—men and women have equal chances of being "husbands" and "wives."[41] NHP would morally prohibit such unequally structured marriage, even though the hierarchy is not gendered or distributed by any group membership. Similarly, NHP prohibits hierarchical same-sex relationships or friendships.

Now, while I have argued that many feminist criticisms of marital hierarchy withstand Landau's critique of NHP, it is evident that many feminists are committed to NHP as well as to the wider systemic critique. Writers as different as Okin and MacKinnon would, I believe, endorse a version of NHP, because they suggest that women's lack of power in marriage is itself bad. They object to power inequality in marriage in itself and not only in its outcomes.

Asking whether marital hierarchy is objectionable in itself will help to illuminate the grounds for NHP's support. If people endorse NHP, as Landau says they do, it is likely not only because hierarchy proceeds from or causes injustice. That is, people likely do not endorse NHP primarily because hierarchy undermines distributive equality or because it was shaped by oppression, but because *it just seems wrong* for an intimate relationship between adults to be rigidly characterized by domination and submission. Plausibly, people who endorse NHP think that hierarchy is wrong in itself as a way of organizing an intimate relationship. NHP likely explains moral disapproval of relationships between much younger and older people, or an intern and a president: even if a 20-year-old is sexually autonomous, the difference in age and position suggests a troubling power imbalance.

Let us return to Landau's defense of hierarchy. He points out that most social groups incorporate hierarchies: chess clubs and country clubs, schools, and workplaces are structured hierarchically, and usually no one opposes this. (Of course, some feminists and social theorists oppose hierarchy in general because the authoritarian structures within our society are inevitably patriarchal, white supremacist, and classist; I set this aside.) If hierarchy is permitted in those associations, what exactly is wrong with it in marriage? If we do not oppose hierarchies in financial partnerships, clubs, schools, and religions, the exceptional opposition to marital hierarchy requires explanation. Landau challenges the defender of NHP to supply principles prohibiting hierarchy in intimate relationships.

Interestingly, Landau includes friendships among the associations in which hierarchy is permitted, citing Holmes and Watson. But friendship seems different in kind from those other associations. *Prima facie*, the purpose of intimate relationships is different from those of the other groups. They are structured to achieve some external goal (winning a chess tournament); hierarchies allow them to accomplish the goal and to persist as individual members change (so it is thought, anyway). Within such organizations, individual members are replaceable; positions endure while persons change.

Personal relationships—friendship and marriage-like ones—are different. A hallmark of such relationships is that the other is not replaceable. A central purpose is the relationship itself; while partners might also have a goal such as running a home, farm, business, or raising a family, the relationship itself is ideally part of their aim. Friendship is perhaps a purer example than marriage of a relationship for its own sake, as it has no institutional form or associated enterprise.

However, the non-fungibility of members of affectionate relationships, although a morally salient difference, does not alone entail NHP. Children are non-fungible to their parents, yet decision-making hierarchy between them is justified. Perhaps the nature of an intimate adult relationship precludes hierarchy—for example, if one sees the friend as another self, one must see her as an equal.[42] However, I will develop the critique of hierarchy in another direction.

To focus intuitions supporting NHP, let's consider an example of cohabiting same-sex friends, Isabel and Madame Merle (after characters in Henry James's *Portrait of a Lady*). Their arrangements are freely chosen and do not produce injustice: they have similar jobs and socioeconomic backgrounds, they had an acceptable range of roommate options, and their time together will not significantly affect their life chances. Imagine now that Isabel chooses to defer to Madame Merle. "Do whatever you like with our jointly used assets," she says. "Use them whenever you want, take first choice, and I'll just use them once you're done. You can shower first, choose the TV shows and music and food. In fact, you're in charge of all our joint activities. I will defer to you in everything. If you want to decide on our leisure activities, or to include me or exclude me, that is the way it should be, all the time!" This arrangement is clearly prohibited by NHP.

An immediate response is to ask why Isabel would choose this: her decision calls for explanation. We might guess that Merle is older and wiser, and Isabel hopes to learn from her, or that Merle supplies more resources, and Isabel wants to compensate, or that Merle has greater charm and charisma, and Isabel wants to secure her friendship. But the example, like Thomas Hill's deferential wife example, prompts the thought that something is wrong: Isabel is a masochist or lacks self-respect, and Merle, if she accepts this offer, is exploitative and disrespectful.[43]

To see what is wrong with intimate hierarchy, let's consider Landau's focal points: hierarchy over jointly used assets and over joint activities. Setting aside considerations of gender equality, what is problematic about hierarchy over jointly used assets? In the case of small household objects, furnishings, clothing, or mementos, some may be more one partner's than another—heirlooms or hobby supplies; NHP is implausible here. But decisions regarding larger assets—a home, car, savings—are likely to affect both parties significantly.

Friends or spouses might choose not to share funds, a car, or a home. However, when lives blend together, even if partners intend to keep assets separate, patterns of use will usually establish reliance and a reasonable expectation of continued use. It would then be wrong for one partner suddenly to deprive the other of what she needs and has come to rely on. Other things being equal, a wrong occurs when one party unilaterally deprives the other of something she needs, uses, and reasonably expects to continue using (such as selling the car). Rather than equal power, the salient moral considerations here are induced reliance and tacit commitments made in shared lives; these prohibit one person's unilateral control over items which the other uses and reasonably expects to continue using.

Indeed, strictly equal power over all jointly used assets seems too strong. While Okin defended "equal legal entitlement" to all household income, this could backfire if it entailed one spouse signing off on the other's loans or expenditures.[44] Such control might prevent an abused spouse from leaving. What is needed is power to access assets allowing each person to pursue her interests, including exit, and which each reasonably expects to be able to use, without the other's unilateral decision preventing it. (Cases of abuse raise special considerations; escaping violence might generate a permission to take the car unilaterally.) The apparent wrong in hierarchy over joint assets can be explained in terms of induced reliance and parties' ability to pursue their interests; NHP is less plausible here.

The more plausible target of NHP is hierarchy in determining joint activities. Again, strict equality is too stringent. People may take turns choosing and hope that decision-making balances without tracking closely who decided more often. Even for major decisions, long-term partners may assume that reciprocation will come in the future—for example, when spouses sacrifice so that one partner can care for an aging parent or weather a work crisis. The problematic hierarchy is not a lapse from strict equality in each decision, but the presumption that one party is the overall decision-maker, that one party's decision is "systematically, structurally final" while the other party enters "decisional slavery."[45] Rather than requiring strict decision-making equality, NHP is better understood as prohibiting the alienation of decision-making power on an ongoing basis.

Hierarchy, as I define it, is not just any inequality in power, but an inequality in decision-making power in which one party holds the deciding voice, binding the other. Such hierarchy may arise explicitly, through a promise to obey, but it may also arise gradually and tacitly. This is the type of hierarchy which is objectionable in itself. What can be said in defense of NHP, thus formulated?

A. Skepticism About Benevolence

One might assume that if one person's choice is wholly subordinate to another person's, her long-term interests will inevitably suffer. If so, hierarchy will fail Hampton's test for fairness in a relationship: "could both of us reasonably accept the distribution of costs and benefits . . . if it were the subject of an informed, unforced agreement in which we think of ourselves as motivated solely by self-interest?"[46] However, *loving* hierarchy, like parenting or benevolent dictatorship, could aim at the good of the subordinate party. Such hierarchy is actually (*contra* Landau) a widespread ideal—for Mormons, Southern Baptists, and Promise-Keepers, for instance, the husband leads or presides over the household. Their teachings on marriage state that "by divine design, fathers are to preside over their families in love and righteousness," and wives are "to subject themselves to their husbands."[47] Kant is only one of many philosophers who paternalistically endorsed gendered marital hierarchy, and belief in the husband's greater competence informed the law of coverture (in which a wife's legal personality was covered by that of her husband's). The subordinate party was to benefit from her husband's making decisions in her best interests.

Even if we set aside claims about gender inequality—thinking back, for instance, to Isabel and Merle—this response faces skepticism that one person, even a loving person, will consistently decide in the best interests of another, especially when interests conflict. There is also an epistemic problem. Even if the dominant partner intended to further the other's best interests, he might not know enough to do so. If even a well-meaning dominant partner may err due to ignorance or weakness of will, we must also remember that not all relationships are loving, and a dominant partner might consistently fail to make benevolent decisions.

A second intimation that hierarchy harms the subordinate is distinct. This is that, even if a preternaturally wise and benevolent decider invariably chose in the other's best interests, *hierarchy itself would constitute a harm to the subordinate partner*; ceding decision-making power is itself a harm. Before developing this thought, I will note a second objection to marital hierarchy.

B. Temporal Duration and Global Effects

Marriages are usually intended to endure, as are some unmarried partnerships. This poses a question about the duration of hierarchy within them. If consent to hierarchy is given at the outset, is it revocable without dissolving the marriage? If not, it is not genuinely consensual in an ongoing sense. Over time, a spouse may wish to alter the balance of power, but the cost—losing the marriage—would be objectionably high. Alienating one's decision-making power indefinitely and irrevocably resembles self-enslavement.[48]

Contrary to Landau's claim that NHP is extraordinary, it is indefinitely alienating one's power to make day-to-day and major life decisions which is in fact extraordinary. A comparable renunciation might only be found in entering a monastic order—even people joining the military expect to exit eventually and to retain some control over their personal lives. The temporal duration of marriage, as well as its global effect on all the quotidian circumstances of one's life and the overall shape of one's life, makes it an exceptional context for alienating choice.

C. Combination of Skeptical and Temporal Objections

The temporal duration of marriage and marriage-like partnerships suggests how hierarchy might itself harm the subordinate. Over time, she may lose her decision-making capacity by alienating her decision-making power. Voltairine de Cleyre suggested this in her attack on marriage and "free unions" as limiting self-sufficiency. de Cleyre argued that the domestically interdependent become unable to fend for themselves:

> . . . after the relation has been maintained for a few years, the interdependence of one on the other has become so great that each is somewhat helpless when circumstance destroys the combination, the man less so, the woman wretchedly so . . . Now this is one of the greatest objections to the married condition, as it is to any other condition which produces like results. In choosing one's economic position in society, one should always bear in mind that it should be such as should leave the individual uncrippled—an all-round person, with both productive and preservative capacities, a being pivoted within.[49]

de Cleyre's Romantic ideal of self-development ignores our necessary interdependence (even the word "crippled" suggests ableism). But she interestingly criticizes the effects of marriage "from the viewpoint that the object of life should be the development of individuality": "[t]hat life may grow, I would have men and women remain separate personalities."[50]

de Cleyre's worry that marriage diminishes self-reliance relates to hierarchy. Decision-making involves independent judgment. If one partner constantly defers to the other, her own judgment may erode. Someone unused to making decisions can lose her own point of view, thinking only of what would please others. Over a long period, hierarchy might harm the subordinate by sapping her capacity to make decisions. Marital hierarchy differs from a workplace, club, or school hierarchy because it concerns decisions about how to live, daily and long-term: whether and how to pursue a career or education, socialize, or spend leisure time. Empirical evidence would be required to make a decisive case; but it is at least plausible that permanently transferring decision-making authority risks diminishing the capacity itself.

D. Autonomy Objection

The preceding objection depends upon psychological speculation. A final objection is normative: no one should give up decision-making power in certain domains. The intimacy of marriage, its involvement of all aspects of life, entails that ceding decision-making power within it differs fundamentally from ceding decision-making power in other associations. Joint activities will inevitably overlap with morally protected choices to such a large extent that decisions regarding them cannot be transferred. Choosing what to eat, where to live, how and when to have sex, whether to pursue an active or sedentary lifestyle, spend or save, have children or pets—the thought is that these kinds of decisions are protected. Again, contrary to Landau's claim that NHP is exceptional, deference in such decisions is only approached in two other social institutions: the military and monastic orders. And in the military, such deference is temporary and limited. The way marriage and other intimate relationships affect the totality of life is what distinguishes them from other social relationships. This might also explain the relevance of personal non-fungibility within them—the whole person is involved in such relationships, whereas only an aspect of the self is involved at work or in clubs. Thus, giving up decision-making power in intimate relationships cedes a greater range of decisions than in other contexts.

Now, I have been assuming that hierarchy in determining joint activities includes major life decisions such as where to live, domestic responsibilities, work-family balance, and daily domestic activities such as meals, chores, and recreation. But many decisions which affect joint activities should not be decided hierarchically *or* equally because they are properly the decision of only one person. For example, a woman may decide to leave her spouse, which affects their joint activities, but he shouldn't have equal or hierarchical power over this decision. The same goes for many personal decisions: medical care, diet, appearance, career, voting, taking roles in community organizations, and so on. A decision to become a vegetarian will affect what and where partners can eat together; a decision to run a marathon will affect how much leisure time one has; decisions regarding birth control will affect how a straight couple can have sex without procreating; and so on. Spouses should not have joint power over these choices because they are choices regarding one person's body which each person ultimately has the right to decide. Hierarchical decision-making on such joint activities would entail abrogating personal autonomy.

This is not to say that partners should disregard one another's wishes. In a caring relationship, parties will take each other's preferences into account. However, a woman's decision regarding contraceptive use, or a man's regarding a vasectomy, should trump the other partner's wishes, since it affects one's body more directly. Once again, this is complicated by shared histories. If someone promises to take the pill for five years in exchange for her partner's promise to get a vasectomy at that point, he is no longer at liberty, morally, to refuse. (Of course, his reasons may have changed, such that his nonperformance is excused or mitigated.) The morality of decision-making in relationships is affected by many factors, including promises. Still, decisions regarding one's own body and independent activities are properly each agent's own.

Thus, decision-making power over joint activities is restricted to activities which are not protected choices about one's own body or activities. Medical, dietary, sexual, and reproductive decisions are protected; but so too are choices about career, friends, and hobbies. This leaves a thin residue. One properly joint decision is the balance of joint versus independent activities: partners must decide how much time will be spent together as opposed to alone or at work or with friends. And this choice seems a paradigmatic example of NHP: one partner should not unilaterally decide how much time will be spent together. Imagine that Merle and Isabel were to agree: "Merle will decide how much time we spend together. Isabel will remain available for whenever Merle wants her, although Merle may stay out until the whim takes her to return home." Intuitively, the choice of how much time to spend together should not be one partner's alone.

This argument needs moral grounding.[51] Each of the choices I have listed as protected may, it seems, be transferred. While arguably decisions leading to irreversible physical harm and regarding sex and reproduction cannot be the subject of promissory obligation, many of the decisions I have described as protected are possible subjects of promise and, hence, can be restricted by another's choice. I can promise (not) to have a medical procedure done, to eat someone's carefully prepared meal, to stay at home, and so on. But while power over individual decisions can be transferred, power over these decisions as a class cannot.

Roughly, a Kantian ethical ideal requires respecting autonomy in oneself and others. Respecting another person's autonomy requires respecting her ability to choose: this is why coercion and deception, which bypass the ability to choose, treat others as mere means. Alienating this ability, submitting one's choice to that of another permanently and globally, fails to respect one's own autonomy; asking another person to do so fails to respect their autonomy. This explains why role-play or daily micro-shifts in power are permissible, but persistent subjugation is not; the wrong is alienating one's power of choice entirely, on an ongoing and open-ended basis.

In some contexts we alienate choice permissibly: we defer to expertise in our plumber, surgeon, or teacher. But here we alienate only one aspect of our choice, and we do not give up our autonomy: our autonomy sets our ends (to have our plumbing fixed) and deferring to expertise is the best means to that end (one hopes). We also defer to club officials or workplace superiors to serve autonomously chosen ends—a hobby or career. In contrast, the decisions made in marriage or other intimate relationships concern the larger ends themselves: how to live, daily and long-term. A hierarchical model of marriage requires the submissive party to alienate her ability to set ends autonomously because marriage involves shared lives, and hence deference within it involves deferring on all the ends of life. We can see this by considering a contrast case, in which one party deferred in order to avoid responsibility—for example, if Isabel, wanting to focus on her studies, happily left all decision-making to Merle.[52] Here, Isabel has chosen an end (her studies) and her deference serves, and is limited by, this end. By contrast, in marital hierarchy the ends of life are left to the dominant party.[53]

Landau might respond that the submissive party has autonomously chosen the end of being in a hierarchical marriage, just as a monk chooses a monastic life.[54] What differentiates such a commitment from an open-ended commitment to a hierarchical workplace or club? Again, social context is relevant. Hierarchy in the workplace, clubs, and so on, is (theoretically) justified by expertise, seniority, and such. In marriage, the explanation has historically been a preference for the male and belief in his greater decision-making ability. But for the sake of argument, let's imagine that spouses spontaneously choose hierarchy in a cultural vacuum. Landau states that this would not conflict with Kantian autonomy, understood as "the ability to choose rationally and freely which options one commits oneself to, without being cheated, manipulated, treated paternalistically or objectified."[55] But respecting one's capacity to set ends requires not alienating it. Transferring the totality of decisions regarding how to live, indefinitely, fails to respect one's capacity of choice. (This does not entail that women pressured into doing this should be blamed.)

Respecting autonomy supports NHP's prohibition of one partner's unilateral controlling joint activities. What is prohibited is the ongoing transfer of significant decision-making power. This entails that, over time, partners should have roughly equal say in decisions which affect their shared lives, except when a decision involves one partner's protected sphere of personal autonomy. Neither partner should have the right to make all decisions regarding joint activities.[56]

4. Non-hierarchical Relations and Marriage Reform

Gender-structured marriage and legal and social institutions surrounding it create hierarchies disempowering women. One response has been to argue for abolishing marriage; others have argued that marriage reform can combat gender hierarchy by legally eliminating gendered spousal roles.[57] As some have argued regarding polygamy, legal recognition may allow regulation impossible when the practice is unrecognized.

A practical question is which arrangement best preserves equal decision-making power in relationships. Reforms such as parental leave and improving women's healthcare would change background social conditions, the context of marital hierarchy. But this essay focuses on the structure of relationships. Notably, friends who cohabit typically do so without hierarchy. Usually, neither is subordinate, nor do they expect one person to bear a disproportionate share of the burdens of shared living.

de Cleyre would likely point out that friends typically have separate as well as joint activities, roles, and friends. Okin reported that reduced exit options increased marital power inequality; maintaining exit options, then, should preserve power equality. Friendships do this because even cohabiting friends tend to have separate aspects of their lives—even deferential

Watson had his own friends, relationship, and medical career. Traditional marriage, by contrast, reflected the unity conception, in which identity was submerged within the relationship with no residue of separateness. Unlike traditional spouses, friends retain independence; there is no social pressure to submerge individuality (or name, or legal identity) within a friendship. Neither friend is expected to be the dominant partner in the relationship. Ideally, friends interact as equals; while friendship may fall short of this ideal, there is no institutionalized form or social pressure encouraging inequality within it.

A long line of feminists has proposed that marital relations be modeled on friendship.[58] While it has been argued that same-sex marriage would break down the last legal entrenchment of gender roles, a friendship model for relationships goes further.[59] Like same-sex relationships, friendships are not defined by gender; moreover, they are not shaped by the union concept which still socially informs marriage. Two people just do not reduce to one; there are two wills, and when marriage is thought of as having only one will, that will has inevitably been the husband's. A feminist egalitarian ideal of marriage could be modeled on friendship, where friends seek one another's good without sacrificing individuality and exit options. Crucial to this model is independence within the relationship.

I previously argued from a political liberal perspective for "minimal marriage," legal frameworks supporting different relationship structures such as polyamorous groups and friend networks. My argument here supports minimal marriage from within a comprehensive ethical doctrine. Modeling marriage (or marriage-like) law on friendship would resemble minimal marriage: supports for caring relationships, with no assumptions about sexual interaction, procreation, number of parties, reciprocity of all legal rights, shared totality of lives, or union. Eroding the legal distinction between marriage and life-structuring friendships will end the last formal legal entrenchment of hierarchy within marriage, the assumption of a shared life in which both parties are subsumed.[60]

Notes

1. For one version of the equality argument for same-sex marriage, see Alex Rajczi, "A Populist Argument for Same-Sex Marriage," *The Monist* 91:3–4 (2008): 475–505.

2. Linda C. McClain, "The Other Marriage Equality Problem," *Boston University Law Review* 93:3 (2013): 921–970.

3. Thanks to Lori Watson for suggesting this clarification. Polyamory and polygamy raise distinct problems of inequality; for discussion, see Peter de Marneffe, "Liberty and

Polygamy" and Laurie Shrage, "Polygamy, Privacy, and Equality," Chapters 6 and 7 in this volume.

4. Friedan's book gives a partial picture of women's oppression, focusing on well-off white women. See bell hooks, *Feminist Theory: From Margin to Center* (Boston: South End Press, 1984), chapter 1.

5. Mothers in this group spent .82 hours a day on housework while fathers spent .26 hours; mothers spent 1.29 hours a day "caring for and helping household members" while fathers spent 0.88 hours. American Time Use Survey, Table A-7, 2007–2011, Bureau of Labor Statistics, accessed at http://www.bls.gov/tus/tables/a7_0711.htm, July 22, 2014.

6. See Susan Moller Okin, *Justice, Gender, and the Family* (New York: Basic Books, 1989), 156–167, for a classic description of this cycle and the effects of economic inequality on decision-making power. It might be responded that a full-time homemaker has a better life than her working-class husband in a tedious or demanding job. For a response, see Anca Gheaus, "Gender Justice," *Journal of Ethics and Social Philosophy* 6:2 (2012): 1–24.

7. Anne Alstott, *No Exit: What Parents Owe Their Children and What Society Owes Parents* (Oxford: Oxford University Press, 2004), 24. Alstott cites a 1998 study; below I set out more recent statistics.

8. Bureau of Labor Statistics, U.S. Department of Labor, *The Editor's Desk*, "Women's Earnings as a Percent of Men's in 2010," accessed at http://www.bls.gov/opub/ted/2012/ted_20120110.htm, January 22, 2014. See also Bureau of Labor Statistics, U.S. Department of Labor, *Highlights of Women's Earning in 2012*, accessed at http://www.bls.gov/cps/cpswom2012.pdf, June 12, 2014.

9. Bureau of Labor Statistics, *The Editor's Desk*, "Happy Mother's Day from BLS," accessed at http://www.bls.gov/opub/ted/2013/ted_20130510.htm, June 12, 2014. See also Marianne Bertrand, Claudia Goldin, and Lawrence F. Katz, "Dynamics of the Gender Gap for Young Professionals in the Corporate and Financial Sectors," Working Paper 14681, National Bureau of Economic Research, Issued 2009.

10. Sreedhari Desai, Dolly Chugh, and Arthur Brief, "The Implications of Marriage Structure for Men's Workplace Attitudes, Beliefs, and Behaviors Toward Women," in *Administrative Science Quarterly* 59:2 (2014): 330–365, p. 330.

11. Quoted in William Alden, "When a Billionaire Speaks Off the Cuff on Motherhood," *The New York Times*, May 23, 2013, accessed online: http://dealbook.nytimes.com/2013/05/24/when-a-billionaire-speaks-off-the-cuff/, July 29, 2014.

12. Simone de Beauvoir, *The Second Sex*, edited and translated by H. M. Parshley (New York: Vintage Books, 1989); see, e.g., p. 425.

13. "A woman, regardless of her age, is under civil tutelage . . . her husband is her natural curator." Immanuel Kant, *Anthropology from a Pragmatic Point of View*, translated by Mary Gregor (The Hague: Martinus Nijhoff, 1974 [originally published 1798]), 7:209 (marginal numbers).

14. Iddo Landau, "Should Marital Relations be Non-hierarchical?" *Ratio* 25:1 (2012): 51–67, pp. 64, 66.

15. Landau, "Marital Relations," 51.

16. Example from Landau, "Marital Relations," 52.

17. Landau, "Marital Relations," 58.

18. Also, not all feminist analyses of injustice focus on distribution. See Iris Marion Young, *Justice and the Politics of Difference* (Princeton, NJ: Princeton University Press, 1990).

19. John Rawls, "The Idea of Public Reason Revisited," *The University of Chicago Law Review* 64:3 (1997): 765–807, pp. 787–791, and Okin, *Justice, Gender*.

20. Okin, *Justice, Gender*, and Okin, "Political Liberalism, Justice, and Gender," *Ethics* 105 (1994): 23–43.

21. "Feminism, Family Law, and the Social Bases of Self-Respect," in *Re-reading the Canon Series: Feminist Interpretations of Rawls*, edited by Ruth Abbey (University Park, PA: Penn State University Press, 2013), 57–74.

22. See Clare Chambers, *Sex, Culture, and Justice: The Limits of Choice* (University Park, PA: Penn State University Press, 2008); Catharine A. MacKinnon, *Toward a Feminist Theory of the State* (Cambridge, MA: Harvard University Press, 1989); my *Minimizing Marriage: Marriage, Morality, and the Law* (New York: Oxford University Press, 2012), chapter 8.

23. See Nancy Folbre, *Who Pays for the Kids? Gender and the Structures of Constraint* (New York: Routledge, 1994), and Susan Maushart, *Wifework: What Marriage Really Means for Women* (New York: Bloomsbury, 2001).

24. Bertrand et al., "Dynamics of the Gender Gap," abstract.

25. Okin, *Justice, Gender*, 149–154.

26. See Richard J. Arneson, "What Sort of Sexual Equality Should Feminists Seek?" *Journal of Contemporary Legal Issues* 9:21 (1998): 21–36, pp. 23–24.

27. Justin Wolfers, interview, "Economists in Love," accessed online at http://www.itsthedishes.com/2343/2011/03/economists-in-love-betsey-stevenson-and-justin-wolfers/ on March 10, 2011.

28. See Ann Cudd, *Analyzing Oppression* (New York: Oxford University Press, 2006).

29. For a different feminist analysis, see Ann Levey, "Liberalism, Adaptive Preferences, and Gender Equality," *Hypatia* 20:4 (2005): 127–143.

30. On abstinence-only curricula, see the report prepared for Sen. Henry Waxman, accessible online at http://www.apha.org/apha/PDFs/HIV/The_Waxman_Report.pdf, accessed July 24, 2014. On children's rights, see Brake, "Feminism, Family Law," and Matthew Clayton, *Justice and Legitimacy in Upbringing* (Oxford: Oxford University Press, 2006).

31. Marianne Bertrand, Emir Kamenica, and Jessica Pan, "Gender Identity and Relative Income Within Households," Working Paper No. 84, Chicago Booth Paper No. 13-08, 2013, 1. The study focuses on the US.

32. Bertrand et al., "Gender Identity," 4.

33. Bertrand et al., "Gender Identity," 27.

34. See for instance MacKinnon, *Toward a Feminist Theory*.

35. UN Entity for Gender Equality and the Empowerment of Women, http://www.unwomen.org/en/what-we-do/ending-violence-against-women/facts-and-figures, accessed July 22, 2014.

36. Cited by the UN Entity for Gender Equality and the Empowerment of Women, http://www.unwomen.org/en/what-we-do/ending-violence-against-women/facts-and-figures, accessed July 22, 2014.

37. UN Entity for Gender Equality and the Empowerment of Women, http://www.unwomen.org/en/what-we-do/ending-violence-against-women/facts-and-figures, accessed July 22, 2014.

38. See Claudia Card, "Against Marriage and Motherhood," *Hypatia* 11:3 (1996): 1–23.

39. Lisa R. Eskow, "The Ultimate Weapon? Demythologizing Spousal Rape and Reconceptualizing Its Prosecution," *Stanford Law Review* 48:3 (1996): 677–709, p. 688. In Chapter 5.i of *Minimizing Marriage* I discuss sexual assault and domestic abuse in greater detail.

40. Thanks to Anca Gheaus for this point.

41. Arneson, "Sexual Equality," 24.

42. This paragraph owes much to Lori Watson. Aristotle's *Nicomachean Ethics* and Kant's *Metaphysics of Morals* have much to add on friendship.

43. See Thomas E. Hill, Jr., "Servility and Self-Respect," *The Monist* 57:1 (1973): 87–104. Hill's discussion has sparked much commentary. Since hierarchy as I understand it need not involve servility, this discussion is orthogonal.

44. Okin, *Justice, Gender*, 180.

45. I owe these phrases to Tamara Metz.

46. Jean Hampton, in "Feminist Contractarianism," in *A Mind of One's Own*, ed. Louise Antony and Charlotte Witt (Oxford: Westview Press, 1993), 227–256, p. 240.

47. Quoting, respectively, " 'The Family: A Proclamation to the World,' The First Presidency and Council of the Twelve Apostles of the Church of Jesus Christ of Latter-Day Saints," accessed at https://www.lds.org/bc/content/shared/content/english/pdf/language-materials/35602_eng.pdf (July 22, 2014); "Christ-Centered Marriages: Husbands and Wives Complementing One Another," by Chad Brand, 1998, accessed at http://www.baptist2baptist.net/b2barticle.asp?ID=230 (July 24, 2014). Of course, many practitioners of these religions treat family members as equals. The Mormon proclamation states that fathers are to "preside," but men and women "are obligated to help one another as equal partners"; Brand argues that male headship is compatible with men and women being equal before God. Examples could be found in other world religions. My point is that major religions endorse gendered marital hierarchy, even though Landau states that NHP is widespread.

48. This paragraph owes much to Tamara Metz.

49. Voltairine de Cleyre, "They Who Marry Do Ill," in *The Voltairine de Cleyre Reader*, ed. A. J. Brigati (Oakland, CA: AK Press, 2004), 11–20, p. 17.

50. de Cleyre, "They Who Marry," 15, 20.

51. I argue within a comprehensive ethical framework and hence am not making a case, within political liberalism, for state action; for a discussion of political liberalism, perfectionism, feminism, and autonomy, see Chambers, *Sex, Culture*, chapter 7.

52. Thanks to Anca Gheaus for this example.

53. A Kantian account could also be developed in terms of shared reasons: for an activity to be joint, the reasons must be shared. Unilateral control is not a reason which can be shared. Thanks to Lori Watson for this suggestion; see Anthony Laden, *Reasonably Radical* (Ithaca, NY: Cornell University Press, 2001).

54. For interesting discussion of whether becoming a nun wrongly alienates autonomy, see Chambers, *Sex, Culture*, chapter 7.

55. Landau, "Marital Relations," 58.

56. It might be objected that this wrongly prohibits BDSM communities. I think it will depend on details: where subordination is temporary and fully consensual, NHP need not prohibit it; when it is long-term, it becomes problematic. Thanks to Laurie Shrage for raising this question.

57. For abolitionists, see Card, "Against Marriage and Motherhood," Martha Fineman, *The Autonomy Myth: A Theory of Dependency* (New York: New Press, 2004); Tamara Metz, *Untying the Knot: Marriage, the State, and the Case for Their Divorce* (Princeton, NJ: Princeton University Press, 2010); and Clare Chambers, "The Marriage-Free State," *Proceedings of the Aristotelian Society* 107:2 (2013): 123–143. For reformists, see Brake, *Minimizing Marriage*, Ann Ferguson, "Gay Marriage: An American and Feminist Dilemma," *Hypatia: A Journal of Feminist Philosophy* 22:1 (2007): 39–57; and Christie Hartley and Lori Watson, "Political Liberalism, Marriage and the Family," *Law and Philosophy* 31:2 (2012): 185–212.

58. See Ruth Abbey and Douglas Den Uyl, "The Chief Inducement? The Idea of Marriage as Friendship," *Journal of Applied Philosophy* 18:1 (2001): 37–52.

59. See Ferguson, "Gay Marriage."

60. I would like to thank Anca Gheaus, Laurie Shrage, Tamara Metz, Christie Hartley, and Lori Watson for many helpful comments and suggestions.

6| Liberty and Polygamy

PETER DE MARNEFFE

POLYGAMOUS COHABITATION SHOULD BE DECRIMINALIZED. There should be no criminal penalties for living as husband and wife with someone other than one's legal spouse, or for being married in a religious ceremony to someone other than one's legal spouse, or for regarding or treating someone other than one's legal spouse as one's husband or wife. Adults have a right to sexual freedom, which includes the freedom to have sexual relations with other consenting adults whatever their marital status. Criminal penalties for polygamous cohabitation violate this right.

It does not follow that polygamy should be legalized, or that it should be possible to be legally married to more than one person at the same time. Whether polygamy should be legalized depends on what the law of marriage should be. This depends partly on what goals warrant the government in recognizing marriage as a legal status in the first place, and partly on what legal rules make the most sense all things considered, taking into account the complexities of family law, inheritance law, tax law, immigration law, and criminal law. If polygamy does not advance the goals that warrant the government in recognizing marriage as a legal status and the legalization of polygamy is not necessary to advance or accommodate other important policy goals, then the legalization of polygamy is unwarranted even if polygamous cohabitation should be decriminalized.

In this essay, then, I have three main goals. First, to explain why criminal penalties for polygamous cohabitation violate a right to sexual freedom. Second, to explain why it does not follow that the nonlegalization of polygamy violates anyone's rights. Third, to explain why it therefore makes sense in principle to hold that polygamy should be decriminalized but not legalized. I do not argue here against the legalization of polygamy or defend an all-things-considered judgment that the government should not legalize polygamy. My aim is much more limited than this. It is simply to explain how a person who takes individual rights seriously can consistently oppose the legalization of polygamy while holding that polygamous cohabitation should be decriminalized.

Why Criminalization Violates Sexual Freedom

Here is a simple argument for decriminalization. The government can criminalize polygamous cohabitation only by criminalizing certain instances of adultery and fornication. Criminal penalties for adultery and fornication violate our rights to sexual freedom. Therefore criminal penalties for polygamous cohabitation violate our rights to sexual freedom and should be repealed.

By *polygamous cohabitation* I mean a situation in which A has an ongoing sexual relationship with both B and C under the following conditions: A and B are legally married, and view each other as husband and wife; A and B also regard C as A's wife although A and C are not legally married; and C regards A as her husband, even though she knows that A is legally married only to B. By *adultery* I mean sex between a legally married person and someone who is not that person's legal spouse. By *fornication* I mean sex between persons who are not legally married to each other. Given these definitions, criminal penalties for polygamous cohabitation necessarily involve criminal penalties for adultery and fornication. Because there should be no criminal penalties for adultery and fornication, the government should not impose criminal penalties for polygamous cohabitation.

Against this argument it might be objected that polygamy is regarded by those who practice it as a marital status, whether it is legally recognized or not, and that it is "a mistake to view marriage in terms of sexual relations alone."[1] Laws prohibiting polygamous cohabitation nonetheless prohibit sexual conduct that should not be prohibited, and for this reason should be repealed.

This simple argument for decriminalization assumes that we have a right to engage in adultery, which some might challenge on the ground that adultery is wrong. But one can grant that adultery is wrong and still hold that people have a right to engage in it. To say that we have a right to do something is not to say that it is right to do it; it is to say that it is wrong for the government to prohibit us from doing it; and this idea is perfectly familiar from other contexts. For example, it is wrong for a politician to cynically misrepresent the position of his opponent for personal gain, but it is also wrong for the government to prohibit him from doing so. This is partly because if the government is permitted to prohibit politicians from misrepresenting the views of their opponents, it is likely to abuse this power and prohibit political candidates from making valid criticisms of those in power. Participants in a democratic political process also have important interests in effectively getting their political message across to voters, and they are likely to be prevented from doing so if those in power are permitted to censor their criticism of opponents. Furthermore, citizens have important interests in being able to make an informed judgment about whom to vote for, and they are likely to be less well-informed if the government is permitted to censor candidates' criticism of each other. Because these important interests are better protected when the government observes a rule prohibiting it from prohibiting political candidates from misrepresenting the positions of their opponents, it would be wrong for the government to prohibit a politician from misrepresenting the position of his opponent even when it would be wrong for him to do so.

The right to sexual freedom can also be explained by reference to important interests. We have important interests in discretionary control over our own bodies and part of having this discretionary control is being at liberty to give or refuse one's sexual consent. Criminal penalties for adultery, which impose criminal penalties for giving this kind of consent, substantially reduce this area of discretionary control. We also have important interests in being able to form emotionally satisfying intimate friendships or romantic partnerships, and also in having adequate opportunity to do so. In some cases, partly due to the difficulty of divorce, it is important to have the opportunity to form an intimate friendship with someone who is married or with someone other than one's legal spouse. Because these interests are so important, laws that prohibit adultery violate a right to sexual freedom.

This is not to deny that adultery is sometimes wrong. If A invites B to rely on A to treat B with respect and consideration, and A promises not to betray or humiliate B, or to act in a way that can be foreseen to result in B reasonably feeling betrayed or humiliated, and A then betrays B or acts in a way that foreseeably results in B reasonably feeling betrayed or humiliated, then, absent extraordinary circumstances, A wrongs B. One can grant this, however, and still consistently hold that the important interests we have in sexual freedom outweigh the interest we have in being protected by the criminal law from being wronged in this way. It is also generally wrong not to keep one's word, but criminal penalties for promise-breaking in our personal relationships would be intolerably intrusive. For this reason it makes sense to hold that although it is generally wrong not to keep one's promises, our interests in managing our personal relationships free of the threat of criminal penalties have greater weight than our interests in being protected by the criminal law from being disappointed by others in this way. A similar line of reasoning makes sense with respect to adultery. Rigorous enforcement of adultery laws would be highly intrusive and change the character of our intimate relationships in objectionable ways. Lax enforcement would not provide an effective deterrent and would therefore not do much to protect us from betrayal and humiliation. In either case our reasons to prefer our situations when there are no such laws decisively outweigh our reasons to prefer our situations when such laws are in place.

The sexual freedom argument for decriminalizing polygamous cohabitation also does not assume that polygamous cohabitation is never wrong. If B marries A on the assumption that both are entering a lifelong monogamous commitment, and A then enters a marriage-like relationship with C without B's consent, or if A secures B's consent only by making certain threats, or if A secures B's consent only as a result of threats made by A's or B's religious leaders, or if A secures B's consent only by some form of dishonesty or misrepresentation, or if A's relationship with C will foreseeably place a heavy burden on the children of A and B, then A's relationship with C might well be wrong. The government would still violate A's rights in imposing criminal penalties on A for having this relationship. This is because wrongs of this kind, although genuine, are not the proper target of criminal penalties, given our weighty interests in sexual freedom.

To claim that adults have a right to engage in polygamous cohabitation is also not to deny that this kind of family arrangement typically threatens the interests of children. If a man who has children with one woman enters a quasi-marital relationship with a second woman and has more children with her, then typically he will have less time for his children from the first marriage and typically will be able to contribute fewer resources to their care. This, however, is equally true of divorce and remarriage. If the interests that children have in receiving good parental care do not justify the government in imposing criminal penalties on their father for having sexual relations with someone other than their mother when their parents are divorced, or for having more children with someone other than their mother after their parents are divorced, then the interests of children in receiving good parental care do not justify the government in imposing criminal penalties on their father for having sexual relations and children with someone other than their mother when their parents are still legally married. Here it is worth adding that the interests of the children of plural unions are not harmed by polygamous cohabitation assuming that their lives are worth living and that they would not have come into existence but for these polygamous relationships.

A plausible rationale for bigamy laws in the nineteenth century was to reduce the desertion of wives and children by husbands and fathers. Most nineteenth-century marriages were characterized by a traditional sexual division of labor, with fathers and husbands working outside the home for money and wives staying at home and taking care of the children and the housework. It was more difficult for women to find satisfying and well-paid employment outside the home, and there was no government aid for families with dependent children. In these conditions, desertion by husbands and fathers typically imposed a serious hardship on mothers and children. If bigamy laws substantially reduced the rate of desertion by making it a crime to live as husband and wife with someone other than one's legal spouse, this was a good reason for them. These laws might also have functioned to protect single women from fraudulent seduction in an era when fornication was illegal and, especially for women, heavily stigmatized. The conditions that make sense of nineteenth-century bigamy laws no longer exist, however. It is now much easier for women to find satisfying work outside the home; there is government aid for families with dependent children; and extramarital sex is no longer subject to criminal penalties or heavily stigmatized. So the good reasons there might have been for criminalizing bigamy in the nineteenth century are no longer good reasons for criminalizing polygamous cohabitation now.

I should now clarify that to ground a right on an important interest is not to claim that this interest trumps all other interests. The important interests that ground our right to freedom of expression, for example, do not trump our interests in not being victimized by a violent mob. So if some people will surely be the victims of violence unless the government prohibits political speech that incites violence against them and they will be safe if the government prohibits this speech, then this policy does not violate any right to freedom of expression. Likewise, if it were necessary to prohibit polygamous cohabitation in order to protect life, liberty, or property, these laws would not violate a right to sexual freedom. Voluntary adult polygamous cohabitation, however, does not threaten anyone's life, liberty, or property, any more than voluntary adult monogamy does. Although there is some reason to believe that there is more child abuse and neglect in polygamous families than in monogamous ones, criminal penalties for polygamous cohabitation are not an effective way to deal with this abuse and neglect. For one thing, these laws do not stop the religious practice of polygamy. For another, their enforcement in the past and their potential enforcement in the future have made members of polygamous communities more mistrustful of government officials than they otherwise would be, and, as a consequence, these laws have made it more difficult for law enforcement and child protective services to protect the children in polygamous communities from abuse and neglect and to ensure that they receive adequate education and health care. Criminal penalties for polygamous cohabitation violate a right sexual freedom, then, because they threaten important interests in sexual freedom *and* they are ineffective and counterproductive in protecting children from abuse and neglect.

The marriage of teenage girls to older men in polygamous cults such as the FLDS in Colorado City, Arizona, is a legitimate object of government concern, as is the expulsion from these communities of disobedient boys. The best approach to these problems, however, is to require that all children receive an adequate education. An adequate education for the children in these communities would inform them of their legal rights as citizens and as children; inform them of state laws against statutory rape and underage marriage; provide them with the skills necessary to gain employment outside these communities should they decide to leave; and inform them of the government agencies and nongovernmental organizations that provide help and support to those who leave these communities. Accomplishing these goals would not necessarily require compulsory public school education, but it would require private schools and homeschooling parents to prove that they are providing an education that achieves these goals. Because neither Arizona nor Utah currently does this, both states are failing to protect the interests of children in these communities adequately. Achieving these educational goals would not stop all girls above the age of sexual consent from deciding against their best interests to enter into plural unions for religious reasons, but there is a limit to what the government may do to prevent these decisions compatible with respecting their rights and the rights of others. Young people above the age of sexual consent sometimes make unwise sexual or marital decisions, whether they live in Colorado City or New York City. So do people who are older. This fact alone cannot justify criminal penalties.

Why Nonlegalization Violates No One's Rights

Although criminal penalties for polygamous cohabitation violate a right to sexual freedom, it does not follow that anyone's rights are violated by the nonlegalization of polygamy. Even if no one is permitted to be legally married to more than one person at a time, no one is thereby prohibited from having consensual sex with another adult, and no one is thereby prohibited from practicing polygamous cohabitation for religious reasons, and no one is thereby prohibited from going through a religious marriage ceremony with someone other than one's legal spouse. If two people wish to have a purely religious wedding—one that does not represent an official government act—and to live together afterward as husband and wife when one of them is already legally married to someone else, they may do so even if polygamy is not legalized.

The nonlegalization of polygamy is also compatible with "the right to marry and to found a family" recognized in the United Nations' Universal Declaration of Human Rights (Article 16). Competent adults have the right to make a consensual marriage-like commitment to each other—at least when they are not already committed in this way to someone else—and to live with each other if they wish to, and to treat each other as spouses if they wish to, and to have and raise children together as parents if they wish to. But they may do all these things even if the government does not recognize marriage as a legal status at all and does not issue marriage licenses to anyone. So although people have a right to marry in the sense just described, the recognition and protection of this right do not require the government to recognize marriage as an official legal status or to issue marriage licenses to anyone, and no government is obligated as a matter of justice to do so. It is therefore possible for the government to respect the right of polygamists to marry and to found a family without legalizing polygamy.

It is nonetheless arguable that, if the government does recognize marriage as a legal status, it is obligated to issue a marriage license to any competent adult couple who applies. It is arguable, for instance, that, although the government is not required to issue any marriage licenses at all, if it does issue them, it must issue them to same-sex couples as well as to opposite-sex couples. Why isn't the government likewise obligated, then, to issue marriage licenses to polygamous couples if it issues them to monogamous ones?

A common argument for same-sex marriage is that it is arbitrary for the government to allow opposite-sex couples but not same-sex couples to be legally married. One might deny this on the ground that opposite sex couples can have biological children and same-sex couples cannot. But opposite-sex couples who cannot have biological children are also permitted to be legally married. Assuming, then, that there is no other relevant difference between them, it is arbitrary to allow opposite-sex couples who cannot have biological children to marry and not same-sex couples. If there is likewise no relevant difference between monogamy and polygamy, it is likewise arbitrary for the government to issue marriage licenses to monogamous couples and not to polygamous ones. The nonlegalization of polygamy might therefore violate a general right not be arbitrarily deprived of a benefit or status that the government provides to others, even if this policy does not violate a right to sexual freedom or the right to marry and to found a family.

It is possible, however, to identify relevant differences between monogamy and polygamy, as I will explain below. A case can therefore be made that the government need not legalize polygamy even if it recognizes monogamous marriage as a legal status. By "a case can be made" I mean that it is possible to give an explanation of why polygamy should not be legalized that is internally coherent and does not rest on any premise that is demonstrably false. Moreover, a case can be made consistent with taking individual rights seriously and so with liberalism in this sense.

Before identifying some relevant differences between monogamy and polygamy, I should emphasize that my aim here is not to demonstrate that polygamy is wrong or that it should not be legalized. I remain open to the possibility that polygamy is the right choice for some people under some circumstances, given their beliefs, life goals, and temperaments, and I remain open to the possibility that the government is warranted in legalizing polygamy, perhaps because this policy is in the best interests of the children of polygamous couples and perhaps because it is in the best interest of plural wives. None of the arguments that follow should be understood, then, as attempting to show that polygamy is wrong or that it should not be legalized. My aims in this essay are much more limited than this. First, I want to make it clear that the question of whether polygamy should be legalized is analytically distinct from the question of whether polygamous cohabitation should be decriminalized and that these policy matters can and should be treated independently. Second, I want to make it clear that it is possible for an informed person who takes individual rights seriously consistently to believe that although polygamous cohabitation should be decriminalized polygamy should not be legalized. Third, I want to make it clear that it is possible for an informed person who takes individual rights seriously consistently to believe that although the government should recognize monogamous marriage as a legal status, it should not recognize polygamy as a legal status.

The Child Welfare Rationale: Scarcity

One argument for the institution of civil marriage is that it promotes the welfare of children. If we can tell a plausible story about how monogamous marriage promotes the welfare of children, and about why polygamous marriage would not generally promote the welfare of children in this way, then we can explain why it makes sense for the government to recognize monogamous marriage as a legal status but not polygamous marriage.

I believe it is possible to tell a plausible story of this kind given the following seven assumptions. I cannot prove that these assumptions are true, but as far as I know none of them is demonstrably false. It is therefore possible for an informed, open-minded, and intellectually conscientious person to accept this rationale for civil marriage, given the current state of our knowledge, while consistently opposing the legalization of polygamy.

(1) Parents are likely to care more about the welfare of their children than anyone else does. So when two people have children with each other and raise them together, their children are being raised by the two people who are likely to care the most about them.

(2) Parents are generally more willing to sacrifice goods for themselves in order to promote the welfare of their own children than they are to sacrifice goods to promote the welfare of other people's children. So when two people have children with each other and raise them together, their children are being raised by the two people who are likely the most willing to make beneficial sacrifices for them.

(3) Children are generally better off when they are being raised by two committed parents who live in the same home with them than when they are being raised by only one committed parent or by only one committed parent in the same home with them. This is because when they are being raised by two committed parents who live in the same home with them they will be getting more care and attention than they otherwise would. I use the term *committed parents* to refer to parents of the following kind: for these parents

the happiness and success of their children is a very high priority and they therefore direct a large proportion of their attention, their mental and emotional energy, and their material resources toward the welfare of their children.

(4) When committed parents have children only with each other, their children will typically receive more from their parents than if one of their parents has, in addition, more children with someone else.

(5) Most people want a long-term romantic partnership; for many this is a high priority; and many therefore spend considerable time and energy and make substantial sacrifices (e.g., in their careers) trying to find a suitable romantic partner and to maintain a relationship of this kind.

(6) The social institution of monogamous marriage functions to identify two people as committed romantic partners; it channels various forms of social support toward maintaining this partnership; and it makes these partnerships psychologically more difficult to end. In identifying spouses as committed romantic partners, the social institution of monogamous marriage satisfies the common human desire for such a partnership even when the relationship is not particularly romantic, or even much fun. In this way it results in these relationships lasting longer than they otherwise would, because many people strongly desire to have a relationship of this kind.

(7) When the government officially recognizes monogamous marriage as a legal status this further supports these romantic partnerships and makes them legally and psychologically more difficult to end and so less likely to end. Note here that the social institution of monogamous marriage could exist in the absence of government sponsorship. The assumption here is that government sponsorship further supports these relationships, more than the social institution alone would.

Given these assumptions, we can elaborate the child welfare rationale for civil marriage as follows. This policy will result in more children being raised in a household by two committed parents who have children only with each other, with the benefits just described. Legal marriage makes official the commitment of two people to a lifelong romantic partnership. In doing so, it supports these relationships and makes them harder to end. If two romantic partners have children, the legal institution of marriage therefore makes it more likely that these children will be raised by two committed parents who live in the same home with them. This will typically result in these children receiving more caring attention from their parents and more emotional and material resources than they otherwise would. In this way, the legal institution of marriage promotes the welfare of children.

A key assumption of this argument is that marriage as a legal status promotes the welfare of children by promoting a certain kind of relationship: a committed romantic partnership of parents. I also assume that by legalizing polygamy the government would increase the number of children who are raised in plural families and proportionately reduce the number of children raised by monogamous parents in the same house. If so, an important question in determining whether polygamy should be legalized is whether this policy would promote an environment for raising children that is just as good as the environment promoted by the civil status of monogamous marriage.

The main reason to think it would not is that polygamy typically results in material and emotional scarcity, a sharp reduction in the material and emotional resources that a family can devote to each child. As a result many children in polygamous families do not get enough of what they need. This is partly because there are so many children in these families and only one father. It is also partly because competition among wives and mothers exacerbates the problem of scarcity for some children—the children of disfavored wives—who then have even less than they would have if goods were distributed equally.

From the structure of polygamy and our general knowledge of human nature we can reasonably predict that polygamy will typically result in emotional and material scarcity. If a man has four children with each of three wives instead of having four children with only one of them, he will then have twelve children instead of four. He must then divide his limited emotional and material resources among twelve children instead of four, which means that each of his children will get less than if he had only four children with only one wife. Furthermore, in this situation the interests he has in the welfare of his children are no longer identical to the interests of the mothers of his children. Moreover, the interests of each mother in the welfare of her children will conflict with the interests of the other mothers in the welfare of their children. When resources are limited, a gain for one mother's child will typically mean a loss for another mother's child. Not only are parents typically less inclined to sacrifice goods for the benefit of another person's child than they are for the benefit of their own children, but in this situation the mothers will actively work to secure more for themselves and their own children, which requires that other children get less than if goods are distributed equally.

These armchair speculations are confirmed by the available empirical evidence. One major sociological study concludes: "Most contemporary plural families struggle financially and are hard put to make ends meet."[2] Another study concludes: "In reality, most men cannot feed and clothe all the children, much less their wives, especially in the impoverished Bitterroot area. They are often not around to help and, when they do contribute, it has to be divided among the different households."[3] These studies are by professional sociologists who strive not to be morally judgmental of polygamy as a social institution, and the second study provides the least negative portrait of polygamy by a sociologist that I have read.

These findings are also supported by personal memoirs of those who have grown up in polygamous families. Brent Jeffs, a nephew of imprisoned cult leader Warren Jeffs, describes his experience of polygamous family life this way:

> While it might seem good in theory, in practice, at least in my experience, it's actually a recipe for misery for everyone involved. In the FLDS anyway, polygamy and its power structure continuously produce a constant, exhausting struggle for attention and resources. In families as large as mine, it simply isn't possible for all the women and children to get their needs met. Just making sure the children are fed, clothed, and physically accounted for is an exhausting challenge. Simply keeping dozens of children physically safe is close to impossible. I'd estimate that maybe one in five FLDS families has lost a child early in life, frequently from accidents that better supervision could have prevented. ... For the father, even though he's at the top of heap in his own family, he must constantly disappoint, reject, ignore, and/or fail to satisfy at least some wives and kids. There's only so much of his time and attention to go around, and supporting such a large family takes many hours, too. At home, if one person has your ear, someone else doesn't. Yes to one wife is no to the others.[4]

Irene Spencer, growing up in another polygamous family, observed in the FLDS community "giant families full of neglected children"[5] and writes of her own family: "Dad was a fireman whose family, understandably, grew much faster than his paycheck—*an almost universal problem among polygamists*" (emphasis added).[6]

Scarcity was also a problem for nineteenth-century Mormon polygamists. A major study of Joseph Smith's plural wives concludes: "The more women a man married, the greater the danger for serious problems in the family, for the husband's time and resources became more and more divided. ... Not surprisingly, therefore, polygamous wives, even those married to prominent, well-to-do men, were often not supported adequately financially. ... Clearly, monogamous men also struggled financially at times, but polygamy exacerbated financial problems."[7] Later in this study the author observes "another characteristic of polygamy: The men often were willing to add plural wives to their families, but after the marriage took place found they were unable to support the multiple families adequately, and the wives often had to depend on siblings and teenage sons."[8] This characteristic of polygamy did not go unnoticed by contemporary observers. For example, the sister of one nineteenth-century plural wife wrote of her polygamous brother-in-law: "I never can like him for he has rob[b]ed my Sister & her family of their just dues by dividing his substance between more than the law allows."[9]

Scarcity was a problem even for families headed by affluent and powerful men. Emily Partridge, one of Brigham Young's many wives, wrote: "I feel quite ashamed to be known as the wife of the richest man in the territory, and yet we are so poor. I do not know why he is so lo[a]th to provide for me. My children are his children. He provides sumptuously for some of his family. If he were a poor man it would be different. ... He manifests a desire to cast me off, and I cannot ask him for anything. What his hired men will let me have I get, but it is like pulling teeth to get that sometimes. I feel very loanly [sic] tonight. I hope I do not sin in my feelings."[10] The author of this study adds by way of explanation that Young hid behind his assistants to avoid having to deal with requests for help from his many wives.[11] The plural wives of Heber Kimball, one of Brigham Young's most important advisors, faced similar difficulties. Although he provided well for his first wife, Vilate, and her children, she was his favorite. Kimball's other wives and children had to look to others for help.[12]

The problem is not only material scarcity, but lack of parental attention and affection, too. Sara Hammon, who grew up in a polygamous family in Colorado City, says in the documentary film *Banking on Heaven*: "I didn't really have a relationship with my Dad. ... He asked me my name every time I met him. ... He once confused me with one of the grandchildren and told me to go home." The chronic absence of fathers is also a common complaint of polygamous children[13] and the first wife of a nineteenth-century polygamist expressed her feelings about it this way:

> How pleased I would be if he would step in, administer to our wants, soothe the cries of my four little ones and do a fathers [*sic*] part. They have looked forward to the time (so long) that they would see their Pa that they think they have no Pa.[14]

Altman and Ginat observe a general phenomenon among modern polygamists: "Fathers generally seemed to treat their children, and to be treated in return, in a distant, cool, and detached way. In some cases, fathers did not know how many children were in the family or how many children each wife had."[15] "In general, husbands in modern plural families are somewhat 'disconnected' from and 'unattached' to their homes. They rarely have a place of their own in family dwellings [such as an office or den], and when they do, the place is often temporary, in a public area, shared with others, and not permanently theirs."[16] "In general, husbands in modern plural families are much less psychologically involved in their homes than are their wives."[17] "We saw wide variations in relationships between fathers and their children in plural families. There were instances of fathers and children having warm, spontaneous, and informal relationships. In most cases, however, we sensed a rather distant, formal and aloof relationship between fathers and children."[18] "Although some fathers displayed warmth and affection toward their children, our general impression is that many men in contemporary Mormon fundamentalist families have somewhat distant and detached relationships with their children."[19]

One cause of material and emotional scarcity is that there are many children and only one father. Another cause is that husbands with multiple wives tend to favor the children of their favorite wife, and the children of the other wives therefore get less than an equal share. According to her biographer, the letters of Martha Hughes Cannon, a late-nineteenth-century plural wife, "display a growing sense of bitterness that she and her children are not being treated fairly, or equally, with his other children and wives."[20] Bennion in her study tells the story of a father who takes only the children of his first wife fishing because she is his favorite.[21] Although some plural wives say that plural marriage fosters a desirable kind of sisterhood among the wives, one of Bennion's informants reported that "co-wives are natural rivals and enemies who 'resent and despise the fact that their husband is having sex with them, is attracted to them, and is taking better care of their children' than their own."[22] Not only do the children of the less favored wives get less, but they are also more often victims of the father's abuse. Carolyn Jessop, who left the FLDS community after growing up in a polygamous family and being a plural wife herself, writes: "But children got caught in the crossfire of these sexual wars. Husbands tended to become more abusive toward the wives they no longer had sex with. They also mistreated the children of those wives."[23]

Given the scarcity of resources and the competition among the wives, it would be surprising if there was not more physical abuse of children in polygamous families than in monogamous ones. There is certainly evidence of widespread abuse and neglect in the FLDS community of Colorado City.[24] It is also a reoccurring theme in the literature on Mormon polygamy that plural wives tend to discipline the children of the other wives more harshly than they discipline their own.[25,26] One book suggests that polygamy is hard on children because all the wives have the authority to whip them.[27] Although being able to share child care with other wives is sometimes cited by sister wives as an advantage of polygamy, some mothers do not want their sister wives to care for their children precisely because they mistreat them,[28] which is an additional source of conflict between the wives.

There is no reason to conclude that plural families are always bad for children. Although Jessop in *Banking on Heaven* describes being a plural wife and mother as "the worst kind of torture" and says that "no human being should have to experience it," she herself comes from six generations of polygamists and does not blame her father for practicing it.[29] This is partly because, unlike her own polygamist husband (and many others), her father was scrupulously fair toward his wives and children.[30] This also seems true of Kody Brown, the polygamous husband presented in the TLC reality television show, *Sister Wives*. The Brown wives seem to get along well and to cooperate effectively with each other, and although they struggle financially at times, the Browns have enough money to meet everyone's needs (especially after being paid an undisclosed amount for appearing in the television show for five seasons, which is not an opportunity that most polygamous families have). Still the Brown teenagers wish they saw their father more and one comments wistfully "we don't ever see Dad now."[31]

The fictional Henrickson family in the HBO television series *Big Love* also seems to function fairly well. Like Kody Brown, Bill Henrickson appears to be scrupulously fair toward his wives and children; his wives seem to get along well; and the Henricksons appear to be even richer than the Browns. But the fictional portrayal of polygamy in Brady Udall's *The Lonely Polygamist* bears a much closer resemblance to polygamy as it is described by some of those who have actually lived it, such as Jeffs, Spencer, and Jessop. Udall is particularly sensitive to the problem of emotional deprivation for all of those involved—the children, the wives, and the husband. Children want to feel special to their parents; wives want to feel special to their husbands; husbands and fathers want to feel they are taking good care of their families. Polygamy makes this all very difficult. Because there are so many birthdays, none of the children can have his or her own party. So they double up, or even triple up.[32] Because there are so many children, each of them has little opportunity to spend time alone with either parent. One of the children expresses his feelings about it this way:

> This was the question every plyg kid was always asking: Can't we ever do *anything* alone? And Aunt Nola said what the mothers always said. "You think I don't have anything else to do? You think you're the center of the universe? You think your life is hard? Well, boo-hoo. Try thinking of somebody other than yourself for once." If there's anything you learned as plyg kid, it was that you were not the center of the universe.[33]

The mothers feel overburdened and neglected. One of them likes secretly to read romance novels, about "ladies who were beautiful and had adventures and boyfriends who loved them and only them . . . none of the ladies in these books had seven children and had to share a husband with three others" or had a husband "who was never around, who paid almost no attention at all to" her.[34]

And the father feels overwhelmed by all his obligations:

> He was tired of the big decisions required of him every day, the momentous life-altering occasions that happened, in this family, at least once a week: the baptisms and birthdays and anniversaries and graduations and band recitals and church plays and 4-H shows. He didn't want to hear about whose junior league basketball game he'd forgotten, or what parent-teacher conference had been missed. He didn't want to see another overdue utility bill or tax notice, didn't want to take any more phone calls regarding feuding wives or lovesick teenage daughters or biblical plagues of chicken pox or pink eye or flu that were always lurking out of sight, waiting to bring the family to its knees.[35]

Novels, films, television shows, as well as personal memoirs, historical accounts, and sociological studies help us to imagine what polygamy is like for those who live it. They do not prove that polygamy is always bad for the children, or the wives, or the husbands. Taken as a whole, however, they do support a conclusion that seems antecedently likely given the structure of polygamy, which is that polygamy commonly results in emotional and material scarcity, and so does not generally provide an ideal environment for raising children.

Not all monogamous families are ideal, to be sure. Children do not always get what they need, emotionally and materially, in monogamous families either. Children are abused and neglected in monogamous families too. So one might think it is unfair to discriminate against polygamous families on the ground that they are not always perfect. But the child welfare argument against legalizing polygamy is not that all monogamous families are perfect. It is that children with two parents who live together and have no children with anyone else are likely to receive more from their parents emotionally and materially than children in polygamous families that have many more children, multiple mothers, and only one father.

It is important to bear in mind, too, that in giving reasons for thinking that polygamy is not an ideal environment for child rearing, I am not giving reasons why polygamy or polygamous families should be legally prohibited. Polygamous families should not be prohibited any more than single motherhood should be prohibited. Adults have rights to sexual and reproductive freedom. As a matter of law, they should therefore be at liberty to have consensual sex with other adults regardless of marital status; to get pregnant as a result; to carry the pregnancy to term; and to raise the children they give birth to (unless they are shown to be unfit). This is partly because we have weighty interests in sexual and reproductive freedom and partly because it is generally in the best interest of children to be raised by their biological parents whether their parents are married or not. The reasons to think that polygamy is not ideal are therefore not given as reasons to think that polygamous families should be prohibited. They are given as reasons to think it is not arbitrary for marriage law to treat monogamy and polygamy differently.

The Child Welfare Rationale: Parental Unity

Another reason to think that legalizing polygamy would not promote the welfare of children is given by part of the hypothesized explanation of why civil marriage promotes it. According to the explanatory hypothesis sketched in the previous section, civil marriage affirms and symbolizes something that most adults want for its own sake: a stable, committed, exclusive romantic partnership. Although the romantic quality of a couple's relationship may diminish once they have children, most parents still want a romantic partner in their lives. The social institution of marriage says in effect, "You have a romantic partner: the other parent of your children." It identifies the other parent of one's children as one's romantic partner even when the relationship is not particularly romantic, an identification that is further supported by social customs such as anniversary celebrations and Valentine's Day. If the relationship falls too far short of a partner's romantic ideal, he or she may wish to terminate the marriage. But the social institution of marriage creates an intermediate position between passionate romance and complete disaffection, which is why it makes such a rich topic for stand-up comics and television situation comedies. The hypothesis sketched in the previous section is that civil marriage supports this intermediate position by supporting the social institution of marriage with its norms of commitment and exclusivity, and so makes the relationship of parents with each other more fulfilling than it might otherwise be.

The social institution of polygamy, in contrast, does not affirm or symbolize the exclusive romantic partnership of parents. It conflicts with the ideal of romantic love that most people endorse, and it violates the norms of exclusivity that most people identify as an essential part of this kind of relationship. Because of this it commonly generates strong feelings of dissatisfaction and therefore does not offer the same kind of incentive for parents to stay together and raise their children together in the same home.

Americans practice polygamy primarily for religious reasons. As one nineteenth-century plural wife put it: "I am sure that women would never have accepted polygamy had it not been for their religion. No woman ever consented to its practice without great sacrifice on her part. There is something so sacred about the relationship of husband and wife that a third party in the family is sure to disturb the confidence and security that formerly existed."[36] Nineteenth-century Mormons practiced polygamy because they believed it was pleasing to God. Fundamentalist Mormons believe the same today and for similar reasons: partly because polygamy was practiced by the Mormon prophet Joseph Smith; partly because it was practiced by the Hebrew patriarchs of the Old Testament; and partly because it involves the renunciation of modern romantic ideals that have no basis in the Bible. Because they believe that God commanded His prophet Joseph Smith to practice polygamy and because this practice has been discontinued by the LDS church, fundamentalist Mormons who practice polygamy today believe they are doing special work for God here on earth, sometimes referred to as "the Work." As one contemporary plural wife explains it: "There is a certain plateau that you reach in the Mormon Church, and you can't go any further or they call you a heretic. . . . We wanted more from the gospel . . . we want to live the fullness of the gospel. So we joined the Work. . . . No one said polygamy was easy. It is the hardest law to live, but it gives the highest rewards."[37]

People also enter into plural marriages for reasons of status.[38] Although it was generally perceived by outsiders as degrading to women, polygamy could increase a woman's status in nineteenth-century Mormon Utah by showing her to be especially righteous and also by being married to a high-status man.[39] Because a woman's status in nineteenth-century Utah was tied to bearing children, polygamy also could enhance status indirectly by providing an opportunity to become a mother.[40,41] Polygamy also gives members of plural families status within contemporary polygamous communities because they are seen to be doing special work for God. A man gains status by having more than one wife, and sister wives gain status, too, by being an essential part of "the Work." A single or childless woman who feels that she has relatively low status within the mainstream Mormon community can also sometimes increase her status by becoming a plural wife in a polygamous community and by bearing children.[42]

Because Americans enter polygamy primarily for religious reasons and reasons of status, one might conclude that the fact that it conflicts with the romantic ideal of exclusivity should not trouble them. This, however, appears not to be the case. As Altman and Ginat observe, many in polygamous families are converts; they didn't grow up that way; they grew up in monogamous families with all the normal expectations of romance and commitment.[43] As a result women join plural families as sister wives often with the expectation, or at least the hope, that they will be the favorite, the husband's single romantic partner, his one true love. They are surprised and disappointed when things do not work out that way. As Bennion reports: "Another women, the first of five wives, said that she watched each subsequent wife go through a state of jealousy and hurt feelings when entering the family. She said that each one thought, when courting her husband, that she would be his favorite and they left the Mormon church to be 'a big fish in a little pond.' But soon after the first couple months of marriage, she said, the wives became relegated to the back burners of family life, no longer able to retain the attention of their husband. They, in effect, became little fish in a little pond."[44] This shows that although one goal is status—to become a big fish in a small pond—romantic love is also a goal. Irene Spencer, too, hoped to become the favorite wife of her husband Verlan. Things didn't work out that way, which is why she entitled her book "Shattered Dreams": polygamy shattered her dreams of romantic love.

Partly because those who join plural families have the expectation or hope of romantic love, polygamy typically causes painful feelings of jealousy and self-doubt. Spencer writes extensively about these feelings. "I wondered how he could ever love me if he were busy making love to her."[45] "The thought of sharing Verlan with Lucy sexually tore me to pieces. . . . Lucy bragged that she had loved Verlan since she was twelve and I feared this might give him reason to love her more than he loved me. Such thoughts were driving me mad."[46] Because Spencer's mother had been a plural wife herself, she tried to persuade her daughter not to enter into a plural marriage. "Please, Irene, I suffered so much trying to live the Principle. Don't do this. You've got a chance to have a husband of your very own."[47] As a headstrong teenager, Irene is sure that her experience of polygamy will be different; she thinks Verlan will really love only her. She is disappointed, then, to discover that she is just one more wife helping her husband to achieve "exaltation" in the afterlife. Discussing how his mother felt when her husband spent nights with his other wife, Brent Jeffs writes: "It's hard for Mom to even talk about how badly that tore her up inside. . . . The pain that this caused still echoes through our family today."[48]

Altman and Ginat describe the conflict between polygamy and ideals of romantic love in the following way: "In some respects the challenges faced by a husband and each plural wife are similar to those of monogamous couples. They must develop a special and unique relationship, acknowledge the distinctive personal qualities of each participant, and keep the intimate and personal 'business' of the relationship to themselves. But meeting these goals is especially challenging for members of contemporary plural families. After all, it is not easy for wives to see their husband in multiple intimate, personal, affectionate relationships while proclaiming the special nature of their own individual relationship. Nor is it easy for a husband to make each relationship with his wives distinctive and unique and to be a 'different person' with each wife. Managing multiple dyadic relationships is difficult for both husbands and wives, and feelings of jealousy, uncertainty, stress, and marital strain are common. So it is challenging for everyone to work out healthy and satisfactory dyadic relationships in modern plural families."[49] Altman and Ginat also observe the phenomenon of jealousy and hurt feelings described by Spencer. "Honeymoons can be a time of emotional upheaval, especially for established wives who are 'left behind' as the new couple goes off on a romantic pleasure trip to celebrate their marriage. Some wives feel abandoned, some are jealous about the husband being with a young and seemingly more attractive woman, some worry that the husband will not love them anymore, and some feel neglected and lonely. A wife who did not have a honeymoon herself may be specially upset and jealous. ... Furthermore, many wives were not raised in plural families, so that the honeymoon of their husband with a new wife contradicts the American monogamous concept of marriage as a unique and intimate bond between one man and one woman."[50] Kimball Young, a distinguished mid-twentieth-century American sociologist (and descendent of Brigham Young), observes that in other societies that practice polygamy there is no ideal of romantic love and that polygamy is particularly problematic in American society where romantic love is so idealized.[51]

Given the conflict between polygamy and ideals and norms of romantic love, it is not surprising that both practicing polygamists and outside observers have concluded that the success of a plural marriage requires renouncing these ideals and norms. One historian of nineteenth-century Mormonism concludes that because polygamy can work only if jealousy can be restrained and exclusivity avoided, polygamy necessitates detachment and emotional distance incompatible with romantic love. "In conclusion, while Mormon plural marriages certainly demonstrated affection and commitment, the record suggests that romantic love as the monogamous, exclusive, sexual relationship of a man and a woman could not be incorporated into the successful practice of plural marriage."[52] Zina Huntington, a plural wife of Joseph Smith and, after Smith was killed, of Brigham Young, reached the same conclusion from her own experience. In an 1869 interview she "ascribed much of the unhappiness in polygamous families to women who expect 'too much attention from the husband and because they do not obtain it, or see a little attention bestowed upon one of the other wives, they become sullen and morose, and permit their ill-temper to finally find vent'. First wives are a particular problem, she observes, as they have a tendency to look upon the husband with a 'selfish devotion' that desires to claim all his time and attention for themselves. The successful polygamous wife, as the marriage develops, 'must regard her husband with indifference, and with no other feeling than that of reverence, for love we regard as a false sentiment; a feeling which should have no existent in polygamy'."[53] By "love," which she identifies as a "false sentiment," Huntington means romantic love,[54] and other Mormon women who publicly defended polygamy in the late nineteenth century agreed with Huntington's assessment of what the successful practice of polygamy requires.[55] Another historian of nineteenth-century Mormon polygamy argues that women had to maintain emotional distance so as not get hurt.[56] And Seth Cooke, living in the Colorado City area, reaches a similar conclusion in *Banking on Heaven*: "Dang near fifty years old, I have never seen what I consider a good example of it. The only way you can survive it is become callous and hard. You think about it. You take one in the bedroom and having sex with her and the other three are in the other room crying. How are you going to feel inside? That's why I decided not to be a polygamist."

The point here is not that exclusive romantic relationships are the only sexual or reproductive relationships worth having. It is simply that polygamy is inconsistent with the ideals and norms of romantic love, and that this is recognized by those who have lived it or observed it. It was also recognized by the founders of the LDS church. Polygamy was endorsed by Mormons partly as a reaction to nineteenth-century ideals of romantic love.[57,58] One historian writes: "Clearly inherent in the system was an assault on the romantic-love ideology which maintained that sexual attraction, reproduction, and companionship could all ideally be obtained in the unique person of the wife. Polygamy quite consciously strove to separate sexual pleasure from sexual reproduction, and sexual love in general from 'spiritual love', or companionship. Such an intent only further increased the instability of the polygamous system."[59] Religious historians characterize Mormonism as a "restorationist" religious movement, one that sought to recreate a social world in America similar to the ancient Hebrew world depicted in the Old Testament, in preparation for the Second Coming of Christ.[60,61,62,63] Nineteenth-century Mormons believed that the modern world was corrupt and that one symptom of this corruption was the assumption that marriage should be based on erotic love or on a special emotional bond between the partners. Marriage, they thought, should be based instead only on a shared commitment to doing God's will, to be fruitful and multiply and to raise righteous children.

It is worth noting, too, that polygamy was practiced by nineteenth-century Mormons and is still practiced by fundamentalist Mormons today as a rigorous spiritual discipline that is believed to be pleasing to God precisely because it involves sacrificing a worldly good that most people strongly desire to have in their lives, namely an exclusive romantic partnership.[64]

Although Joseph Smith and Brigham Young did not practice polygamy as a form of asceticism, when one reads about the genuine hardships polygamy imposed on ordinary Mormons, particularly the women, and why they thought it was nonetheless the right choice for them, it is hard to avoid the conclusion that they believed their willingness to practice polygamy was pleasing to God precisely because it involved the sacrifice of personal goods that most Americans were unwilling to sacrifice at the time.[65,66] As one historian puts it: "Plural wives often saw the trials of polygamy as opportunities to overcome character defects such as jealousy and/or selfishness, thereby hastening their purification and redemption."[67] Helen Mar Kimball Whitney, a fourteen-year-old plural wife of Joseph Smith and later of Orson Whitney, stressed the primary importance of religious renunciation in the service of higher goals as the motivation for entering into polygamy.[68] Another nineteenth-century plural wife wrote: "There is nothing in the world so good as polygamy to make people unselfish, once they have made up their minds that they will live it for the rest of their lives."[69]

The picture of polygamy as a form of religiously motivated renunciation is further supported by testimony from contemporary Mormon polygamists. For example, Jessop writes: "Granma . . . taught me that I had been blessed by God with an opportunity to come into a family where generations of women had sacrificed their feelings and given up the things of this world to preserve the work of God and prove worthy of the celestial kingdom of God."[70] Another contemporary plural wife describes her experience this way: "We all lived in this euphoria. . . . We felt all this suffering, sackcloth-and-ashes and humility was part of a big plan. We were all going to be greatly rewarded for it. Every day we were imbued with the feeling that what we were doing was spiritually important. We were the chosen people of God having our mettle tested."[71] Another observes: "It's an ascetic deprivation thing. Whoever gives up the most is the highest."[72] Mormon polygamy requires plural wives to renounce their desire for an exclusive romantic partnership with their husband; to surrender any claim to being the unique object of their husbands' romantic or sexual attention; to renounce the feelings of possessiveness, jealousy, and resentment that people commonly feel when their intimate partner is regularly having sex with another person; to accept the feelings of betrayal, humiliation, and rejection that this commonly involves; and to see these feelings as spiritual faults rather than as grounds for legitimate complaint. Whether or not this renunciation results in spiritual development, it makes vivid the incompatibility of polygamy and norms of romantic love.

The fact that polygamy is inconsistent with ideals and norms of romantic love is not a good a reason to prohibit it. Nor is the fact that it is structurally inegalitarian, with the husbands sometimes playing the role of kings and plural wives playing the role of fawning, backstabbing courtiers.[73,74] Monks practice celibacy as a form of self-denial and other organized religions are inegalitarian, in permitting men but not women to become priests, for example. These are not good reasons to prohibit these spiritual practices or religions. The claim here is simply that civil monogamous marriage offers parents something that polygamy does not: a civil institution that affirms and symbolizes a kind of relationship that most parents want in their lives. According to the hypothesis, it therefore makes it more likely that parents will raise their children together in the same house. Obviously polygamy also affirms and symbolizes something that is important to fundamentalist Mormons, a commitment to doing God's special work here on earth. But in doing this it does not promote the welfare of children in the way that the child welfare argument supposes that monogamous marriage does.

Exclusive Life Partnerships as a Distinctive Human Good

A predictable objection to the child welfare rationale for civil marriage is that promoting the welfare of children is not the only purpose of marriage. This is surely true if by purpose we mean an aim that people actually have in getting married. People get married for all sorts of reasons: to solemnize their commitment to each other, to make their parents happy, to become eligible for various government benefits, to help a friend get a green card, and so on. What we are concerned with here, however, is not the aims that people actually have in getting married, but the goals that might actually justify the government in establishing and maintaining the institution of civil marriage. Even if people have aims in getting married other than promoting the welfare of children, promoting the welfare of children might still be the only rationale that can justify the government in maintaining this institution.

It is not the only possible rationale, however. One can also argue that the institution of civil marriage promotes a certain kind of human relationship that has distinctive value, which I will call an *exclusive life partnership*. What I mean by this is a long-term sexual relationship of two people in which the partners make joint decisions as equals about where they will live, what their living space will be like, how to use their money, how best to advance their separate careers, whether to have children, how to raise their children if they have any, how to conduct their sexual relationship, and whether to have sexual relationships with other people, a relationship in which each partner recognizes the other as the only person entitled to make joint decisions with them in these important areas of life. Suppose that having this kind of relationship is a distinctive human good, or, in other words, that having this kind of relationship makes a person's life go better for him or her in distinctive ways that other kinds of relationship do not duplicate or replace without loss. Suppose, too, that the legal institution of monogamous marriage promotes this good by making it more likely that people will have long-term relationships of this kind, and that the legalization of polygamy would not make this more likely. Then it is possible to defend the government policy of recognizing monogamous marriage as a legal status but not polygamy in the following way: By recognizing monogamous marriage as a legal status, the government promotes valuable relationships of this kind, whereas legalizing polygamy would not have this effect.

Someone might of course deny that exclusive life partnerships are in fact a distinctive human good, but this should not worry us much. Someone might also deny that consistency is good, or that truth is good, or that rationality is good, or that knowledge is good, or that doing the right thing is good, or that liberty is good, or that equality is good, or that fairness is good, or that justice is good. The mere fact that someone denies that something is good is no reason to doubt that it is. If something seems to us to be good, and it continues to seem good to us upon ongoing critical reflection, and the belief that it is good is consistent with our other beliefs, then we are justified in believing that it is good unless there is some reason to doubt it. If someone shows us that our belief that exclusive life partnerships are a distinctive human good is based on faulty information or on faulty reasoning, then we will have some reason for doubt, but no one, to my knowledge, has shown this or shown that exclusive life partnerships are not in fact a distinctive human good.

The belief that exclusive life partnerships are a distinctive human good is also consistent with the three general conceptions of human welfare that are most commonly discussed in the philosophical literature: hedonism, desire-satisfaction, and objective list (or substantive good).[75,76] According to hedonism, pleasure is the only thing that is intrinsically, or non-instrumentally, good for us. Because exclusive life partnerships seem to produce a distinctive kind of pleasure and also to be a source of pleasure that is not easily replaced by other kinds of relationships, the claim that exclusive life partnerships are a distinctive human good is consistent with this kind of view. According to the desire-satisfaction view, nothing is non-instrumentally good for us other that states of affairs that we desire for their own sakes. Because many people seem to desire an exclusive life partnership for its own sake, the claim that this kind of relationship is a distinctive human good is consistent with this kind of view as well. According to objective list or substantive good views, a state of affairs other than pleasure can be non-instrumentally good for us and can be good for us even if we do not desire it. If something has a property that provides a good reason for someone to want it for himself and this reason is not outweighed by any reason for him to want not to have it, then having it contributes to his welfare even if he does not happen to desire it. Because exclusive life partnerships have properties that make them distinctive, and these properties seem to provide good reason for people to want these relationships for themselves, the claim that this kind of relationship is a distinctive human good is consistent with this kind of view as well.

From these considerations I conclude there is no obvious error in thinking that exclusive life partnerships are a distinctive human good. Nor is there an obvious error in thinking that the institution of civil monogamous marriage promotes this good, by making it more likely that people will have this kind of relationship in their lives. Nor is there an obvious error in believing that the legalization of polygamy would not have this effect. A case can therefore be made that the government ought to recognize civil marriage as a legal status in order to promote relationships of this kind, but that it should not legalize polygamy for this reason because this policy would not have the effect of promoting relationships of this kind.

The limited claim so far is that it is not arbitrary for the government to treat monogamy and polygamy differently because it makes sense to believe that monogamy promotes a distinctive human good that polygamy does not promote. Even if this distinction is not intellectually arbitrary, however, it is arguable that treating citizens as equals requires the government to remain neutral toward different conceptions of a good life and that any government policy that is justified partly by the assumption that exclusive life partnerships are a distinctive human good fails to be neutral in the relevant sense.[77,78,79]

There are two ways to respond to this objection. One is to reject the requirement of neutrality as invalid. The other is to argue that, although valid, the principle of neutrality does not exclude this consideration as a basis for marriage policy.

When Ronald Dworkin first defended the idea that the government should be neutral toward different conceptions of the good life, he presented it as one possible interpretation—the liberal interpretation—of the principle that the government should treat all its citizens with equal concern and respect.[80] He did not argue that this was the only possible interpretation of the equality principle. In fact, he recognized that there was an alternative interpretation—a "conservative" one—that would not entail government neutrality. He suggested only that a liberal interpretation of the equality principle would require this kind of government neutrality. After the publication of Dworkin's essay, however, a number of political theorists who see themselves as liberals, and not as conservatives, rejected the requirement of neutrality as invalid, arguing that it was not warranted by the fundamental principle of equal concern and respect that Dworkin identified as the basis of our rights.[81,82] These anti-neutrality liberal positions are internally coherent and have been defended by intellectually serious, well-informed, and theoretically sophisticated political philosophers. Furthermore, no one has clearly and convincingly explained why taking individual rights seriously entails a general commitment to neutrality. So it is possible for someone who takes individual rights seriously, and so who is a liberal in this sense, consistently to reject the requirement of neutrality as invalid.

It is not necessary, though, to reject the neutrality principle in order to defend civil marriage as promoting exclusive life partnerships. One can deny instead that the government would violate the neutrality principle in justifying its marriage policy in this way. On one possible interpretation, the principle of neutrality prohibits the government from adopting a policy under the following conditions: the policy can be justified only by counting a certain reason in its favor and counting this reason in its favor implies that someone's way of life is bad or worthless (and implies this regardless of whether this way of life involves the violation of others' rights) or that someone's conception of a good life is false (and implies this regardless of whether this conception of the good life requires or permits the violation of others' rights). Suppose, for the sake of argument, that the government policy of issuing marriage licenses to monogamous couples but not to polygamous ones can be justified only on the following assumptions: (a) exclusive life partnerships are a distinctive human good, (b) the legal institution of monogamous marriage results in more people having this kind of relationship, and (c) the legalization of polygamy would not have this effect. One might think that assumption (a) violates the principle of neutrality on this interpretation because counting this as a reason implies that the lives of polygamists are bad or worthless or that polygamists' conceptions of the good life are false. But assumption (a) does not in fact have this implication.

To see this, consider whether assumption (a) implies that the monastic lives of monks and nuns who are committed to celibacy are bad or worthless. No, it does not. Could a monk or a nun who believes that a celibate monastic life is the best life for him or her consistently believe that exclusive life partnerships are a distinctive human good? Yes. To identify something as a distinctive human good implies that a life that contains it is for that reason better, at least for some people. It does not imply that a life that does not contain it is bad or worthless. Identifying something as a distinctive human good would imply that any life that does not contain it is bad or worthless only if every good or worthwhile life must contain every distinctive human good. Not only is it hard to see why this should be, it seems practically impossible for *any* human life to contain *every* distinctive human good. So unless every human life is inevitably bad or worthless, it is not the case that every good or worthwhile human life must contain every distinctive human good. Consequently, it is consistent to hold that celibate monastic lives are good and worthwhile, and even the best kind of life for some people given their beliefs, life goals, temperaments, and circumstances, while also holding that exclusive life partnerships are a distinctive human good.

It is likewise consistent to hold that polygamous lives are good and worthwhile, and even the best kind of life for some people given their beliefs, life goals, temperaments, and circumstances, while holding that exclusive life partnerships are a distinctive human good. As a consequence, the rationale for distinguishing monogamy and polygamy sketched above does not violate the requirement of neutrality in implying that polygamous lives are bad or worthless. It implies only that exclusive life partnerships are a good worth promoting, that monogamy as a legal institution promotes it, and that legalizing polygamy would not.

The exclusive life partnership rationale is also consistent with another interpretation of neutrality. On this interpretation, a policy violates the principle of neutrality under the following conditions: the policy can be justified only by counting a certain reason in its favor, and counting this reason in its favor implies that some particular conception of the good life is true or that some particular comprehensive moral, philosophical, or religious doctrine is true. By a *conception of the good life* I mean a philosophical conception of what makes a person's life go well. Hedonistic, desire-satisfaction, and substantive good conceptions of individual welfare

are all conceptions of the good life in this sense. Because these conceptions differ from each other and yet they are all consistent with the claim that exclusive life partnerships are a distinctive human good, as explained above, this claim does not imply that any *particular* conception of the good life is true. Nor does this claim imply that only one way of life is good, a married life as opposed to a celibate monastic life, for example. To the contrary, this claim is consistent with the pluralistic view that different ways of life are good for different people, given their different beliefs, life goals, temperaments, and circumstances. By a *comprehensive doctrine* I mean a general view about the meaning, value, and purpose of human life, combined with general prescriptions about how to live that are based on this general view and that provide practical guidance about how to act in a wide range of situations. An example is this: we are valuable because created by God; our purpose on earth is therefore to live in a way that is pleasing to God; we please God when we act in accordance with His will; we act in accordance with His will when we act in accordance with certain moral prescriptions that are stated in the Bible. The belief that exclusive life partnerships are a distinctive human good is not itself a comprehensive doctrine in this sense. Nor does it rest on, presuppose, or imply the truth of any particular doctrine of this kind. It is consistent with many different views about the meaning, value, and purpose of human life. It is consistent with many different views about how best to live. It is consistent with many different sets of prescriptions about how to act. Therefore, a government policy justified by reference to this good does not violate the principle of neutrality on this interpretation either.

There are no doubt other interpretations of neutrality that would exclude the exclusive life partnership rationale for civil marriage. Why, though, should we believe that the neutrality principle is valid on any such interpretation? Although some have recently suggested that government policies that aim to promote monogamy or marriage, as opposed to other kinds of human relationship, cannot be justified by "public reason" or consistent with "political liberalism," these theorists typically begin their arguments by assuming that these constraints on policy justification are valid without fully explaining why.[83,84,85] For this reason, their arguments do not conclusively address the possibility that although these policies violate these constraints, these constraints are not in fact valid.[86]

Dworkin's primary aim in introducing the idea of neutrality was to explain what liberalism is. He thought that any decent person would agree that the government should treat its citizens with equal concern and respect, but that decent people might disagree about what this requires. Liberalism, according to him, is the view that equal concern and respect requires government neutrality; conservatism is the view that it does not. There are other ways, however, to understand what liberalism is. One might understand liberalism instead as the thesis that individuals have certain rights combined with a certain conception of the content of these rights.[87] More specifically, one might say that liberalism holds that individuals have certain rights to freedom of thought, freedom of expression, freedom of conscience, sexual and reproductive freedom, the freedom to vote and run for political office, freedom of movement, freedom of contract, a right to own personal property, and a general right against unwarranted searches and seizures of person and property. Conservatives also believe that individuals have these rights, but they believe they have different content, and so allow more government interference in some areas and less government interference in others.[88] My main claim here is that it is possible for someone to accept these rights on a liberal interpretation and consistently to believe that polygamous cohabitation should therefore be decriminalized because criminal penalties violate a right to sexual freedom, but that polygamy need not be legalized because nonlegalization violates no one's rights.

It can also be argued that criminal penalties for polygamous cohabitation violate a right to religious liberty or to freedom of conscience[89] and some might think that the nonlegalization of polygamy violates these religious rights, too, even if it does not violate sexual freedom. I think this is also false. Religious liberty is the liberty to engage in the religious practices that one believes one ought to engage in and to make the religious commitments one believes one ought to make. Freedom of conscience is the freedom to do what one sincerely believes one has a duty to do. Some people sincerely believe they ought to practice polygamy because this will please God or bring them closer to God. Some people sincerely believe they have a religious duty to practice polygamy. In neither case, however, does the religious practice of polygamy require its legalization. It requires only that polygamous cohabitation and the religious ceremonies that solemnize plural unions not be prohibited. This the government can easily accomplish without legalizing polygamy, and this in fact is all that religious polygamists in this country have asked for.

Conclusion

The main analytical claim of this essay is that the decriminalization of polygamous cohabitation and the legalization of polygamy are separate policy issues and should be evaluated separately. One can therefore consistently hold that polygamous cohabitation should be decriminalized but polygamy should not be legalized. The main substantive claim of this essay is that someone who takes individual rights seriously and who accepts a liberal view of the content of these rights can consistently believe that polygamous cohabitation should be decriminalized without believing that polygamy should be legalized, and can consistently believe that polygamy should not be legalized even if the government continues to recognize marriage as a legal status. To illustrate this possibility I've identified two possible rationales for marriage as a legal status—the child welfare rationale and the exclusive life partnership rationale—and explained why it makes sense to think that although they warrant the civil institution of monogamous marriage, they do not warrant the legalization of polygamy. Perhaps neither rationale is sound. Perhaps they both rest on false empirical or evaluative assumptions. If so, it is doubtful there is any sound rationale for the institution of civil marriage. If not, this is no reason to legalize polygamy. It is a reason for the government to cease recognizing marriage as a legal status altogether.

Note that although I've defended the intellectual coherence of the position that polygamy should be decriminalized but not legalized, I have not presented an all-things-considered argument against legalization. As I observed at the outset, when considering what marriage law should be we must consider both the justifying purposes of civil marriage and what policies are warranted all-things-considered, taking into account the complexities of family law, inheritance law, tax law, immigration law, and criminal law. Even if the government does not violate anyone's rights in not legalizing polygamy, it is still possible that legalization is the best policy all-things-considered. I take no position on this complex issue here.

The distinction between policies that are intellectually defensible as a matter of principle and policies that are best all things considered is also relevant to the issue of divorce and remarriage, which I touched on only briefly. I have given as a possible rationale for not legalizing polygamy that it commonly results in emotional and material scarcity for children and someone might point out that divorce and remarriage commonly have a similar effect. Although divorce and remarriage is sometimes called "serial monogamy" it might also be called "asynchronous polygamy." Doesn't the child welfare rationale for not legalizing polygamy suggest, then, that it should also not be legally possible to remarry a second or third spouse while one's first spouse is still alive? If so, isn't this a problem for the child welfare argument?

An important difference between polygamy and divorce and remarriage is that second and third monogamous marriages are still monogamous. Consequently they offer the same potential benefits to the children of second and third marriages that first marriages offer to the children of first marriages, provided that these marriages last. Like first marriages, second and third marriages also give people something they want independently of having children—a committed, exclusive, romantic partner—which can function as an incentive for parents in second and third marriages to bring up the children they have with each other together. Costs and benefits, however, are also relevant. The government could take a position on divorce and remarriage that is similar to that of the Catholic Church: although no one will be prosecuted for having sexual relations or children with someone other than his or her legal spouse, adults can be legally married only once (while their first spouse is still living); no relationship to someone other than a person's first spouse will be legally recognized as a marriage while the first spouse is still alive. It is conceivable that in the long run this policy would be in the best interests of children because it would create incentives for those who wish to be legally married to choose their spouses carefully and to work out difficulties in this relationship rather than leaving the marriage. But it is also possible that in the long run this policy would not be in the best interests of children because it would result in the relationships of their parents, including stepparents, being less stable. Suppose, for the sake of argument, that the benefits for all those involved of allowing legal divorce and remarriage decisively outweigh the costs, but that the same is not true of legalizing polygamy. In this case, there is no inconsistency in defending legal divorce and remarriage while opposing the legalization of polygamy, even if one accepts the child welfare rationale for civil marriage sketched above.

Thinking intelligently about marriage law ultimately requires weighing the costs and benefits of different policies. But it is helpful too to have some idea of the range of positions that one can consistently hold as a matter of principle. Here I have argued that one position open to those who take individual rights seriously is that polygamy should be decriminalized but not legalized.[90]

Notes

1. Thom Brooks, "The Problem with Polygamy," *Philosophical Topics* 37:2 (2009): 110.

2. Irwin Altman and Joseph Ginat, *Polygamous Families in Contemporary Society* (New York: Cambridge University Press, 1996), 84.

3. Janet Bennion, *Women of Principle: Female Networking in Contemporary Mormon Polygamy* (New York: Oxford University Press, 1998), 72.

4. Brent Jeffs, *Lost Boy* (New York: Broadway Books, 2009), 8–9.

5. Irene Spencer, *Shattered Dreams: My Life as a Polygamist's Wife* (New York: Hachette, 2007), 102.

6. Spencer, *Shattered Dreams*, 10.

7. Todd Compton, *In Sacred Loneliness: The Plural Wives of Joseph Smith* (Salt Lake City: Signature Press, 1997), xiv.

8. Compton, *Loneliness*, 199.

9. Compton, *Loneliness*, 377.

10. Compton, *Loneliness*, 421.

11. Compton, *Loneliness*, 420.

12. Compton, *Loneliness*, 127, 135.

13. Jessie L. Embry, *Mormon Polygamous Families: Life in the Principle* (Salt Lake City: University of Utah Press, 1987), 159.

14. Paula Kelly Harline, *The Polygamous Wives Club* (New York: Oxford University Press, 2014), ix.

15. Altman and Ginat, *Polygamous Families*, 424.

16. Altman and Ginat, *Polygamous Families*, 255.

17. Altman and Ginat, *Polygamous Families*, 258.

18. Altman and Ginat, *Polygamous Families*, 246.

19. Altman and Ginat, *Polygamous Families*, 432.

20. Mari Grana, *Pioneer, Polygamist, Politician: The Life of Dr. Martha Hughes Cannon* (Guilford, CT: TwoDot, 2009), 98.

21. Bennion, *Women of Principle*, 82.

22. Bennion, *Women of Principle*, 38.

23. Carolyn Jessop and Laura Palmer, *Escape* (New York: Broadway Books, 2007), 226.

24. Jessop and Palmer, *Escape*, 32–40, 238–240.

25. Bennion, *Women of Principle*, 140.

26. Jeffs, *Lost Boy*, 30.

27. Ben Bradlee, Jr. and Dale Van Atta, *Prophet of Blood: The Untold Story of Ervil LeBaron and the Lambs of God* (New York: Putnam, 1981), 101.

28. Bennion, *Women of Principle*, 33.

29. Carolyn Jessop, *Triumph: Life After the Cult, A Survivor's Lesson* (New York: Broadway Books, 2010), 147.

30. Jessop, *Triumph*, 150.

31. Season Four, Episode Eight, at minute 6:50.

32. Brady Udall, *The Lonely Polygamist* (New York: Norton, 2010), 289–290.

33. Udall, *The Lonely Polygamist*, 421.

34. Udall, *The Lonely Polygamist*, 297.

35. Udall, *The Lonely Polygamist*, 128.

36. Lawrence Foster, *Religion and Sexuality: Three American Communal Experiments of the Nineteenth Century* (New York: Oxford University Press, 1981), 208.

37. Bennion, *Women of Principle*, 98.
38. Bennion, *Women of Principle*, 65–66.
39. Foster, *Religion and Sexuality*, 211–212.
40. Foster, *Religion and Sexuality*, 211–212.
41. Harline, *Polygamous Wives*, 25.
42. Bennion, *Women of Principle*, 5–6, 65–66.
43. Altman and Ginat, *Polygamous Families*, 9, 150.
44. Bennion, *Women of Principle*, 107.
45. Spencer, *Shattered Dreams*, 44.
46. Spencer, *Shattered Dreams*, 164.
47. Spencer, *Shattered Dreams*, 60.
48. Jeffs, *Lost Boy*, 28.
49. Altman and Ginat, *Polygamous Families*, 357.
50. Altman and Ginat, *Polygamous Families*, 149–150.
51. Kimball Young, *Isn't One Wife Enough?* (New York: Holt, Rinehart and Winston, 1954), 205.
52. Joan Smyth Iversen, *The Antipolygamy Controversy in U.S. Women's Movements, 1880–1925: Debate on the American Home* (New York: Garland Publishing, 1997), 66.
53. Compton, *Loneliness*, 108.
54. Compton, *Loneliness*, 108.
55. Harline, *Polygamous Wives*, 76–77.
56. Foster, *Religion and Sexuality*, 212.
57. Louis J. Kern, *An Ordered Love: Sex Roles and Sexuality in Victorian Utopias—the Shakers, the Mormons, and the Oneida Community* (Chapel Hill: University of North Carolina Press, 1981), 179–180.
58. Iversen, *Antipolygamy Controversy*, 64.
59. Kern, *Ordered Love*, 179.
60. Kathryn M. Daynes, *More Wives than One: Transformation of the Mormon Marriage System, 1840–1910* (Urbana and Chicago: University of Illinois Press, 2001), 18.
61. B. Carmon Hardy, *Solemn Covenant: The Mormon Polygamous Passage* (Urbana: University of Illinois Press, 1992), 338–339.
62. Compton, *Loneliness*, xiii, 287, 312.
63. Jan Shipps, *Mormonism: The Story of a New Religious Tradition* (Urbana: University of Illinois Press, 1985), 61–62.
64. Martha Sonntag Bradley, *Kidnapped from That Land: The Government Raids on the Short Creek Polygamists* (Salt Lake City: University of Utah Press, 1993), 62.
65. Daynes, *More Wives*, 28.
66. Compton, *Loneliness*, 468.
67. Iversen, *Antipolygamy Controversy*, 62.
68. Foster, *Religion and Sexuality*, 208.
69. Young, *One Wife*, 213.
70. Jessop and Palmer, *Escape*, 19.
71. Bradlee and Van Atta, *Prophet*, 76.
72. Bradlee and Van Atta, *Prophet*, 167.

73. Jessop and Palmer, *Escape*, 8, 138.

74. Jeffs, *Lost Boy*, 61, 80–81, 94.

75. For a standard discussion see Shelly Kagan, *Normative Ethics* (Boulder, CO: Westview, 1998), 29–41.

76. For the term "substantive good" and the reasons to prefer it over "objective list" see T. M, Scanlon, *The Difficulty of Tolerance* (New York: Cambridge University Press, 2003), 173.

77. Elizabeth Brake, *Minimizing Marriage: Marriage, Morality, and the Law* (New York: Oxford University Press, 2012), 144.

78. Cheshire Calhoun, "Who's Afraid of Polygamous Marriage? Lessons for Same-Sex Marriage Advocacy from the History of Polygamy," *San Diego Law Review* 42 (2005): 1034.

79. Clare Chambers, *Against Marriage: An Egalitarian Defence of the Marriage-Free State* (Oxford: Oxford University Press, forthcoming 2016); see chapter 2, "Marriage as a Violation of Neutrality."

80. Ronald Dworkin, *A Matter of Principle* (Cambridge, MA: Harvard University Press, 1985), 192.

81. Joseph Raz, *The Morality of Freedom* (New York: Oxford University Press, 1986), 161–162.

82. George Sher, *Beyond Neutrality: Perfectionism and Politics* (New York: Cambridge University Press, 1997), 92–97.

83. Brake, *Minimizing*, 134–148.

84. Chambers, *Against Marriage*, chapter 2, "Marriage as a Violation of Neutrality."

85. Andrew F. March, "Is There a Right to Polygamy? Marriage, Equality and Subsidizing Families in Liberal Public Justification," *Journal of Moral Philosophy* 8 (2011): 247.

86. Chambers does not even accept "political liberalism" herself (see *Against Marriage*, chapter 2). She wants to show that political liberalism is inconsistent with state-recognized marriage only because she is opposed to state-recognized marriage and believes that many political philosophers who identify themselves as liberal accept some form of political liberalism.

87. Peter de Marneffe, *Liberalism and Prostitution* (New York: Oxford University Press, 2010), 159–160.

88. Dworkin's principle of neutrality can be understood as an attempt to provide a theoretical explanation of the content of these rights on a liberal interpretation. As I have argued elsewhere, however, the notion of neutrality is too vague and ambiguous to play this theoretical role in a theory of rights and so cannot play the kind of theoretical role in liberal theory that Dworkin at first imagined (Peter de Marneffe, "The Possibility and Desirability of Neutrality," in Roberto Merrill and Daniel Weinstock, eds., *Political Neutrality: A Re-evaluation* (New York: Palgrave Macmillan, 2014, pp. 44–56), 50–51.

89. Martha Nussbaum, *Liberty of Conscience: In Defense of America's Tradition of Religious Equality* (New York: Basic Books, 2008), 179–198.

90. My thanks to Elizabeth Brake, Steven Reynolds, Konden Smith, and James Weinstein for helpful comments on an earlier draft.

7| Polygamy, Privacy, and Equality

LAURIE SHRAGE

> *It was not just that white American Mormons were engaging in a*
> *practice thought to be characteristic of Asiatic and African peoples who*
> *were believed, at the time, to be civilizationally and racially inferior, . . .*
> *but also, as a practice of such peoples, "polygamy leads to the patriarchal*
> *principle," which, "when applied to large communities, fetters the people*
> *in stationary despotism"—another racist or orientalist observation about*
> *this Mormon practice based in the "scientific" perspective of the day . . .*
> *White American Christians, the Court implied, legislate monogamy . . .*
> *In other words, the social harm was introducing a practice perceived to be*
> *characteristic of non-European people—or non-white races—into white American*
> *society.*
>
> —Judge Clark Waddoups, December 13, 2013[1]

1. Introduction

Are laws that restrict polygamy in the US based on ignorance, fear, and prejudice? An influential legal ruling on polygamy, *Reynolds v. U.S.* (1879),[2] which upheld a criminal conviction for polygamy (in the Utah territory), is notable for its openly racist assumptions. In a recent ruling involving marriage law in the state of Utah, *Brown v. Buhman* (2013), Judge Waddoups (a George W. Bush appointee) calls attention to the racist and imperialist notions that framed this nineteenth-century US Supreme Court case. Citing extensively Edward Said's important work on orientalist discourse, as well as work by other scholars exposing *Reynolds*'s imperialist underpinnings, Judge Waddoups concludes "the court believes that *Reynolds* is not, or should no longer be considered, good law . . ."[3]

While *Brown v. Buhman* neither invalidates laws that ban bigamy,[4] nor requires states to provide access to civil marriage to units larger than two,[5] it does invalidate laws that prohibit cohabitation for polygamist adults who are living with partners to whom they are not legally married.[6] Appealing to *Lawrence v. Texas*, Judge Waddoups argues that Utah's restrictions on cohabitation violate our constitutionally protected right to privacy. Essentially, Waddoups dismisses *Reynolds* for its blatant racism, and removes cohabitating unmarried adults from the law's reach by appealing to a ruling that decriminalized gay sex. Could a progressive (like me) ask for more than we were given in this ruling (by a W. Bush appointee, no less)?

Importantly, Waddoups's opinion leaves two questions wide open: whether the state has a legitimate interest that justifies the criminal prosecution of bigamists, and whether denying polygamous families access to civil marriage violates their constitutionally protected rights. Because this opinion reminds us that we cannot justify our current legal preference for monogamy with imperialist, racist, parochial, or ethnocentric arguments, we must be sure that any arguments we construct against bigamy or polygamy are free of such bias. In this essay, I will explore two concerns or reservations that are commonly deployed to justify the disparate legal treatment of bigamists and polygamists: that the practices of bigamy and polygamy promote the subordination of women, and they inevitably lead to the loss of critical forms of privacy necessary for forming stable marital bonds. I will argue that legal bigamy and polygamy could be structured in ways similar to civil monogamy, so that their impact on gender equality and marital privacy would be, at worst, neutral and, at best, empowering for all involved.

In the next section, I will situate *Brown v. Buhman* in a very brief historical trajectory in order to illuminate some aspects of this ruling. In section 3, I will examine and address the concern that polygamy and bigamy are socially harmful because they are inconsistent with the full equality of women, and because these practices exclude adults who are not heterosexual. In section 4, I will address the objection that polygamy and bigamy are incompatible with maintaining forms of privacy that are necessary for marital happiness and stability. In section 5, I will draw out the implications of my arguments and consider whether bigamy should be decriminalized in cases where there is no fraud and coercion involved, and whether doing this will be sufficient to give polygamists access to civil marriage.

2. The Right to Marry

In 1948, the UN General Assembly passed the Universal Declaration of Human Rights, partly in response to the genocidal acts that the world had witnessed in that decade. Article 16 of this Declaration addresses marriage: "Men and women of full age, without any limitation due to race, nationality or religion, have the right to marry and to found a family. They are entitled to equal rights as to marriage, during marriage and at its dissolution."[7] Article 16 proclaims that the right to marry is a right we have based on our humanity, and not only our citizenship. It calls upon all governments to respect and protect this right, and not to limit this right based on a person's "race, nationality or religion."[8]

Loving v. Virginia (1967), the Supreme Court ruling invalidating anti-miscegenation laws, echoes the spirit, if not the exact words, of Article 16:

> Marriage is one of the "basic civil rights of man," fundamental to our very existence and survival. . . The Fourteenth Amendment requires that the freedom of choice to marry not be restricted by invidious racial discriminations. Under our Constitution, the freedom to marry, or not marry, a person of another race resides with the individual, and cannot be infringed by the State."[9]

In this passage, those writing for the majority assert that marriage is both a human right and also a civil right, guaranteed by our Constitution, and a right not to be limited on account of a person's race.

In 1993, the State Supreme Court of Hawaii ruled that denying same-sex couples access to marriage potentially constitutes sex discrimination, which is prohibited by the state constitution's Equal Rights Amendment. Moreover, the court concluded that, because marriage is a basic civil right, the government must provide a compelling state interest to justify limiting this right due to the sex of potential participants.[10] The majority opinion then appealed to the *Loving* ruling to challenge the argument that bans on same-sex marriage treat men and women alike, and therefore are not discriminatory. In *Loving,* the Court rejected the state's argument that anti-miscegenation laws treat blacks and whites equally, and acknowledged that laws aiming to keep racial groups separate were based on pernicious racist ideas. Similarly, laws banning same-sex marriage are predicated on sexist ideas about gender role complementarity that serve to marginalize women (gay or straight) and gay men.

In *Brown v. Buhman*, the state was not able to provide a compelling state interest that could justify banning cohabitation among adults who are not legally married to each other. In his opinion, Judge Waddoups states "the Supreme Court has over decades assumed a general posture that is less inclined to allow majoritarian coercion of unpopular or disliked minority groups, especially when blatant racism (as expressed through Orientalism. . . [or] imperialism), religious prejudice, or some other constitutionally suspect motivation, can be discovered behind such legislation."[11] Because Utah's anti-polygamy statute was used to prosecute "religious cohabitation," which targets a particular religious group (fundamentalist Mormons) but not other unmarried adults who cohabitate, the Court applied the strict scrutiny standard and found that this provision of the law violated the plaintiffs' right to the free exercise of their religion and to private forms of intimacy. However, the Court found the parts of the statute prohibiting bigamy to be neutral and generally applicable, and therefore did not apply the higher standard of review to this part of the law.

Today, criminal laws that ban bigamy appear to be operationally neutral, as they are used to prosecute Christians, Muslims, Jews, and members of other religious groups alike. Opponents of bigamy and polygamy are less likely to support their case by invoking racist or Orientalist stereotypes, and more likely to invoke progressive ideals of gender equality and individual privacy.[12] If bigamy and polygamy necessarily "lead to the patriarchal principle" of authoritarian and anti-egalitarian social relationships and government, laws criminalizing bigamy or denying polygamists access to civil marriage are probably justified. In the next sections, I will investigate whether bigamy or polygamy, in principle and practice, undermine gender equality or individual and marital privacy. I will argue that many of the reservations progressives have about polygamy are based on inexperience with societies in which polygamy is permitted, rather than animosity toward particular racial or religious groups.

3. Equality in Marriage

Thom Brooks and Stephen Macedo both argue that, because polygyny has been the most common form of polygamy, both historically and globally, legally recognizing polygamy or permitting bigamy will primarily translate into empowering patriarchal religious communities that want to practice polygyny.[13] Moreover, until same-sex marriage is permitted in most places, recognizing polygamy will default to recognizing another form of heterosexual marriage. For these reasons, legal polygamy will promote several forms of inequality. First, it will direct social resources to support gender-structured marriages in which a husband's relationship with each wife is not symmetrical with each wife's relationship with him. If there are two or more wives, each wife will contractually have non-exclusive rights to his sexual attention, reproductive capacities, and property, while the husband will have exclusive rights over each wife's sexual attention, reproductive capacities, and property.[14] Second, because of the structural asymmetry mentioned above, the husband would play a more central role in the marriage than each wife (even if he was not their "head and master"), thus relegating each wife to a somewhat peripheral (if not subordinate) role. That is, each wife might have an equal say over her own sphere, while the husband has an equal say in every sphere of the marriage, giving him greater power in marital decision-making. Third, because polygamy in its known forms is gender structured (polygyny or polyandry), gay men and lesbians would be excluded from participation, even where same-sex monogamy is legally recognized.

While I am quite sympathetic to the concerns behind these objections, I think each objection can be satisfactorily addressed. To begin with, we need to remember that civil monogamy has, for most of its history, been gender structured. For example, English and US law for many centuries imposed a system of coverture in which a wife's legal identity was subsumed by her husband, along with her right to enter contracts, own property, live separately, and so on. Until the mid-twentieth century in the US, many states had "head and master laws" that gave husbands exclusive control over all the couple's property. Today, bans on same-sex marriage are the primary legal remnant of the belief that marriage must involve people of different gender, even though spouses now have identical formal rights and duties. So the relevant question is as follows: can the inequalities that result from the gender structuring of marriage be eliminated from polygamy as they mostly have been from monogamy? In other words, are there forms of polygamy that do not impose a gender-structured set of roles, rights, and duties on spouses, and in which each spouse has equal standing under the law?

Because we are discussing equality within a legal marriage, we need to consider which aspects of marriage the state should regulate and which it should not. Under US law, wives and husbands are formally equal, but nevertheless many couples live in gender-structured marriages.[15] Should the state do more to "dis-incentivize" traditional gender divisions of domestic labor, income earning, and financial management in marriage? For example, in 2002, the Swedish government introduced a program that provides 480 days of paid parental leave for each child born or adopted. Yet, in order for parents to qualify for the full amount of paid leave, each parent is required to utilize 60 days of the leave and cannot transfer this benefit to the other parent.[16] By contrast, in the US our income-tax laws often incentivize gender-structured marriage, in that they discourage a lower-earning spouse from working outside the home. This is because the lower income of a married person is taxed at a significantly higher rate (based on the combined earnings of the couple), and the net income received from the additional lower income may be less than the value of the lower earner's labor in the home, especially when child care costs are factored in. When the lower income earner is the wife, as it often is in many marriages, the tax system structures personal choices in ways that make the traditional gender division of labor seem most rational.

Given how state policies can support or destabilize historically entrenched divisions of labor in marriage, it is not unreasonable to think that state policies should cover more than the entry and exit requirements of marriage. As the Swedish government has shown, the state can create programs that mitigate the social subordination of women, which marriage often perpetuates. At a minimum, governments can revise their social security and tax policies so that they do not incentivize wives to become economically dependent on their husbands. When wives stay out of the paid work force, they gamble their future well-being on the increasingly slim odds that their husband will be able to provide adequately for their needs, even if they stay married (which many do not). Few men today can earn a "family wage," and close to half of all marriages end in divorce in the US. The inequalities of economic and social status that develop during a marriage can leave a woman worse off after a marriage ends than she was before she entered it. Even while her marriage lasts, a wife's economic dependence places her in a weak bargaining position in relation to her spouse, which can limit her ability to get her needs met, or exit her marriage and form new and sustaining social relationships.

So can we ensure that neither monogamy nor polygamy will promote the social subordination of women, or render wives economically and socially dependent on their husbands? We need to consider both the formal legal constraints on marriage, as well as some of the informal constraints that perpetuate the narrowing of economic and social opportunities for wives. Regarding the formal legal constraints, the terms of a civil marriage can and should assign spouses identical rights and duties, without regard to their gender, and whether there are two spouses, or three or four. That is, the state should not assign central and peripheral roles to spouses in a polygamous marriage, and therefore differential rights and duties based on such roles. All spouses would have a claim to an equal or equitable share of all property acquired during the marriage, the same exit rights, and the same next-of-kin rights vis-à-vis all other spouses.[17] No spouse would have exclusive claim to another's spouse's affection or share of that person's economic assets.[18]

Moreover, just as the state does not dictate whether spouses in a monogamous marriage are sexually active or procreative, the state should not dictate whether and which spouses in a plural marriage could be sexually active or procreative. Furthermore, the state could impose a cap on the number of spouses over a lifetime that would be recognized for purposes such as immigration preference, testimonial privilege, tax relief on inheritance, or social security benefits. This number could be the same for serially married and divorced monogamists as it is for polygamists. Finally, to remove all gender structuring from marriage, there should be no entry requirement that mandates that marital units include spouses of different sex.

Even with these rules, some married people will live within gender-structured marriages.[19] The gender structuring in some marriages might conform to patriarchal norms, while in other marriages, the informal patterning of roles and responsibilities might follow a feminist or queer logic. The worry that Brooks and Macedo have regarding the likelihood that most polygamous marriages would be structured by patriarchal polygynous norms seems to overlook how marriage customs continually evolve in response to broad social transformations, such as the social integration of blacks, straight women, lesbians, gay men, and eventually perhaps people who defy easy categorization. If plural marriage were to become attractive to feminists and polyamorists, as it has at earlier historical moments, then the forms it could take would be more diverse than religious polygyny.[20]

My discussion of legal polygamy primarily pertains to a form that some call "polyfidelity." This type of polygamy could involve a single marriage contract (license) issued to multiple spouses, or multiple "monogamous" contracts (bigamy) where each spouse is legally married simultaneously to every spouse who is a spouse of one of their spouses. In a polyfidelitous arrangement, spouses make comparable commitments to all spouses and to no other person outside their marriage(s). Another form of legal bigamy would involve simultaneous "monogamous" marriage contracts that would not require transitivity among all spouses. So A may marry B, B may marry C, but A and C would not be spouses. A could marry another person, but A might choose not to exercise this right. One problem here is figuring out A's relationship to C. Clearly these people will have an impact on each other's lives, but no legal relationship with one another. If all spouses have the same legal right to additional simultaneous marriages, whether they exercise this right or not, there is some degree of equality among them. Yet, such an arrangement could, in practice, generate informal inequalities if, say, only men took additional spouses. So I am less certain that this form of bigamy or polygamy could be structured in ways that genuinely protect and promote equality and privacy.

Before I switch to the subject of privacy and marriage, I will briefly comment on the question "what about the children?" which often surfaces in debates about marriage reform. In a recent ruling upholding Canada's anti-polygamy laws, BC Supreme Court Judge Robert Bauman pointed to evidence involving "higher mortality rates of children born into polygamous families, the dangers of early sexualization of girls, gender inequality, and the problem of so-called lost boys—young men turfed out of polygamous communities as a result of competition for young brides."[21] While it is beyond the scope of this essay to address these important findings, we need to ask whether the detrimental effects of polygamy on children are due to the social isolation faced by polygamous families and ethnic groups, and the social stigma that children from polygamous families suffer. Moreover, researchers studying the impact of polygamy on children need to control for variables such as poverty and the prevalence of authoritarian patriarchal norms, which can have a detrimental impact on children and girls in monogamous families. Opponents of same-sex marriage have made claims about the detrimental effects of such marriages on children, and their claims have been challenged by further and broader scientific research. There are many questions to address in regard to studies comparing the outcomes for children of different marriage forms, including whether they should compare outcomes in countries where polygamy is legal to those in which it is not, and whether they should compare outcomes for patriarchal polygynous families with those for egalitarian polyamorous units. In short, this kind of research is difficult to do well, and the results are likely to be quite controversial.

In a traditional gender-structured marriage, wives assume the greater share of responsibility for caring for children, whether the marriage is monogamous or polygamous. When the division of labor and responsibilities in a marriage is not determined by the gender of a spouse, then these duties can be divided up in a variety of ways that suit the preferences and needs of all spouses. In a plural marriage of the polyfidelity type, there would simply be more options for creatively distributing care work (assuming there is a single household or family to manage). As with monogamy, the roles and responsibilities of nonbiological parents (stepparents) would need to be worked out, and the rules could vary in ways that make biological ties more or less significant. The rules for second- and third-parent adoption would need to be worked out for polygamous marriages in ways that are similar for nonbiological parents in a monogamous marriage. In other words, I don't think the issues here are fundamentally different for polygamy than they are for monogamy. The primary difference is that children in a polygamous family are more likely to have more than two primary parents at any given time, and this is not necessarily bad.[22]

4. Marital Privacy

The concern polygamy poses for privacy is readily captured by the expression: "two's company, three's a crowd." The sentiment here is that a third person can disrupt the romantic-sexual bond between two people that is necessary for the stability of an intimate and marital relationship. In a polygamous arrangement, this third person may also have a romantic-sexual relationship with one or both halves of a couple. So how can this work?

There is a legitimate concern here that cannot be answered by simply asserting that a person can love (in a romantic sense) more than one person at a time, and therefore there is no reason to feel threatened if one's lover is capable of this. Intimate relationships typically involve some sharing of sensitive information about ourselves, and some lowering of the emotional and bodily boundaries that we've established for non-intimate associates. Moreover, intimate partners may shape each other's decisions and plans in ways that would seem intrusive for non-intimate partners. So how can intimacy work when there are more than two people involved in a marriage?

I will focus on the following questions. Does polygamy generally translate into less control over one's personal information, personal space, and ordinary but important decisions about one's life? Does monogamy afford us more control over these things, or only an illusion of greater control? Consider, for example, that when a marriage ends, it's not uncommon for each spouse to lose control over sensitive information they have shared. Sadly, it's not uncommon for intimate partners (former and current) to seek revenge simply by making public some amount of private and personal information about each other.[23] Moreover, partners in any marriage may find that other relatives and close friends intrude upon their physical space and hard-won agreements. So are monogamous partners better able to keep relatives and close friends from interfering in their relationship than polygamous partners?

Intimate partners typically have rules (implicit and explicit) about (i) when to share sensitive information about each other, (ii) how to preserve some separate living space where they can openly interact with each other, and (iii) which decisions should be made by themselves without interference from others. The rules among intimate partners in a polygamous marriage may be more complex than the rules for those who live monogamously, but polygamists (and ethical polyamorists) nevertheless have rules about respecting and protecting each other's privacy. The challenge for polygamous unions is perhaps how to balance the privacy needs of each spouse while maintaining various kinds of transparency and openness that appear necessary for establishing trust and emotional closeness.

In a monogamous relationship, there is only one other adult who has privileged access to our private lives, sexual selves, living space, and personal deliberations. The relationship we have with this one person is different from those we have with any others, and some feel that this is an important part of romance and intimate companionship. However, the uniqueness of this relationship can also heighten the emotional and social stakes involved should the relationship be harmed or lost. One advantage of polygamy is that married people do not need to place their happiness or future into the hands of just one close companion. When problems arise in the relationship between any two spouses, there is at least one other spouse who can help mediate and diffuse tensions (or, of course, possibly make things worse). If one cannot get a particular spouse to cooperate with an endeavor or with solving the problems of the family, there are other spouses to whom one can turn. One may feel less alone or isolated, which of course could be a problem for those who prefer to spend time alone or to be more isolated from others.

The question, though, for the purposes of this essay is whether the state should have a preference for one model of intimacy over the other. If some adults want to pursue forms of marital intimacy that involve more than two, should the government get in the way? Some social conservatives may object to marriages in which there is no commitment to sexual exclusivity between two people. For example, David Brooks contends, "Anybody who has several sexual partners in a year is committing spiritual suicide. He or she is ripping the veil from all that is private and delicate in oneself, and pulverizing it in an assembly line of selfish sensations. But marriage is the opposite. Marriage joins two people in a sacred bond. It demands that they make an exclusive commitment to each other. . ."[24] Brooks's concern about sexual exclusivity applies equally to "open" monogamous marriages as to polygamous ones. Yet many conservatives today see more evil in having the state police the sexual habits of married people than in restricting the state's authority to punish non-exclusive sexual behaviors among consenting adults. Most liberal democratic states have decriminalized adultery, as well as birth control, and this suggests that there is some consensus around minimizing the state's intrusion into the bedrooms of its subjects. So given that the state does not mandate and enforce sexual exclusivity between two people in a monogamous marriage, it should not prosecute polygamous families for failing to practice sexual exclusivity between two spouses, or among three or four.

The only perhaps-legitimate reason the state could have for preferring a model of marital intimacy that limits such relationships to two is that such marriages are more stable, and therefore contribute more positively to maintaining civil peace and harmony, and sustaining strong and thriving families. When families break up, they become civil adversaries in ways that can damage their members, and leave their dependents without proper care and resources. People from so-called "broken families" can become a burden to society in a number of ways, for example, if they access greater social resources such as the civil court system or social welfare programs, or engage in antisocial or criminal activity. I will contend that the conviction that monogamous marriages are more stable is based on the lack of experience with, and understanding about, how plural marriages work. As with same-sex marriages, the more understanding we have of polygamous marriages, the less likely we are to see them as inferior, or as detrimental to their participants and society.

As I've indicated above, polygamous and polyamorous partners generally follow rules in order to protect the privacy and decisional autonomy of their members and their relationships. As with a monogamous couple, adherence to these rules can promote the stability of adult relationships and families. Those of us who have lived in societies that promote monogamy can probably articulate many of the rules that couples follow, or are urged to follow, in order to promote trust and strengthen their relationship. I am not claiming that many of us follow these rules well, or that the rules are always clear, but we have some understanding of the basic rules, and we can determine when they have been violated.

For example, we have rules about what constitutes appropriate or inappropriate sharing of information about one's spouse or intimate partner. Intimate partners may further elaborate these rules among themselves.

Many may place limits on sharing the details of their sex lives, health problems, or finances with others. People usually place limits on sharing criticisms or negative assessments of one's intimate partner with others. Polygamous and polyamorous intimate partners will generally observe similar rules, but will also need some rules about sharing sensitive information among simultaneous intimate partners. They may agree, for instance, to be maximally transparent with each other about health and financial matters but not about the details of their respective sexual lives. They may also set limits on sharing negative assessments of a spouse, both with other spouses and with non-spouses.

Married people and intimate partners generally have rules about sharing domestic space. We have "master bedrooms," and rules about knocking before entering rooms, which allow family members some spatial separateness within a single domestic setting. Homebuilders could redesign homes to meet the needs of polygamous families. There might be several master bedrooms that are allocated on a timeshare basis, much like a vacation residence shared by several couples. Wealthier families may prefer to provide each adult with a separate sleeping space that could accommodate more than one person, or even separate apartments or houses. In short, the design of homes or apartment complexes need not be tailored only to the needs of one kind of family.[25]

Married people and intimate partners also have rules about how to make decisions on important matters affecting their relationship or family. This may be the most difficult issue on which to address the "three's a crowd" worry. Do we really want our decisions about children, the acquisition or disposal of personal property, vacations, visitors, and so on to involve more than one other person? Some may not find this attractive, and poly intimacy is not for everyone, as Elizabeth Emens has pointed out.[26] But for those who don't find the prospect of group decision-making on private matters too daunting, they are likely to have rules for going about it.

Rules about decision-making among intimate partners often place limits on interference from outsiders (however this is defined, e.g., friends, in-laws, etc.). They may divide authority for making decisions on some matters, thereby giving one partner greater control over certain domains of their common life. They may adopt basic rules about fair distributions and arrangements, so that decisions which violate these rules can be challenged and scrutinized. They may establish a process for resolving disputes, grievances, tensions, and hurt feelings. When there are only two people in an intimate relationship the decision rules sketched above may be less explicit, but generally there are some such rules. In poly units, the rules may need to be more explicit, only because more people are involved and the partners may need to be sure all are on the same page. But if the rules for an intimate relationship are made more explicit, and perhaps occasionally re-evaluated and negotiated, this would not necessarily be a bad thing.

Given that both monogamous and polygamous families can develop and articulate adequate rules for protecting the informational, spatial, and decisional privacy of all members, I don't think that the contention that the latter are inherently less stable can be maintained. Those of us who have lived mostly in monogamous families can benefit by learning about how non-authoritarian and egalitarian polygamous families work.

5. Decriminalizing Bigamy

In the US and many other countries, bigamy is a criminal offense.[27] Intentionally marrying someone while one is legally married to another is a crime, even when no fraud or coercion is involved. Do these laws serve a legitimate state purpose? Does someone who practices bigamy or polygamy with the consent and full knowledge of all spouses pose a serious threat to society?

It seems reasonable to impose criminal or civil sanctions on bigamists when fraud or coercion is involved. When bigamists fail to inform an existing or new spouse of all their current marriages, or when the existing spouses have not given consent and have a new spouse forced upon them, it seems reasonable to prosecute such cases of bigamy under the criminal or civil law.[28] But if all the spouses are fully informed and agree to bigamous arrangements, where is the harm?

Our current laws may reflect the assumption that no one would agree to be married to a bigamist, and therefore that fraud and coercion are always involved. But this assumption is certainly false. People who choose to practice polygamy may desire to have multiple separate marriage contracts, especially if they cannot obtain a single plural marriage license. Criminally prosecuting consensual bigamy only serves the purpose of allowing a majority to impose its marriage customs on a minority. Whether people practice polygamy or bigamy for religious or secular reasons, they have the right to equal treatment and due process.

The state might defend its anti-bigamy laws by arguing that they treat polygamists equally and do not infringe their fundamental right to marry, because, like everyone else, they can marry one other person at a time.

Yet this reasoning seems to suffer from the same flaw as the argument that anti-miscegenation laws do not involve racial discrimination because they apply to both blacks and whites, or that bans on same-sex marriage don't involve sex discrimination because they apply to both men and women. Bigamy laws are based on the notion that polygamy is an inferior form of marriage. If my arguments that civil polygamy can be restructured so that it does not subordinate women and undermine valuable forms of marital privacy are sound, then there is no reason to hold that polygamy is inherently inferior to monogamy, other than irrational prejudice. While I do not regard the desire for plural marriage to be based on an immutable identity trait, such as a disposition toward polyamory, I also do not think this is relevant to the issue of decriminalizing bigamy. People may desire bigamy or polygamy for cultural reasons, and if the practice is not harmful to the individuals involved or to society, then there is no justification for criminalizing it.

Decriminalizing open and consensual bigamy would essentially provide polygamists access to civil marriage, as polygamous spouses could form separate legal marriages with all other spouses in the unit.[29] Yet governments could also issue a single marriage license to a polygamous unit, which may facilitate polygamy of the polyfidelity type. A single license issued under the rules of one governing power would mean that all spouses would be subject to the same marriage laws, and could be granted the right to approve or contest the entry or exit of any other spouse. That is, this arrangement might make it easier to ensure that no spouse takes a new spouse without the notification and consent of all existing spouses. Moreover, the government would recognize the spouses as a single family, rather than multiple but overlapping families. I am undecided about whether the government would have legitimate reasons to prefer polyfidelitous polygamy over other kinds of poly families (e.g., where A is married to B and C, but B and C are not married to each other). As I mentioned above, I worry that the latter arrangement would support greater informal inequalities and loss of decisional privacy than the polyfidelitous kind. But I'm open to being proven wrong.

Even if one accepts that some forms of polygamy are just and fair, legal polygamy may require an unmanageable degree of governmental administration, particularly in terms of the distribution of marital entitlements.[30] For example, how would governments handle inheritance claims, or the preferred status that spouses receive for immigration purposes, when dealing with polygamous families? Governments, of course, already address complicated entitlement distributions, for example, when the US federal government calculates social security retirement benefits for former and current spouses. As I suggest above, legal recognition for polygamy may necessitate some caps on inheritance tax relief, immigration preference for one's spouses, and so on. Adrienne Davis argues that the default rules that have been well established in commercial partnership law provide legal norms and models that could be adapted to multi-partner marriage. These rules cover the entry and exit requirements for partners, divisions of property, and unanimity norms for adding or expelling a partner, while allowing any partner to voluntarily and unilaterally exit (as with no-fault divorce). Davis claims, "In the eleven community property states, the law has already recognized these similarities, explicitly incorporating commercial partnership norms into its default principles."[31] By recognizing the similarities between a marriage and a commercial partnership, and then applying similar default rules, the law can help to stabilize partnerships as they add or lose members, and accordingly adjust the rights and responsibilities of each member. A marriage and a commercial partnership of course have different ends, which may determine how extensive or intrusive the formal default rules become. For example, will they define who makes the coffee, or the process for making a major purchase? Libertarians will prefer that the general default rules be quite minimal in both cases, allowing each partnership maximum room to define its own rules. Whether we decide that the default rules for marriage and commercial partnerships should be basically the same or significantly different in some respects, treating them as analogous should prove helpful for exploring this question.

Removing criminal sanctions from bigamy and providing polygamists access to civil marriage can protect the interests of those who live in polygamous or polyamorous households. Elizabeth Emens discusses the case of a mother whose parental rights were violated because she was living in an informal polyandrous relationship with two men, one of whom was her legal husband. The judge's decision was based on his objection to the mother's alternative lifestyle, which he made explicit during the court hearings. The judge then ordered the removal of her son from her care and awarded custody to the child's paternal grandmother, against the advice of experts who were called upon to assess whether this would be in the child's best interest.[32] The precarious situation of mothers who live in consensual polyamorous families is similar to the situation that existed for gay parents when some US states had and enforced anti-sodomy laws, or bans on same-sex marriage. Victimless and harmless acts that subject parents to criminal prosecution or loss of custody because of the moral disapproval of others (including judges) disrupt the bonds between parents and children. Similarly, states that ban polygamy make it difficult for polyamorous intimate partners to adopt each other's biological children. Because criminalizing bigamy and banning polygamy socially marginalize people who live in open and consensual polygamous households and infringes their basic civil rights, we need to provide weighty reasons to justify retaining these state policies.

Some theorists, such as Andrew March and Tamara Metz,[33] argue for replacing civil marriage with a more secular "civil union" status for all spouses in order to give adults more control over how to structure their families and households. I have argued elsewhere that privatizing marriage and replacing it with a more minimally restrictive civil union contract[34] would not sufficiently protect vulnerable or weaker parties in a marital contract. Private marriage structures that are inegalitarian or authoritarian, such as patriarchal polygyny, are unlikely to be mitigated by a civil union contract that provides formally equal rights to all spouses.[35] Instead, by reforming the institution of civil marriage so that it becomes a more just institution, we can promote more individual freedom and social equality for a greater number of people. For this reason, I think the government should not "get out of the marriage business," but instead regulate marriage in ways that reflect less irrational prejudice and bias.

6. Conclusion

I have explored whether imposing criminal sanctions for bigamy and excluding polygamists from civil marriage can be justified without appealing to parochial prejudice or intolerance. I have argued that two general worries based on widely shared political commitments to equality and individual autonomy do not provide good reasons for preserving statutes that criminalize bigamy or ban polygamy. It is not that I do not share these worries or values, but rather, it's that I think when these worries are investigated, they will be dissolved. If we've learned anything from marriage reform movements of the last century, it is that marriage reform has been responsive to and part of larger social revolutions involving the political rights of blacks, women, lesbians, and gay men. Decriminalizing bigamy and legally recognizing polygamous families will likely gain more support as the demands of the polyamorous community (gay and straight), as well as religious minorities, are heard and met. They will also gain support when we recognize that we can meet these demands for inclusion without compromising our beliefs about the nature of just institutions or a just society.[36]

Notes

1. From *Brown v. Buhman*, Case No. 2:11-cv-0652-CW, 18–20, accessed March 13, 2014; https://ecf.utd.uscourts.gov/cgi-bin/show_public_doc?211cv0652-78.

2. *"Reynolds v. United States,"* The Oyez Project at IIT Chicago-Kent College of Law, accessed March 13, 2014; http://www.oyez.org/cases/1851-1900/1878/1878_0.

3. *Brown*, 22. See also, "A Utah Law Prohibiting Polygamy is Weakened," John Schwartz, *The New York Times*, December 14, 2013: http://www.nytimes.com/2013/12/15/us/a-utah-law-prohibiting-polygamy-is-weakened.html (accessed March 14, 2014); and "Federal Judge Strikes Down Part of Utah's Polygamy Ban," Eyder Peralta, *National Public Radio (NPR)*, August 28, 2014: http://www.npr.org/blogs/thetwo-way/2014/08/28/343953743/federal-judge-strikes-down-part-of-utahs-polygamy-ban (accessed September 1, 2014).

4. Under Utah law, "(1) A person is guilty of bigamy when, knowing he [*sic*] has a husband or wife or knowing the other person has a husband or wife, the person purports to marry another person or cohabits with another person. (2) Bigamy is a felony of the third degree." http://le.utah.gov/~code/TITLE76/htm/76_07_010100.htm (accessed May 5, 2014). Presumably, the cohabitation clause of this statute is no longer enforceable.

5. Currently, a legal marriage can only be formed between two adults, but one way to legally recognize polygamous units would be for the state to issue a single marriage license to marital units of two or larger, rather than requiring separate licenses for each pair of a polygamous unit. The exit rules could allow for one spouse to leave without dissolving the marriage among the remaining spouses.

6. Sometimes these informal marriages are called "spiritual marriages." For an interesting discussion of *Brown v. Buhman*, see http://onpoint.wbur.org/2013/12/23/polygamy-utah-sister-wives-gay-marriage.

7. http://www.un.org/en/documents/udhr/index.shtml (accessed March 13, 2014).

8. It's interesting to think about what would be included in this list, if Article 16 were revised today. In addition to race, nationality, and religion, the list (at a minimum) should be expanded to include sex, gender, sexual orientation, incarceration or economic status, and disability. Claiming that marriage is a basic human and civil right does not determine what rights, privileges, or obligations the state should confer on those who enter marriage. The language of Article 16 focuses on the equal right to marry, and not on the content of this right. An interesting question is whether the state can protect the equal right to marry if it were to privatize marriage, and allow private civil groups to regulate the terms of marriage.

9. The phrase "basic civil rights of man" is taken from *Skinner v. Oklahoma* (1942), a case dealing with compulsory sterilization penalties. http://supreme.justia.com/cases/federal/us/388/1/case.html (accessed March 13, 2014).

10. "In Hawaii, Step Toward Legalized Gay Marriage," Jeffrey Schmalz, *The New York Times*, May 7, 1993, http://www.nytimes.com/1993/05/07/us/in-hawaii-step-toward-legalized-gay-marriage.html (accessed March 14, 2014).

11. https://ecf.utd.uscourts.gov/cgi-bin/show_public_doc?211cv0652-78, 11 (accessed March 14, 2014).

12. Ron Den Otter suggests that the recent *Windsor* decision, striking down important provisions in the federal DOMA law, in part because the law's aim or effect demeans lesbians and gay men in violation of the Constitution's equal protection guarantees, could apply to bans on polygamy, if their aim or effect is to demean a sexual minority or religious minority. "Legally, No Different from Same-Sex Unions," *The New York Times*, December 17, 2013: http://www.nytimes.com/roomfordebate/2013/12/17/should-plural-marriage-be-legal/no-constitutional-difference-between-plural-and-same-sex-unions.

13. Thom Brooks, "The Problem of Polygamy," *Philosophical Topics* 37.2 (2009): 109–122; and Stephen Macedo, *Just Married: Same-Sex Couples, Monogamy, and the Future of Marriage* (Princeton,NJ: Princeton University Press, 2015). See also John Corvino, "Enough with the Scare Tactics," *The New York Times*, December 17, 2013: http://www.nytimes.com/roomfordebate/2013/12/17/should-plural-marriage-be-legal/enough-with-the-scare-tactics.

14. Gregg Straus usefully maps out different kinds of symmetrical and asymmetrical polygamous relationships in his essay "Is Polygamy Inherently Unequal?" *Ethics* 122 (2012): 516–544.

15. I'm not convinced that polygyny in its most patriarchal forms is significantly worse than monogamy in its most patriarchal forms. Where monogamy is the norm, there is often toleration for husbands, but not wives, to have extramarital romances. Non-patriarchal polygamy and monogamy can take many different forms, but primarily wives would have full equality with husbands.

16. "Gender Equality in Sweden," http://sweden.se/society/gender-equality-in-sweden/; "Parental Leave: The Swedes Are Most Generous," *NPR*, August 8, 2011: http://www.npr.org/blogs/babyproject/2011/08/09/139121410/parental-leave-the-swedes-are-the-most-generous; "In Sweden, Men Can Have It All," *The New York Times*, June 9, 2010: http://www.nytimes.com/2010/06/10/world/europe/10iht-sweden.html; "For Paternity Leave, Sweden Asks if Two Months Is Enough," *The Wall Street Journal*, July 31, 2012: http://online.wsj.com/news/articles/SB1000087239639044422690457756110020336384.

17. For a discussion of the importance of providing formal exit rights to women in polygamous families, see Cheshire Calhoun, "Who's Afraid of Polygamous Marriage? Lessons for Same-Sex Marriage Advocacy from the History of Polygamy," *San Diego Law Review* 42 (2005): 1023–1042.

18. For an interesting ethnography on the practices of American polygamists, see Janet Bennion, *Women of Principle: Female Networking in Contemporary Mormon Polygyny* (New York: Oxford University Press, 1998). Many women in the families she studied provided income and services for each other as well as their common husband. With more spouses, there are more adults in a household who can contribute their waged and unwaged work, and increase the family's economic assets and security.

19. For an interesting discussion of how much informal or private inequality a liberal state should tolerate, see Andrew March, "Is There a Right to Polygamy? Marriage, Equality and Subsidizing Families in Liberal Public Justification," *Journal of Moral Philosophy* 8.2 (2011): 246–272.

20. Libby Copeland observes that the modern polyamory movement, as far back as the nineteenth-century Oneida Community, has had progressive attitudes about women and gender roles. Libby Copeland, "Making Love and Trouble: The Surprising Woman-Friendly Roots of Modern Polyamory," *Slate*, March 12, 2012: http://www.slate.com/articles/double_x/doublex/2012/03/polyamory_and_its_surprisingly_woman_friendly_roots_.html.

21. "Canada's Polygamy Laws Upheld by B.C. Supreme Court," *CBC News*, November 23, 2011: http://www.cbc.ca/news/canada/british-columbia/canada-s-polygamy-laws-upheld-by-b-c-supreme-court-1.856480 (accessed May 5, 2014). For helpful discussion of this objection in regard to polygamy, see March, "Is There a Right to Polygamy?"

22. I have argued elsewhere that, because the modern marriage contract leaves unspecified how child care responsibilities will be divided between parents, both married and unmarried parents should formalize some kind of co-parenting agreement. This agreement would lay out the terms of cooperative parenting, and would be operative even when the relationship between the parents undergoes a significant change (such as separation or divorce). "Is the State's Promotion of Marriage Bad for Children?" (unpublished ms.).

23. Some of the most egregious examples of this can be found on "revenge porn" websites.

24. "The Power of Marriage," *The New York Times*, November 22, 2003: http://www.nytimes.com/2003/11/22/opinion/the-power-of-marriage.html.

25. For a recent work about how domestic space is shaped by changing views about privacy, see Peter Ward, *A History of Domestic Space: Privacy and the Canadian Home* (Vancouver: University of British Columbia Press, 2009).

26. Elizabeth Emens, "Monogamy's Law: Compulsory Monogamy and Polyamorous Existence," Public Law and Legal Theory Working Paper No. 58 (Feb. 2003), 27–29, http://www.law.uchicago.edu/files/files/58-monogamy.pdf.

27. http://definitions.uslegal.com/b/bigamy/.

28. I concede that judging genuine consent is likely to be difficult, especially when the spouses have unequal social standing. But for the sake of argument, I am assuming that under some circumstances, we can determine that consent to a bigamous arrangement is given freely and without undue coercion. The challenge then is to develop practices and procedures to ensure that a person consenting to bigamy is giving genuine consent. At a minimum, there could be mandatory disclosure laws concerning existing legal marriages before a couple could obtain a marriage license. In addition, there could be mandatory counseling requirements to insure that potential spouses understand their rights and potential legal obligations. Transparency and consent are important to protect the autonomy of each spouse with respect to freedom of association and privacy.

29. So if there were three partners, each partner would form two marriages with the other two partners. I'm assuming that if bigamy is not a crime, those who are legally married to more than one person would gain the rights and obligations of civil marriage in relation to each spouse. I suppose the state could approve laws or regulations that involve treating a second marriage differently than a first marriage, say, with respect to inheritance or property rights. But if the state did not do this, then presumably

the state would follow some other kind of rule, as it does with successive spouses and social security entitlements.

30. See also March, "Is There a Right to Polygamy?"

31. Adrienne Davis, "Regulating Polygamy: Intimacy Default Rules and Bargaining for Equality," *Columbia Law Review* 110:8 (2010): 2005.

32. Emens, "Monogamy's Law," 27–29.

33. March, "Is There a Right to Polygamy?"; Tamara Metz, *Untying the Knot: Marriage, the State and the Case for Their Divorce* (Princeton University Press, 2010).

34. See also Elizabeth Brake, *Minimizing Marriage: Marriage, Equality, and the Law* (Oxford University Press, 2012).

35. L. Shrage, "Reforming Marriage: A Comparative Approach," *Journal of Applied Philosophy* 30:2 (2013): 107–121; and "The End of Marriage," *The New York Times*, November 4, 2012: http://opinionator.blogs.nytimes.com/2012/11/04/the-end-of-marriage/.

36. Acknowledgment: I would like to thank Elizabeth Brake and Thom Brooks for their insightful and helpful comments on an earlier draft of this essay. I would also like to thank the Princeton University Center for Human Values, where I wrote drafts and outlines of several essays on marriage, including this one.

8| Temporary Marriage

DANIEL NOLAN

OST MARRIAGES BEGIN WITH AN agreement that the relationship be permanent: "till death do us part," or various equivalents. It is widely recognized that such agreements are not always kept, and in societies where divorce is common, the partners may even reasonably suspect the arrangement will not last until one of the parties dies. Still, marriage until one of the partners dies is the norm.

Legal recognition of marriage in most countries reflects this expectation that marriage is a permanent arrangement. Few jurisdictions recognize explicitly temporary marriages: a marriage that automatically expires at the end of five years, for example. If a couple wants their marriage to expire after five years, they must engage in the usual "permanent" marriage and then later initiate divorce proceedings to end the marriage.

Marriages limited to a pre-established time period are a special case of marriages that are specified in advance to automatically end upon some condition obtaining (other than the death of a partner). While the more general topic of conditional marriages is an interesting one, the focus of this essay will be on marriages that, when entered into, are due to expire after a fixed amount of time. These are what I will call "temporary marriages." By "temporary marriages" I thus mean something more specific than marriages that *in fact* last a period of time less than the remaining life of the spouses: any marriage that ends in divorce is a "temporary marriage" in this more general sense. I also mean to include marriages that contain an option to be extended for another period of time or even an option to be made permanent: as long as the marriage automatically would end after a period of time fixed in advance (unless actively extended), I will count it as a "temporary marriage." For want of a better term, I will refer to the more usual marriage, contracted as lasting until the death of the first partner, as "permanent marriage," even though of course many such marriages are dissolved before death.

There are several interesting questions about temporary marriages, so specified. One is whether they are, or would be, genuinely *marriages*, or whether alleged temporary marriages are really temporary arrangements of a different sort ("quasi-marriage," perhaps). A second is whether it could be moral to enter into such an arrangement, and if so when is it morally permissible. A third is whether the state should recognize such marriages performed in its jurisdiction as genuine marriages: whether, for example, the state should recognize marriages that expire after a certain length of time fixed on the occasion of the marriage, without requiring divorce proceedings, even when both parties are still alive.

Of these three questions, my focus will be on the third: I will argue that the state should recognize temporary marriage, and offer temporary marriage as another form of marriage registered in the same sort of way that standard "permanent" marriages are. I will not much discuss the question of whether it would be morally permissible to enter into a temporary marriage, were one available. I think it is very plausible that temporary marriages are morally permissible in general, whatever moral problems there might be with particular special cases; but I will not try to defend this here. The question of whether temporary marriage is genuinely marriage is one I will discuss below, where I will defend the view that these arrangements are indeed marriages: but for most of the purposes of the essay, if a reader wants to interpret my talk of "temporary marriage" as talk of "temporary quasi-marriage," or the like, this should not make much difference. Even if so-called temporary marriage is only temporary quasi-marriage, I still want to argue that it should be recognized by the state in the way marriage is.

What am I calling for when I call for state recognition of temporary marriage? One important thing is that the state record these relationships, when appropriately solemnized, as "marriages" in marriage registries in the way that permanent marriages are recorded.[1] I also think states should have provisions for automatically registering when temporary marriages have expired: it would not be good enough to allow only permanent marriage and require divorce for couples wishing to have a temporary marriage. As well as this symbolic equality, many jurisdictions confer substantial financial and other benefits on married couples. Not all of these will be appropriate for temporarily married couples: paying a survivor's pension well past the original expiry date of the marriage, for example. But many of these financial and other arrangements will be appropriate, and where appropriate they should be extended to temporarily married couples. (I shall have a little more to say about some of the rights and benefits of marriage below, but my focus here is not on the minutiae of exactly how best to implement temporary marriage regulations.)

There are weaker forms of recognition a state could extend that would also be steps in the right direction. For example, a state could recognize couples as married when they are in a temporary marriage that was contracted validly in the jurisdiction in which they married, even if that state does not allow people in its jurisdiction to *enter into* temporary marriages. A number of states take this attitude to certain marriages: some states recognize same-sex marriages contracted elsewhere, even when they do not themselves allow same-sex marriage. Some states recognize polygamous marriages which are validly contracted elsewhere. Some states recognize marriages, contracted validly elsewhere, where one of the partners would be considered too young to be allowed to contract marriage in the state. And so on. So far as I can tell, most Western countries *do* recognize certain child marriages but *do not* recognize temporary marriage. A forty-year-old who marries a fourteen-year-old in New York State can have his marriage recognized throughout the US and most of the rest of the world,[2] but two twenty-five year olds who wish to enter into a five-year temporary marriage cannot. The law in the United States, at least, takes a considerably less dim view of marriage to children than it does of temporary marriage.[3]

I mean the argument in this essay to be a general argument that all states should recognize temporary marriage, but I will mainly have liberal democracies in mind. My examples of the current situation will mostly be from English-speaking Western countries, especially Australia, the United Kingdom, and the USA, since I am most familiar with the situation in those countries.

I will begin with a discussion of what seem to me some of the more important arguments in favor of state recognition of temporary marriages, followed by discussion of arguments against temporary marriage that are important to address (either because of their strength or because of their influence). Then I will address the question of whether what I am calling temporary marriage is a kind of marriage. Finally, I will discuss what immediate practical consequences my discussion might have: even if we accept that ideally the state would recognize temporary marriages, is it worth trying to produce that change in current institutions?

Temporary marriages have received very little discussion in contemporary English-language philosophical literature, despite the distinctive questions they raise about the role of the state in marriage and the nature of marriage itself. This essay is one step in rectifying that deficiency.

Arguments for Recognition

The first argument I will offer for recognition of temporary marriages is an argument from marriage equality. One tempting marriage equality principle is that we should recognize marriages that people are in, or wish to enter, unless there is a significant social reason not to. This does not mean that there should be complete carte blanche: it seems to me that there are good reasons not to recognize involuntary marriages or marriages with children below a certain age, for example, and arguably there are good reasons not to recognize, and perhaps even to forbid, marriage with non-humans, polygamous marriages,[4] incestuous marriages, and so on. This principle of marriage equality does provide an initial presumption in favor of recognizing marriages, however, and insofar as there is something good about recognizing marriages that people want to enter into (even if that good can be outweighed), this general appealing feature of recognizing the marriages people wish to contract should carry over to the temporary marriage case.

The reason this is a principle of marriage *equality* is that it is a principle that, at the level of state action, there should be a presumption of not treating one marriage, or intended marriage, as privileged over another. The mere fact that one form of marriage conforms better with what is ordinarily done, or what has historically been done, should not be enough of a reason to refuse to recognize the marriages of people who want to do things differently. The standard of restricting marriage only where there are significant social reasons to do so seems to me a non-arbitrary standard, and does not seem incompatible with the sorts of equality we care about. (Compare: we can have *both* equality before the law *and* a legal code where some actions are illegal and others not, when there are non-arbitrary reasons for the illegal actions to be illegal.)

One limitation of appealing to marriage equality is that it might be in dispute whether so-called temporary marriages could be *marriages* at all. (Presumably some opponents of same-sex marriage do not see themselves as opposed to "marriage equality" because they do not think those relationships could be marriages in the first place. Likewise, perhaps, for some opponents of plural marriage.) I will have something to say about whether such relationships can count as marriages below, but I think the thrust of the principle of marriage equality often does not depend on the fine points of what can count as a marriage. The principle of "marriage-like" equality is also a strong one. I think, for example, that permanent, exclusive same-sex sexual relationships, with a public ceremony like a marriage ceremony, should be treated by the state just as marriages are treated: and this seems very plausible *even if* our current word "marriage" does not cover such cases. I both happen to think our current word does cover such cases, and other same-sex relationships besides—but I think the relevant principle of equal treatment does not depend on this for its application.

A principle of near-marriage equality, as far as state recognition goes, primarily concerns which relationships deserve the kind of recognition, support, and benefits the state currently extends to some marriages (for example, the ones Australia recognizes in the Commonwealth Marriage Act.) I think the most plausible principle is that the state should extend this sort of recognition and benefits to relationships that are sufficiently like marriage, when couples in those relationships so desire and apply for such recognition, *unless* there are sufficiently good social reasons not to do so. Depending on exactly what the word "marriage" means in English, this may include some non-marriages. I think it will very likely *exclude* some marriages as well, since I suspect the English word "marriage" applies to some relationships that the state rightly declines to extend recognition and benefits to.[5] One thing that may potentially cause confusion is that it might be that the *stipulative use* of a word like "marriage" in an act of parliament might vary its application from its ordinary English use. I see no problem with stipulative uses of statutory language in this way, and it would be a mistake in general to confuse interpretation sections of statutes with any attempt to change the meaning of words in their ordinary English use.

Once we have a principle that any relationship that is sufficiently marriage-like ought to receive the same general kind of recognition that the state extends to marriage, unless there is sufficient social reason not to, debate about temporary marriage should focus on two things. One is whether it is even enough like marriage to trigger the operation of the equality principle. The second, more pressing matter for debate is whether there are good reasons not to recognize temporary marriage. I am inclined to think that evaluating arguments against temporary marriage should not occur in a vacuum: we should look at comparative costs and benefits, to see whether there are any serious harms that are not already the sorts of things we tolerate from other arrangements. And we should also consider what benefits there are to temporary marriage: if it had some drawbacks but sufficiently important social and individual benefits, it could be fit for recognition on balance. Establishing the principle of marriage equality I mentioned above provides a framework for the rest of this defense of temporary marriage.

While many might already be convinced of a marriage equality principle somewhat like the one I have articulated, others may wish for a justification of it. If a justification is to be convincing, it should be tailored to the values and principles of the person demanding the justification, so what I will say here will not please everyone. But let me offer a few of the more general defenses. A principle of not arbitrarily denying some groups privileges given to others seems like a fairly general principle of social justice, and this is particularly so when the rights involved are important and intimate rights like marriage. (For what it is worth, the right to marry is recognized as a fundamental human right in Article 16 of the United Nations Universal Declaration of Human Rights.) General considerations of liberty can also be invoked: at a first pass, people should be free to enter into the arrangements they want to, unless there are good reasons to prevent them. If we are to have a state-recognized institution of marriage at all, considerations of liberty suggest that we should not be unduly restrictive in who can participate in the institution and how. Respecting and accommodating the lives of others is one of the great goods of a liberal society, and we should not impair this good without a good reason. We should be reluctant to disparage people's important human relationships without good cause. It is possible to subscribe to these general principles and yet resist marriage equality: it is usually possible to find a way to endorse a general principle and resist any particular proposed application of that principle. Nevertheless, I think it is plausible that the principles of justice, liberty, and respect indicated here are best understood as supporting the sort of ideal of marriage equality (and near-marriage equality) articulated above.

A final limitation of the argument from marriage equality should be noted. It is consistent with marriage equality, even in my formulation, to hold that the state should not recognize *any* marriages. This might be because someone thinks the state has no role here, or even that the state has a role, but the state ought to discourage or suppress marriage. I will not have much to say here to defend the state's recognition of marriage, since that would take me rather too far afield.[6] I concede that those who think it is on balance best for the state not to recognize marriages in general are unlikely to be convinced that the state should recognize temporary marriages in particular.[7]

Another consideration in favor of recognition of temporary marriage stems from the role it plays in some religious and cultural traditions. Perhaps the best-known form of temporary marriage is *mutah* (*sigheh* in Persian), a form of temporary marriage traditionally recognized in Shia Islam, and which has legal recognition in Iran. In this form of temporary marriage, a marriage contract for a definite period of time is entered into, and a well-established body of religious law governs these arrangements. *Mutah* is sometimes vilified as a front for prostitution, and indeed *mutah* contracts for an hour or a night or a weekend with a significant cash payment sometimes might serve that purpose, but there is no evidence that this is the main purpose, or even among the main purposes, to which *mutah* is put. (It is true that the man in a *mutah* arrangement often gives the woman some money or property. But the requirement for the husband to give a dower (mahr) to the wife is a Koranic requirement (4:24) common to most traditional Islamic marriages, and by itself no more signals prostitution than dowers and dowries in other marriage traditions.)

Mutah does not just exist in Iran: with the fall of Saddam Hussein, it is becoming more common in Shia areas of Iraq as well, for example. And Shia Islam is not the only religious tradition that recognizes temporary marriage. A number of contemporary neopagan communities practice temporary marriage, though without state recognition. Temporary marriage also arguably existed for a time in late-medieval and early modern Scotland, though this is disputed.[8] A contemporary example of neopagan temporary marriage is *handfasting*: this commitment ceremony is often treated by the participants as marriage and can be done for a fixed period of time (a year and a day, or two years, for example) though sometimes time-limited handfasting is treated more as a betrothal or engagement than as a marriage.[9] Of course, it is not a conclusive argument for allowing a social arrangement, let alone giving some kind of legal approval of such an arrangement, that it is part of a religious tradition, even a large religious tradition. It is no part of my argument that religious mores are immune to challenge. However, it is a serious cost to a policy if it bars a part of someone's religious or cultural tradition, unless there is a good reason to do so.

Furthermore, we might hope for evenhandedness between religious traditions, as much as practical, in secular law. The current secular institution of marriage in Western Europe and countries such as Australia or the USA is historically an outgrowth of Western Christian traditions concerning marriage. This runs the risk of *de facto* privileging Christian religious understandings of marriage over rival religious traditions. Those who object to using secular law to privilege one religion over another should be especially sensitive to this effect of the status quo. Legal recognition of temporary marriage would (in a small way) undermine this privileging of Western Christianity by our secular institution of marriage, and would extend more recognition to the marriage practices endorsed by some alternative religious traditions. Secularism and religious tolerance both give us some reason to do so. Those reasons might even be sufficient in the absence of sufficiently good reasons to prohibit temporary marriage: "religious accommodation" per se seems valuable given the important role religion plays in people's lives.

Benefits to the Participants in Temporary Marriages

Concerns for equality, whether equality of treatment of marriages, or equality of treatment of religious and cultural traditions, are not the only kind of reason to recognize temporary marriages. There are also the benefits which would be gained by those who consider themselves to be in temporary marriages, or who are not in temporary marriages but who would like to be in recognized temporary marriages. These couples are unlikely to enjoy the state giving the impression that they are not in a "real" marriage. If marriage benefits anyone, it is hard to see why it would not benefit some who wish to enter into a temporary marriage. Unless, that is, the only benefits of marriage come from its intended permanence, but this is not so for many of the benefits of marriage. Temporary marriage might be of use in providing some reassurance through relationship troubles, for example, just as traditional marriages do. A public ceremony of commitment in the presence of friends and family is something many couples who marry think is worth the trouble and expense of the ceremony: the happiness that can come with a couple's big day would be there in marriage ceremonies celebrating temporary marriages too. Furthermore, marriage is in fact something valued by people other than the couple involved: many parents hope to see their children happily married, and many children value their parents' marriage. Some traditionalist parents might not be pleased by a temporary marriage in the way they might be by a permanent marriage, but many other parents want to be at their son's or daughter's wedding, and would be happy for their children to marry in the way their children want.

Perhaps it might be argued that any of these benefits could be secured at least as well, or to a higher degree, by some other mix of institutions (permanent marriage, or publicly recorded engagements, or something else). The fact that other arrangements might also be beneficial does not undercut the claim that temporary marriage would sometimes be, but it might be thought to undercut the claim that the benefits it brings give us a reason to recognize these arrangements (or otherwise encourage them). But there are reasons to think that these benefits are not as available without temporary marriage. It should be familiar from the same-sex marriage debate and the attempt to placate demands for same-sex marriage with a "civil union" surrogate that this is not seen as good enough by many of those who want to marry and to be considered married. It is widely perceived as conferring only a second-rate status or as signaling that the state does not fully respect the relationships which the partners themselves often see as marriage. No doubt sometimes these "separate but equal" legal statuses are created with good intentions: but the fact that they are perceived, both by same-sex couples and society at large, as not being "real marriages" or full marriage recognition is enough by itself to ensure that they do not play the same role as full state recognition of relationships *as marriages*. Just as in the case of same-sex marriage, fobbing off those who wish to publicly enter a temporary marriage with a status that is not seen as amounting to marriage would upset and hurt the participants, and tend to produce and support a societal attitude that those relationships were somehow ersatz and inferior. This is not a claim that this would have to be the outcome as a matter of necessity: just that as attitudes currently are, this would be the foreseeable result. So nothing less than recognition of temporary marriage *as marriage* would bring all the benefits of recognition of temporary marriage. (This is not to deny that recognition of temporary civil unions might bring some benefits, of course.)

Another legal benefit to recognizing temporary marriages flows from the fact that in many jurisdictions, purporting to go through a ceremony of temporary marriage may amount to a criminal offense. Section 103 of Australia's Marriage Act, for example, makes knowingly going through an unauthorized ceremony of marriage a criminal offense, punishable by a fine or up to six months in prison. Purporting to solemnize a marriage without the authority to do so is also grounds for a fine or up to six months prison (sections 100, 101). While the law *criminalizes* forms of marriage it does not recognize, those seeking to go through a ceremony of marriage, even if they do not want state recognition, run a serious legal risk. There does not seem to be a history of this sort of law being enforced against those engaging in temporary marriage ceremonies in Western countries, but removing the risk of prosecution and potential criminal penalties would still be a clear benefit for those wishing to enter into temporary marriages.[10]

Some will respond that this only means that we should decriminalize some or all of the marriage-like ceremonies not authorized by the state. There is an argument to be had about whether the state should regulate marriage at all (though I think some regulation is desirable), but at least given that in fact many states have frameworks which criminalize all unauthorized marriage, authorizing temporary marriage seems more desirable than criminalizing it.

One reason sometimes suggested for temporary marriages, particularly those with the possibility of renewal, is that the fact that they have to be positively renewed contributes to their value. This might be because partners are less likely to take each other for granted. Or it might be because it minimizes the risk that partners will stay married merely due to inertia. (Many people would rather not be in a relationship that the other person stays in only because it is too much trouble to get out of.) Many couples in traditional marriages are unlikely to think that *their* relationships would be better in these ways if their marriages were temporary. But if some couples estimate that they will derive benefits, or avoid risks, from the requirement to positively renew the marriage in order for it to continue, I am inclined not to substitute the judgment of the state for their own judgments of these matters.

Some people find it difficult to honestly promise that they will stay married to another person for life. This might be because of misgivings about the institution of permanent marriage, or beliefs about themselves and their future, or even because they find it difficult to predict or empathize with their situation in the future. Many people in their early twenties do not have much confidence in their judgments of what they will be like in their early sixties, and some at least will have this lack of confidence in judgments about what they will feel about their current romantic partner at that distance. Not everyone has this difficulty, and some who do willingly choose nonetheless to engage in a permanent marriage. But at present people who do not feel they could make this commitment honestly either must risk dishonesty in their wedding vows, or miss out on marriage altogether. It may well benefit some people who find themselves in this situation to have the option of temporary marriage, and greater confidence they can live up to the commitment that requires. This is not the claim that *everyone* who finds themselves with these doubts would be better off engaging in temporary marriage than permanent marriage: only that some may well be.

Specific benefits for temporary marriage in particular may be available in specific situations. One recent proposal for temporary marriage in Mexico City[11] suggested two-year temporary marriages might reduce the divorce rate, with a connected benefit of reducing pressure on family courts. Jeremy Bentham, in unpublished manuscripts, claims that young adults in particular might benefit from short-term marriages, before maturing to the point where "one feels the need for a companion of all moments."[12] Whether speculative benefits like these, or others, would flow from temporary marriage is an open empirical question[13]—but we might want to leave the decision about how best to guard against risks and pursue benefits of marriage and marriage-like relationships up to the couples involved, as much as is feasible.

Arguments Against

The Slippery Slope

One argument against temporary marriage, familiar from the debate over same-sex marriages, is the slippery slope argument. If you allow temporary marriage, the argument goes, you will "weaken marriage" somehow, so after a few more steps down the "slippery slope" some loathed social arrangement occurs, or occurs with societal sanction, at the bottom of the slippery slope. (The infamous argument attributed to Rick Santorum that recognition of same-sex marriage would somehow lead to "man-on-dog" sex, or perhaps "man-on-dog" marriage, whatever that might be, is perhaps the best known version of this argument,[14] though there are slippery slope arguments worth taking at least a little more seriously.)

The general problem with slippery slope arguments is that it is hard to make plausible that there is a slope like this. Even after some steps have been taken away from a starting point, this does not do much to show that the "slide" is irreversible, let alone unstoppable. And one obvious way to draw a red line of how far to go in expanding marriage recognition is to draw it in terms of what marriages would be good to recognize, all things considered. If we thought that line would hold, then the slippery slope argument has no force against proposals to recognize forms of marriage that it would be good to recognize, apart from worries about slippery slopes.

I suspect what some advocates of the slippery slope argument have in mind is a fear that allowing marriage rights to people who deserve them will not stop there: somehow, political momentum or social change will steamroller us into going too far. In general, this seems like a poor piece of political prediction. Almost any political or legal institution can be put on a hypothetical spectrum of alternatives, and it can be seen that the institution is not yet at one of the extremes. We stop in the middle of hypothetical slippery slopes *all the time*. It is also true that social changes sometimes go too far—but even in those cases, the powers of reaction are not helpless and social trends can move in the opposite direction. Of course any social change *might*, somehow, go too far, as might any attempt to keep a status quo. The mere possibility of undesirable downstream consequences does not seem to be an argument for or against any social movement, or any lack of social movement, in particular.

So I think we must examine temporary marriage on its merits, and resist those who try to raise the prospects of radically different forms of marriage, that we do oppose for good reasons, in an attempt to derail the discussion. If temporary marriage is desirable, embracing it need not and should not lead us to embrace undesirable marriage institutions. And if temporary marriage is undesirable, it can and should be opposed on its own merits, without ungrounded assertions that recognizing temporary marriage would somehow force us to recognize a parade of horrors.

Won't Someone Think of the Children?

Some temporary marriages will result in children. When those temporary marriages end, those children may be left without married parents. If this led to bad outcomes for these children, that would count against the desirability of temporary marriages, and so perhaps form the basis of a public policy argument against recognizing such marriages.

The welfare of children is important, and protecting children from unwise decisions of their parents is an area where most agree society has a role to play, though that role should be traded off against our interest in respecting and protecting the autonomy of parents. There is a lot of research that shows that certain positive outcomes for children are more likely for children of (permanently) married couples who stay together. Statistically, it is more likely that such children will do better in various ways (e.g., finishing high school, avoiding emotional and developmental problems, and so on) than children of cohabiting couples, or children of single parents, or children who live in families that go through divorce while they are growing up. However, it is hard to tell whether marriage per se helps with these outcomes. When these studies are controlled to compare like with like (e.g., controlling for the effects of race or poverty), much of the correlation between marriage and positive outcomes disappears: a recent large study in the UK, for example, concluded "Once we take these factors into account, there are no longer any statistically significant differences in these child outcomes between children of married and cohabiting parents."[15] This study by Goodman and Greaves compares non-divorcing married parents and never-married cohabiting parents, but similar reductions in the statistical differences between different child-rearing arrangements can be found when we control for other factors that might predict child welfare.[16]

Even when studies suggest that there are positive differences for children of permanently married couples that survive controlling for observable features of parents such as race or class or age, it remains very difficult to rule out common-cause explanations of the correlation between marriage and positive outcomes for children: maybe those who engage in permanent marriage are also likely to have traits that make for good parenting, and it may be that permanent marriage itself makes little contribution.

Many children who are born in marriages but grow up outside marriage do so because of divorce. It is relatively hard to know how much the divorce process is a cause of later problems, rather than the absence of marriage between parents. (There is some evidence that children brought up outside marriage because of the death of a spouse do much better than children of marriages that end in divorce,[17] which suggests the divorce itself is part of the problem, especially when it is remembered that having a parent die is also a traumatic experience for most children.) Temporary marriages, in which children are born in a marriage but the marriage does not end in divorce, might, for all the research shows, be considerably better for children than being born into a marriage that ends in divorce before the children are grown.

I can see no particular reason to think that children of temporary marriages will do worse, on average, than children of never-married parents. They may even do better. Children of the never-married often do very well, of course, and circumstances like child poverty are much better predictors of trouble for children than the marital status of children's parents. More research can be usefully done on what child-rearing arrangements are good for children, and if temporary marriage is legally recognized it will make sense to do research on its effects. The most negative conjecture that would be reasonable on the available evidence, it seems to me, is that children of temporary marriages might be slightly worse off, on average, than children of low-conflict permanent marriages where there is no divorce (even when factors like poverty are controlled for). The relatively slight difference in average child welfare does not seem sufficient to bar recognition of temporary marriage. It has not seemed a good enough reason to bar recognition of *de facto* relationships, for example.[18] If research that shows that children raised by lesbian couples have better average outcomes even than children in low-conflict permanent heterosexual marriage, for example, that would not justify the banning of recognition of permanent heterosexual marriage. Likewise, even if research suggested that permanent (heterosexual) marriage of parents was slightly better for children, that would by itself be little reason not to recognize other child-rearing arrangements as legitimate.

Note that all of the concerns discussed above are reduced further for children born in temporary marriages that last until the children are adults. There is no evidence I know of that shows that children in families where the parents divorce after children reach adulthood have worse outcomes than those in which their parents stay married. (Of course, such divorces might still be hurtful or traumatic for some adults whose parents divorce: but there is little evidence that in general the sons and daughters suffer worse life outcomes.) We are free to speculate that a long-term temporary marriage somehow is worse for children's upbringing, because of children's attitudes to their parents' marriage, parents' attitudes to each other, or other factors, but this speculation is at present not based on any firm evidence, and I do not see how it could be made terribly plausible to someone not already casting around for a rationalization of their distaste for temporary marriage.

It would make sense for those entering temporary marriages to be clear with each other, and perhaps publicly clear, in agreeing what will happen to any children conceived or born during the relationship. Perhaps there is even a case for this to be legally mandated. But it is hard to find a reason, based on considerations of child welfare, for banning temporary marriage outright, or barring its recognition.

Are the Temporarily Married Missing Out?

One might suspect that temporary marriage is an inferior rival to some other arrangements. If so, then perhaps recognizing temporary marriages, especially if this has the effect of encouraging temporary marriage, will lead to people foregoing the better option in favor of temporary marriage. If temporary marriage tends to make people worse off than they would be with another alternative, that *prima facie* is a reason to discourage it.

One could think that temporary marriage is inferior to being single, or inferior to standard *de facto* relationships. But I suspect that the main line of response that will be developed along these lines will be from those who think there is something superior about permanent marriage. Something about the relationship being unconditional in various ways might be adduced, perhaps, or something about its suitability for raising children (though a temporary marriage of a long enough duration to last beyond where children are raised is not obviously very different as a relationship for child raising).

One kind of response to claims that permanent marriage has special features that temporary marriages lack would be to argue that, on the contrary, temporary marriages would not lack anything very valuable that permanent marriages typically have. Temporary marriages can be expressions of commitments that are of central importance to the parties involved, can provide public affirmation by families and friends of an intimate and loving relationship, can provide the framework for joint projects of living together and raising children, and so on. A claim that permanent marriage brings some benefit with it so important that temporary marriages should not be recognized by the state requires evidence, and the case has not been made that temporary marriages cannot have the virtues that permanent marriages have.

Even if it could be shown that permanent marriage has special benefits that temporary marriages must lack (and that there were no sufficiently important compensating benefits to temporary marriage), more would need to be done to show this should motivate non-recognition. One serious problem with this style of argument is that the paternalism it embodies will be objectionable to many: there should be serious limits to the extent to which we should use the law to pressure people into doing things we think would be good for them. The most serious problem with this style of argument however, it seems to me, is that even if it is shown that permanent marriage is best for some people who permanently marry, it would not follow that it is the best option for everyone, at every stage of their adult lives. Whether it is a good idea for someone to get permanently married depends on who their potential marriage partner is, whether the other person wants to marry, and a host of other factors. *Even if* the very-best-off people are permanently married, it does not follow that everyone else ought to immediately engage in permanent marriage. Among the people who are currently best-off not immediately permanently marrying, there may well be some who would be best-off engaging in temporary marriage.

This does not entirely end the argument: one could try to argue that, for example, being single is best for everyone who would not be best served by immediately engaging in permanent marriage. Or that temporary marriage would have the overwhelming effect of leading people who would be better off permanently marrying settling for temporary marriage instead. These speculations about what is best for people do not seem to me strong enough to justify withholding marriage recognition from those who want it, even if they might justify, for instance, advocacy campaigns encouraging permanent marriage.

Social Complications

A final concern about recognizing temporary marriages is that a lot of decisions will need to be made and implemented about what legal and institutional mechanisms go along with this social status. Decisions will have to be made about superannuation and pension laws, laws about child custody, immigration rules for temporary spouses, taxation rules, inheritance when the parties do not have valid wills, and so on. What sorts of property rights are vested by temporary marriage, or divorce from temporary marriage, would need to be decided. The question of whether a streamlined divorce system should be offered for the temporarily married would have to be answered, and so on. Just as it is not entirely uncontroversial what these rules should be for married people now, it is unlikely to be entirely uncontroversial how to treat temporarily married couples.

As well as institutional questions, there are questions about informal social norms as well. There is a social norm that married people are considered "taken," ought not be courted by others, and so on. (Not every subgroup or every individual adheres to this custom, and how it is adhered to varies very widely even by those who recognize it.) But what should the conventions be about someone who is nearing the end of the time limit of a temporary marriage? How do we treat friends whose temporary marriage ended: in the typical way when a relationship ends, or somehow differently? Are couples who were formerly married treated like divorced "exes," or in a different way?

Neither the formal nor informal decisions that would need to be made about the institutions and conventions of marriage seem to me serious obstacles to allowing temporary marriage. Many of the legal rules for temporary marriages can be modeled on the existing rules for *de facto* relationships, which already provides answers for what happens to these couples when they pay tax, immigrate, have children, and so on. Some changes might be appropriate, but a handful of competent lawyers could draw up reasonable changes in the laws in a matter of days. Informal conventions are harder to put in place, but again there seems little problem in principle in these growing up. It would be absurd to continue the ban on temporary marriage on the grounds that the temporarily married might need others to extend existing informal conventions to form expectations in dealing with them.

Is "Temporary Marriage" Marriage?

Most of the arguments for or against temporary marriage discussed above do not rely on temporary marriage being a kind of *marriage*, as long as it is at least enough like marriage in relevant respects. But it is an interesting question in its own right whether "temporary marriages" really are, or would be, genuine marriages. (At least, the question will be interesting to some philosophers.) In my view, many, perhaps all, would be. I doubt this can be made uncontroversial, since there is a wide range of deeply held views around about what is required for genuine marriage. However, in this section I will offer some considerations in favor of taking them to be genuine marriages that might at least sway those who do not already have a firm view.

Let me start with two relatively straightforward points. The first is that institutions like *mutah*, seventeenth-century Scottish "marriage for a term of years," and the like, are called marriages by competent people, including marriage experts, anthropologists, specialist historians, and the like. The interminable debates about *mutah* in the Islamic jurisprudential tradition are about whether it is allowed to Muslims, not whether it is marriage at all. Insofar as we should be guided either by the practice of competent speakers or of the usage of experts, this suggests that our expression "marriage" would cover temporary marriage as well as the more usual marriage-until-death. Note that you can get a fair idea of the kind of social relationship intended just from the expression "temporary marriage," or slightly longer descriptions like "marriage when it is decided ahead of time that it will only last for a fixed duration," and those descriptions do not strike most people as paradoxical. Of course it might *be* paradoxical even if it does not seem so to apparently competent users of the expression "marriage": but it seems to me the plausible starting assumption should be that it is a coherent possibility when it seems so to both laypeople and experts.[19]

The second point is that paradigm "temporary marriage" is very similar, in a vast range of cases, to many paradigm permanent marriages. It tends to go with couples cohabiting, forming a household, being publicly recognized to be committed to each other, often sexual exclusiveness, and an array of other similarities. Of course, not all temporary marriages have all these characteristics, or would have, and neither do all permanent marriages. But as social relationships go, there are wide and deep similarities. It is true, of course, that there are non-marriages that are similar to marriages (more or less wherever we draw the line between them). But "temporary marriage" is at least a prime candidate to be a kind of marriage, whereas sharing an ice cream or working in the same occupation or even mere cohabitation are not.

Thirdly, recall that there are bad marriages that are nevertheless genuinely marriages. Sometimes spouses are unhappy, sometimes they are neglected, sometimes they are unfulfilled. Marriages can persist in the face of adultery, social disapproval, lack of trust, withholding of property, long physical separation, and so on. *Even if* you think that temporary marriage lacks some valuable features that your idea of an ideal marriage would possess, do not forget that relationships that genuinely are marriages need not be ideal ones.

To say something more, it might be worth at least briefly discussing some accounts of what marriage amounts to. (These remarks will be brief, partly because this is not a "what is marriage?" essay, and partly because relying on a controversial general theory of marriage is unlikely to be very persuasive.) The first general conception of marriage I want to discuss is a "positivist" or "institutional" one, according to which marriage is basically whatever the law or other institutional rules say it is. A view need not entirely defer to the law or other institutions (such as established churches), of course: one might think that not even the law or a church can marry someone to a non-agent, or without the awareness or consent of the marriage participants. But even a mixed theory will be effectively positivist about a given case insofar as that case is resolved by deference to the law or other institutions.

According to this positivist criterion, we only need to look at the marriage law, and perhaps look at some law-like rules of institutions such as major churches, to determine whether temporary marriage is genuinely marriage. And the answer in most Western countries (barring a few exceptions extended for ambassadors and the like) is that they are not. According to this positivist conception, even if couples in the Western Isles of Scotland wish to engage in the "inveterate Celtic practice of marriages for a term of years" through ceremony to that effect, they would not be genuinely married, because of current Scottish law (or would perhaps be accidentally permanently married, depending on the ceremony and paperwork). It is a tougher question whether temporary marriages are genuine marriages in the USA, since there is a colorable argument based on the Fourteenth Amendment to the US Constitution that temporarily married couples, like same-sex married couples, have a right to have their marriage recognized, given recognition extended to permanent heterosexual marriages.[20]

While the positivist criterion rules out temporary marriage as genuine marriage, it does suggest that if temporary marriage received legal recognition it would at that point *become* genuine marriage. Once the law says a couple is married for a term of years, that will be decisive for a positivist. So a positivist conception of marriage should allow that temporary marriage *would be* marriage, once it secured recognition.

My own view is that while marriage laws and institutions are somewhat relevant, they do not by themselves settle the question of whether a marriage exists. A racist government that tomorrow declares all mixed-race marriages in its jurisdiction dissolved, for example, does not seem to me successfully to dissolve all such marriages (though it does remove state recognition of those marriages, and the legal status associated with marriage for those couples). There is no need to take a stand for or against positivism about marriage for current purposes, but I think it worthwhile to discuss a rival account of marriage. Let me label this rival the "functional" theory of marriage.

According to functional theories, a relationship is a marriage provided that relationship plays enough of the key roles of marriage.[21] Some of these roles might be public: marriage is typically a public commitment to another person, and influences not just the spouses' treatment of each other, but others' treatment of those spouses. Some of the important roles concern spouses' treatment of each other. Functionalists could recognize legal and institutional features of relationships as being among the relevant functional roles, too. Some might concern joint property, roles of children conceived by the spouses, and so on. In determining the functions of marriage, some attention should be paid to the goals of marriage: how it contributes to other social organizations, how it contributes to typical desires and intentions of marriage partners, and so on. Particular functional accounts may well vary in the importance they attribute to different aspects of marriage. Functionalism of this sort seems particularly appealing when we consider the anthropological exercise of discovering whether a community has practices that deserve the name "marriage."

For functionalists, the question of whether temporary marriage would be a kind of marriage becomes the question of whether it would play enough of the roles of marriage, and in particular whether it would serve the social ends marriage serves. Given its similarity to permanent marriage, it is hard to see how it could fail to play those roles pretty well and serve the same purposes. This is particularly true when we consider societies with "permanent" marriage but high rates of divorce: it is hard to see, for instance, how a twenty-year temporary marriage which successfully raises children, and involves sexual exclusiveness, cohabitation, shared property and projects, and the like, would perform important roles worse than a permanent marriage without children that results in divorce after two years filled with acrimony and physical abuse, let alone a two-week "Vegas marriage" ending in divorce, which the participants would not have agreed to sober. Set the functional criteria to be restrictive enough to rule out temporary marriage, and they will rule out many permanent marriages: on the other hand, set functional criteria keeping in mind the imperfection of many genuine marriages, and many temporary marriages will pass that hurdle.

Functionalism should not be uncontroversial, but it is a plausible enough approach to be worth serious consideration. And since temporary marriages apparently can play enough of the functional roles that permanent marriage does, that suggests temporary marriage is, or at least could be, genuine marriage.

Ralph Wedgwood offers a significantly different picture of the "essence of marriage," or rather the "essence of Western marriage."[22] It is a little difficult to know what he means by "essence" here, since he allows there are genuine marriages (and even genuine Western marriages) that do not have all of these features. Whatever he has in mind, he offers four criteria which are arguably at least relevant to determining whether a relationship is fit to be considered a genuine marriage. The first is a legal criterion, somewhat similar to the sort of positivist criterion discussed above: "marriage law is essential to our modern Western conception of marriage."[23] The rest of the "basic core," somehow essential to Western marriage, are three "generally shared expectations": "that a married couple's relationship typically involves the following three elements: (1) sexual intimacy; (2) domestic and economic cooperation; and (3) a voluntary mutual commitment to sustaining this relationship."[24] Wedgwood has much to say about the legal criterion and his three criteria of general shared expectations. I doubt any of his three "generally shared expectations" really are essential to the institution of marriage: scenarios where only a minority of marriages had all three can easily be envisaged, and scenarios where many people *did not know* whether or not a majority of marriages conformed to all three are even easier to imagine. And I suspect that many married couples, presented with the opinion that it is essential to their marriage what people they have never met expect about that couple's sexual practices, would find the suggestion either risible or offensive.

Even if Wedgwood's three expectations are not essential to marriage, they might still be useful, if fallible, indicators of the sort of relationship that counts as marriage (or even "Western marriage"). It is easy to see that temporary marriages could easily have all three features, and be expected to have such features once awareness of temporary marriages were sufficiently widespread. Of course, a voluntary and mutual commitment to sustaining the relationship might come with a time limit, but that hardly makes it not voluntary, or means that such relationships do not call for maintenance. As discussed above, if legal recognition is required for marriage, temporary marriages in many Western countries do not yet exist. Whether or not they currently do, legal recognition would remove this barrier, so with the recognition I am arguing for, temporary marriages would meet Wedgwood's four criteria for genuine marriages.

Conclusion

Even though I have argued in this essay that the state should recognize temporary marriages, and that they are indeed genuine marriages, I doubt this essay will trigger legal changes anytime soon. Still, if I am right about what form of marriage equality we should support, and that this is indeed a case where some can be given the freedom to have the marriage they want without terrible side effects, it might serve as one of the early steps in a long march to more-principled marriage laws. Working out what the state should do in principle seems to me a worthwhile project even when this does not hold out the immediate practical prospect of change.

Consideration of temporary marriage raises a number of further issues of philosophical interest, beyond the interest of the case itself. One is the more general question, if we are to expand recognized marriage beyond permanent marriage, of what sorts of conditional marriages should be recognized: what sorts of conditions are appropriate, and what are not? Another interesting philosophical question is the question of what, if anything, is particularly valuable about marriage, and to what extent nontraditional marriages might have less of this value, or for that matter which nontraditional options may better realize these values. A third question of interest is what social relationships are appropriately temporary, in the sense that they might be appropriately entered into with a pre-established expiry date. Business arrangements are appropriately temporary, parent/ child or sibling relations are ordinarily thought not to be: but where do the boundaries in the middle lie? (Is friendship ever appropriately temporary in this fashion?)

Rational reflection on our social institutions is likely to be a never-ending project, but the search for generally defensible principles about how to organize society has often served us well, and plays a valuable role in our social thinking as well as reacting to particular new social pressures with particular ad hoc adjustments. There is not currently an outcry in the West demanding respectful treatment for temporary marriage, but the principles that should support our recognition of it are no less correct for that.[25]

Notes

1. Many states are under international obligations to register marriages under the United Nations Convention on Consent to Marriage, Minimum Age for Marriage, and Registration of Marriages.

2. See the *New York Code* Article 3 sections 15 and 15a.

3. The situation in many other Western countries is often about as lenient when it comes to recognizing marriages to children, particularly ones contracted in jurisdictions favorable to child marriage.

4. See de Marneffe, Chapter 6 in this volume, and Shrage, Chapter 7 in this volume, for more comprehensive discussions of polygamy.

5. Some plausible examples: marriage by the already married undertaken behind the back of their current spouse, some marriages of children, or some marriages between close relatives, for instance father-daughter marriages.

6. One strong argument for state recognition of marriages, it seems to me, is the need to take state action *against* some forms of marriage. If we are to require consent for marriage, or prevent marriage of young children, or marriages between close relatives, state involvement in marriages is needed: and one natural way to involve the state is to require, by legislation, that certain standards must be met for a marriage to be valid.

7. It is worth discussing the connection between the principle of marriage equality outlined in the text and a "minimal marriage" proposal recently defended by Elizabeth Brake in "Minimal Marriage: What Political Liberalism Implies for Marriage Law," *Ethics* 120:2 (2010): 302–307. Brake argues that political liberalism allows for very few restrictions on which marriages are recognized by a liberal state, and that such a state should have a marriage law that allows for extensive disaggregation of the different obligations and benefits traditionally associated with marriage. "The central idea is that individuals can have legal marital relationships with more than one person, reciprocally or asymmetrically, themselves determining the sex and number of parties, the type of relationship involved, and which rights and responsibilities to exchange with each" ("Minimal," 303).

While Brake does require "publicly justifiable grounds" for marriage laws, she adopts a particular philosophical conception of what sorts of grounds they can be, grounded in the sort of liberalisms defended by writers such as John Rawls and Joseph Raz (see Elizabeth Brake, "Minimal," 313–315). I do not wish to rely on such specific premises, but I hope that the principle of marriage equality I articulate will be of wider appeal. Nevertheless, Brake's principle would support state recognition of temporary marriage, as far as I can tell, and a Brake-style liberal about marriage should be able to agree with something like the principle I enunciate, with perhaps a specific understanding of what sorts of "significant social reasons" ought to be considered when deciding whether to recognize particular marriage relationships.

8. Marriages for a term of years were declared illegal in Scotland in 1609. The Statutes and Band of Icolmkill, more often called the Statues of Iona, declared "the suppression in particular of the inveterate Celtic practice of marriages for a term of years" (Statute 1). This very strongly suggests that marriages for a term of years were occurring before (and perhaps after) the legislation was passed. See the "Register of Privy Council of Scotland," Vol. IX, 1610–1613 (1889).

9. See, e.g., K. V. Hovey, *Handfasting* (Avon, MA: F+W Publications, 2008).

10. It is not obvious such a prosecution would succeed, but the risk that it would, together with the threat of arrest and trial even if followed by an acquittal, seem to me disadvantages already.

11. A. Leff, " 'Til 2013 Do Us Part? Mexico Mulls 2-Year Marriage," *Reuters*, September 29, 2011, http://www.reuters.com/article/2011/09/29/us-mexico-marriage-idUSTRE78S6TX20110929.

12. M. Sokol, "Jeremy Bentham on Love and Marriage: A Utilitarian Proposal for Short-Term Marriage," *The Journal of Legal History* 30:1 (2009): 13.

13. Laurie Shrage, "Reforming Marriage: A Comparative Approach," *Journal of Applied Philosophy* 30:2 (2013) discusses in Section 2 a number of examples of benefits participants in temporary marriages have said they have derived from those marriages. The empirical case that some people derive some benefits they value from temporary marriages is firmly established by the sort of evidence Shrage provides, in my view: though the relative value of any particular benefit versus overall benefits that might be gained from alternative arrangements might be harder to establish.

14. The issue of exactly what point Santorum intended to make with his remarks on the relevant occasion is controversial.

15. A. Goodman and F. Greaves, *Cohabitation, Marriage and Child Outcomes* (London: Institute for Fiscal Studies, 2010), 5.

16. Once apparently confounding factors are controlled for, there can be some real surprises. In the USA, higher percentages of children born outside marriage drop out of high school than those who grow up with married parents. However, K. Finlay and D. Neumark suggest that once we control for some other influences, some data from the USA suggests that, in the case of Hispanic mothers, "never-married motherhood *reduces* the likelihood that children drop out of high school [compared to mothers who marry], and the estimates are often statistically significant" ("Is Marriage Always Good for Children? Evidence from Families Affected by Incarceration," *The Journal of Human Resources* 45:4 (2010): 1079). Any particular study will be controversial, of course, and Finlay and Neumark's focus on groups sensitive to male incarceration might just show

that Hispanic mothers who have a choice between remaining unmarried and marrying a man likely to be incarcerated may do better remaining unmarried. Still, the fact that sometimes when we control for other factors relevant for the success of children we can get a statistically significant *negative* correlation between marriage and child outcomes illustrates how cautious we should be in inferring much about the role of permanent marriage per se in children's welfare.

17. M. Parke, "Policy Brief No. 3: Are Married Parents Really Better for Children? What Research Says About the Effects of Family Structure on Child Well-Being (Annotated Version)," *Center for the Law and Social Policy*, May 2003, <www.clasp.org>.

18. *"De facto"* relationships have different names in different jurisdictions (this is the standard label for them in Australia). Confusingly, in England and Wales they are often informally known as "common law marriages," despite not being recognized as marriages by English and Welsh common law. The status known as "common law marriage" in Canada and most of the USA is similar, though it arguably differs in being a form of marriage (as its name suggests), and in some US states "common law marriage" is treated as a permanent state, only terminated by death or divorce. "Domestic Partnership" is perhaps the closest equivalent to the status I am talking about in the USA.

19. By the same token, the fact that same-sex marriages in traditional societies were referred to as "marriages" by explorers, anthropologists, and others seems to me a good argument that the English word "marriage" does not by definition rule out same-sex marriages, even though the view that marriage is by definition between opposite-sex couples is sometimes encountered.

20. See the reasoning in *Perry v. Brown* for the case of same-sex marriage.

21. An example of such an account in the literature can be found in A. A. Wellington, "Why Liberals Should Support Same-Sex Marriage," *Journal of Social Philosophy* 25:3 (1995): 5–32.

22. R. Wedgwood, "The Fundamental Argument for Same-Sex Marriage," *The Journal of Political Philosophy* 7:3 (1999): 225–242.

23. Wedgwood, "Fundamental," 229.

24. Wedgwood, "Fundamental," 5.

25. Thanks to the audience at the ANU MSPT seminar, Elizabeth Brake, Rachael Briggs, Anca Gheaus, Dana Goswick, Holly Lawford-Smith, Laurie Shrage, and Nic Southwood for feedback.

9 | The (Dis)value of Commitment to One's Spouse

ANCA GHEAUS

1. Introduction

Marriage is about commitment: future spouses typically say—among other things—to each other, and to the world, that they are willing to remain in a close relationship "for better or for worse, for richer, for poorer, in sickness and in health." That is, they declare that the survival of their relationship will not depend on whether the relationship will turn out to be convenient and that their marital intentions do not depend on their future life circumstances. Whether marriage vows are to be understood as a promise, as an attempt to promise, or as a mere statement of intention, they express the future spouses' commitment to each other. Common sense usage links commitment with a promise to do something or an intention to be loyal to someone or something. Entering marriage with somebody usually involves all senses of commitment.

Many believe that marriage is the paradigmatic case of an attitudinal commitment to another person or to a relationship. Throughout this essay I discuss (marital) commitment as being "to a relationship or to a person," rather than settling for any of these. Philosophical literature on close relationship and love in general sometimes focuses on the value that a relationship has for an agent, and sometimes on the value that another person can have for an agent. There is clearly a difference between being committed to a relationship—and therefore being willing to do what it takes to protect that relationship and help it flourish—and being committed to a person—and therefore being willing to do what it takes to protect that person and help her or him flourish. In happy circumstances the two sets of actions will coincide. I believe that the second attitude, rather than the first, reflects love; this may be contentious however, and therefore I do not try to adjudicate here whether love-based marital commitment is to relationships or to persons.

Of course, various people in non-marital relationships can be and are committed to each other. But marital relationships are different from other intimate relationships because they are assumed to be permanent and their purpose is comprehensive and not limited to a certain number of pre-established activities—some of the marital commitment is open-ended. Together, these features of marriage make marital commitment a very high-level commitment and, therefore, a central case of commitment to persons or relationships. First, because marriage is not meant to be limited to a definite amount of time, the promise or intention to stay married is unusually demanding; friends, too, may hope that their friendship will endure, but the level of commitment in friendship is usually lower than in marriage. Second, marital commitment is very comprehensive: spouses typically share their lives with each other, rather than embark together on specific, and clearly delimited, projects. People engage in common long-term, even lifelong projects other than marriage (think for instance, of coworkers in domains from which one never really retires, such as subsistence agriculture or various crafts) but the scope of marriage is unusually broad. As long as it preserves permanency and comprehensiveness marriage remains a paradigmatic case of commitment even if one extends the definition of marriage beyond the usual requirements of heterosexuality and monogamy.

Intimates' commitment to each other is usually assumed to be highly valuable and marital commitment enjoys special praise in most cultures; indeed, commitment is often considered to be *the* feature that makes marriage admirable.[1] Moreover, popular culture sometimes represents the value of marital commitment as a moral value, casting doubts on the character of spouses who break their marriages for trivial reasons—therefore indicating a lack of commitment—and even providing some *pro tanto* justification to the continuation of marriages that are otherwise morally objectionable such as, for instance, abusive or neglectful relationships. One reason why marital commitment is praised is that it is thought to indicate the depth of the love for one's spouse.

In this essay I aim to question these beliefs. I advance and give some support for two claims, one weaker and one stronger. Both claims unfold against a background analysis of the general good of commitment, discussed in the second section. Much of this argument draws on Cheshire Calhoun's analysis of commitment, which I discuss in the second section. I hope to contribute to the discussion by taking Calhoun's analysis further to suggest that, since commitment has no intrinsic value, and since it is by definition a form of cost, we must welcome situations when the goods to which commitment is usually instrumental can be realized in its absence.

The third section applies the previous section's conclusion to the case of marital commitment. It explores the weaker claim: that we ought to praise marriage and marriage-like relationships only for the good they contain, and not for the fact that spouses are committed to each other. Commitment is only instrumentally valuable; it does not as such add any value to the relationship. Commitment has costs: it partially forecloses the future, and so it makes one less attentive and less open to life's possibilities; therefore, it would be desirable for people to achieve the same goods without commitment. If the marital goods achieved thanks to commitment—and which would be unachievable without it—are less important than the goods one foregoes by being committed, then the price of commitment is not worth paying. (As individuals who intentionally avoid commitments to relationships or individuals must believe.)

The second, and more ambitious, suggestion—which I explore in the fourth section—is that commitment in general, and marital commitments in particular, are problematic instruments for securing the good of romantic and sexual love. It makes sense to prefer that another person's (perhaps, especially romantic or sexual) love for you is sustained by their spontaneous inclination, rather than by their commitment.[2] Moreover, the pragmatic reasons for commitment are weak when it comes to activities that, ideally, are process-oriented rather than goal-oriented—such as love for another person. Marriage and marriage-like relationships in particular depend on commitment in order to help individuals cope with the often tedious or irritating routines of shared everyday life. As much research suggests, this kind of routine is inimical to romantic and erotic love. Marital commitment may save the relationship and many of the goods it sustains, but it is unlikely to save romantic and erotic love.

The last section discusses some of the implications of my position for the goods of marriage and for the desirability of marriage reforms that aim to break the connection between marriage and permanence (such as temporary marriage) or between marriage and the comprehensive sharing of one's life (such as minimal marriage).

2. The Value and Costs of Attitudinal Commitments

Following Calhoun,[3] I understand commitment in general to be a species of intention. Agents who commit themselves intend to follow through on the object of commitment even under future circumstances that are such that, had the agents not been committed, it would be rational for them to revise their intention. Commitment, as discussed here, is active rather than passive, although in everyday language we sometimes refer to commitments that are not actively assumed (and even to unconscious commitments). One type of commitment is to the performance of particular acts, as in promises, contracts, and resolutions. Another type is attitudinal commitments, that is a form of dedication to things that are very important to the agents' sense of who they are and to their idea of what a good life is. Examples of the latter sense include normative commitments (that is, commitments to values), but also substantive commitments: to hobbies, causes, persons and relationships, etc. Marriage most likely encompasses both kinds of commitments. Marriage itself is a contract: spouses-to-be promise each other future performances and they sometimes devise and enter specific marital contracts; and the everyday realities of married life contain numberless instances of promises and resolutions. But certainly what distinguishes marriage from other contractual relationships is its attitudinal commitment component. Spouses typically see each other and their relationship as central to their idea of a good life, and, at least in love-based marriages, to their identity. It is the underlying attitudinal commitment that is supposed to support, and give meaning to, the commitment to the particular performances specified by the marriage contract (and often to the specific everyday promises spouses make to each other).

The value of making promises and entering into contracts is relatively straightforward: both are necessary for creating trust and legitimate expectations, on which people's well-being depends. They, unlike attitudinal commitments, are also not likely to be attributed intrinsic value or be moralized. Therefore promises and contracts as such are not the subject of this essay, but in the end I will indicate how claims about the marital attitudinal commitments bear on what sorts of marital contracts ought to be available. Here I address the question of the value of substantive attitudinal commitments in love-based marriages. Why is it important that people commit to those individuals and relationships that are central to their self-identity and to their beliefs about a good life?

Before starting to address this question, I indicate one more feature of commitment: it comes in degrees, depending on how radical the change of circumstances must be in order to challenge the agent's intention. At one end there is no commitment, but rather mere intentions, or very provisional plans: any new desire is a potential trigger for a cost-benefit re-evaluation of what one should do.[4] Non-committed rational agents should be ready to revise their mere intentions or very provisional plans as soon as better alternatives come along. An intention to have dinner at a particular location, for instance, may change as soon as a better possibility comes along. At the other extreme there is blind commitment, when a cost-benefit analysis of the intention that forms that commitment is off the table under any circumstances. Commitments can be so deep that agents are willing to hold on to them not only in spite of prudential reasons (when overall more convenient alternatives present themselves) but even in spite of value changes. Someone may be so deeply committed to a friend, for instance, that she will continue to remain loyal to the relationship or the person even if, over time, their moral values evolve and become incompatible.

As Calhoun herself notes, commitment enjoys popular praise; committed lives are believed to be better lives for the individual who lives them, and an ability to make commitments is usually considered the marker of maturity. Popular wisdom encourages individuals to commit themselves. But what is the value of commitment to the committed individual?

An obvious value of commitment is pragmatic, or instrumental. Given the limited resources of which individuals dispose, such as time and energy, commitment seems necessary for the achievement of non-immediate goals. In the pursuit of such goals better alternatives are likely to present themselves and the non-committed, or feebly committed, agent is likely to become distracted from the initial goal. But this seems to be an overly simplified picture. First, as Calhoun notes, better options do not always present themselves. Second, and more important, even when better options do appear, agents who have already invested significant time and effort in the pursuit of a goal tend to be reluctant to waste these resources and hop onto a new, more appealing, project. Even if I am not committed to learn German, but I merely intend to, discovering that I like Russian better will not necessarily convince me to change course. Since I am well advanced with German (a language which turns out would not be the language of my first choice, should I make that choice *now*), I will likely stick to it: doing otherwise may mean that I have wasted the resources that I put so far into learning German. (Just as commitment, mere intention may work by ignoring the so called 'sunken costs fallacy'—that is, by treating past investments as a reason to continue pursuing a goal even when changing course is more likely to yield better outcomes for the agent.) Switching back to an understanding of commitment as the reluctance to engage in a cost-benefit analysis, we do not always need commitment in order to pursue long-term goals: often no new data comes up to challenge the initial cost-benefit assessment. In other cases past investment makes it irrational to change course mid-way. And when new options really are sufficiently attractive to outweigh one's reluctance to waste past investment, it is not clear why it is rational *not* to change course midway and why commitment would be at all desirable.[5]

Perhaps, however, more should be made than Calhoun does of the following fact: commitment is often needed to achieve non-immediate goals not because without it we would change course and pursue *other* goals, but because in the pursuit of non-immediate goals we are likely to encounter significant adversity. Without commitment we might rarely if ever achieve non-immediate goals because of failures such as weakness of the will or mistakenly discounting the future, rather than due to an abundance of attractive opportunities. The frustrations of learning German may, in the absence of commitment, cause me to postpone my next assignment indefinitely even while I recognize the irrationality of my behavior. And while procrastinating I may end up doing next to nothing rather than pursue an alternative, worthwhile goal such as learning Russian. Calhoun's analysis of the pragmatic value of commitment touches on this point when she notes the popular belief that life without commitment may well turn into a life lived from moment to moment. But she does not pursue this thread to consider what, if anything, is wrong with such a life. For the remainder of this essay I shall leave to one side the question of whether living from moment to moment can be a valuable way of leading one's life, if only one could afford to. (On a hedonistic view of well-being it probably is.) Instead, I concede that non-immediate goals are important to a good life and that most often commitment is necessary for attaining them. As I show in the next section, this consideration applies to the case of marital commitment and is a plausible argument in favor of the instrumental value of commitment in marriage.

The second way in which commitment is usually said to be valuable is non-instrumental: many believe that commitment is constitutive of a good life because without commitment it is difficult to see in which way one's self and one's life can be said to be one's own creations. Making attitudinal commitments—to values, causes, individuals, and relationships—is *the* way in which we take an active stance in determining who we are and what projects give meaning to our lives.[6] However, as Calhoun argues, it is enough to have normative, rather than substantive, commitments, in order to ensure unified agency and life plans. Someone who lacks substantive commitments—that is commitments to particular people, relationships, or projects—can nevertheless be the author of their life in the sense usually employed by those who think that having a life plan is essential for a good human life. And some normative commitments—like deliberately seeking the satisfaction of one's strongest desires—are in fact incompatible with substantive commitments.[7]

But how likely is it, in the first place, that the best lives are guided by a life plan? Some philosophers, such as Charles Larmore, draw on the European Romantic tradition to argue that the aspiration to exert control over the shape of one's life, reflected by a life plan, is itself misguided. According to Larmore, the well-being "that life affords is less often the good we have reason to pursue than the good that befalls us unexpectedly"[8] because "we are never in a position to grasp in advance the full character of our good, even in its broad outline."[9] In any case—whether or not having a life plan contributes to or diminishes one's chances to a maximally good life—substantive attitudinal commitments, of which marital commitments are an example, do not seem necessary. Normative attitudinal commitments are enough.

A last reason to believe that substantive attitudinal commitments are constitutive to a good life is that in the absence of such commitments one's life is less likely to have meaning. It may be true that most of the things that give meaning to people's lives are those to which they are usually committed. But commitment does not seem to be necessary for meaning; being engaged with people and activities about which one cares is enough. Not all caring amounts to commitment, since not all caring is accompanied by an active intention to pursue what one cares about while making sure that the caring will continue in the future. One may instead care about projects, people, relationships, and causes—and derive meaning from them—without dedicating oneself to them. Following Calhoun again, a person's life can be meaningful because she spends enough time in the company of people she loves, pursuing causes she thinks are worthy and engaged in activities she finds valuable, even while thinking she might as well spend her time with other people she loves and doing other worthy things.

While substantive commitments may not be constitutive of a good life—because self-identity, life plans, and meaning are all possible without them—they may however be indirectly instrumental to leading a meaningful life. Most people may be better able to care for complex, rather than simple, activities and it is unlikely—for the reasons given above—to successfully pursue complex activities without some level of commitment. If so, then commitment is indirectly instrumental to meaningful lives, because without it individuals are less capable of successfully pursuing complex activities. If I am better able to care about activities which require that I exercise high levels of skill, commitment to acquiring skill will often be necessary if I am to have access to activities about which I care.

This consideration, however, does not apply with the same force to another source of meaning, human relationships. We typically do not need to master complex skills in order to pursue the relationships that we care about. Having good relationships may require dispositions such as attentiveness, respectfulness, communication skills, patience, or tolerance which can, to some extent, be learned; but one does not have to learn them within the particular relationship the pursuit of which one values. Perhaps a long history of practicing these dispositions in the past is helpful—or even necessary—for having a good relationship now. If so then at most one may need to be committed to cultivating good relationships in general in order to be in a good position to have a good relationship with a particular person.[10] This however doesn't show that good relationships require substantive—as opposed to normative—commitments. Therefore, commitment to a person or relationship does not seem in any way necessary in order to for the relationship to be meaningful. As I discuss in the next sections, commitment is often necessary to sustain marital relationships over time but it seems particularly necessary when other kinds of motivation—like love—are insufficient to sustain the marriage.

Calhoun explains the attractiveness of the view that commitment is valuable by appeal to typical human psychology: many or most people seek familiarity and making commitments affords one more familiarity in how one relates to one's future. Because being committed to something includes the intention to continue to be motivated by that thing's value, commitment can function as a sort of roadmap. But in virtue of what makes it appealing, commitment is also a highly costly attitude for the committed individual. In order to sustain commitments, agents must foreclose certain future possibilities. Whoever wants to follow a map must refrain from roaming too far out of the mapped area: commitment has an inbuilt opportunity cost. In Calhoun's own words, it

> involves refraining from putting oneself in the way of temptation, refraining
> from cultivating activities, attitudes, and ways of life that are incompatible

with sustaining one's commitment, repressing commitment-threatening emotions and desires, and resisting the live option of reconsidering the reasons for having the commitment. That is, commitment entails readiness to engage in a set of refusals.[11]

On this account of commitment, part of its value is as an instrument to realizing long-term goals, and part of its value is its contribution to individuals' well-being by responding to their need for familiarity. The latter source of value is also dependent on contingent (and by no means universal) psychological factors. But given the high opportunity cost involved in commitment, it seems that it would be desirable if people were less inclined to seek familiarity and therefore less reliant on commitment for their well-being. Calhoun notes that people are willing to pay the cost of foreclosing future opportunities in order to secure familiarity; but the foreclosing of opportunities is likely to also entail foreclosing one's own development—in terms of experience, intellectual gains and, more generally, openness to the world. Hence, if personal development is itself desirable independent of one's psychological inclinations, then it is regrettable that some such inclinations—like the desire for familiarity—can be satisfied only at the cost of limiting it. Less need for commitment would be desirable at least in cases when it is not in fact necessary for securing other goods—such as the acquisition of complex skills, the advancement of worthy causes, and the cultivation of long-lasting good relationships—because individuals are sufficiently motivated by, say, curiosity or love.

The next section applies this analysis to the case of marital commitment.

3. How Does Commitment Contribute to the Value of Marital Relationships?

An exceptionally popular TV miniseries from the 80s, *The Thorn Birds*, tells the story of the long-lasting love between a woman called Maggie and a man called Ralph. They first meet when Maggie is still a teenager. In spite of the mutual affection, attraction, and respect they feel for each other, they never become an established couple because Ralph is a Catholic priest. Yet, they remain in touch and throughout their long and winding lives occasionally reunite as lovers. Maggie and Ralph never marry each other because he chooses priesthood over family life; she not only regrets, but is also critical of his choice, yet does not sever her relationship with him. The mutual love that unites them seems to be, until the end, stronger than her hurt for being rejected and his commitment to celibacy.

Maggie and Ralph are united in a lifelong romantic relationship that survives without them being committed to each other, and in spite of various commitments that each of them has (Maggie marries another man). Stories of lifelong lovers who are kept together by love alone rather than by commitment abound (and many of them are about real, rather than fictional, characters). I have chosen the fictional story of Maggie and Ralph because the narrative setup makes it clear that, in this case, commitment is least likely to have played any role in whatever goods their relationship realizes, including its longevity. They dedicate themselves neither to each other nor to their relationship, and they incur no contractual long-term obligations to each other. Therefore their relationship obviously lacks any kind of commitment. Some will think this kind of relationship is less desirable for this reason (and all other things equal). But others will find particular value precisely in the fact that some people succeed in having a long-term intimate relationship that endures entirely due to love. Here I will explore this latter possibility.

Maggie and Ralph's love relationship is different from a usual love-based marriage in its lack of comprehensiveness: Maggie and Ralph do not share a household, do not raise children together, do not provide companionship, economic security, or social embedding for each other, and do not support each other in everyday small and large endeavors. Unlike most good marriages, in which mutual love is one of the several goods realized in the relationship, the relationship between Maggie and Ralph only realizes the good of mutual love. This may be an explanation of its endurance in spite of their lack of commitment to each other, or to their relationship.

By contrast, comprehensive relationships like marriage are less likely to endure in the absence of commitment. Commitment to one's spouse is one way of ensuring a long-lasting, mutually supportive relationship. One reason why commitment is generally necessary for the endurance of many marriages is of the kind discussed by Calhoun in her general analysis of commitment: other, more attractive partners or valuable activities that are incompatible with partnered life may present themselves to spouses. In such cases commitment to one's spouse or one's marriage can prevent spouses from abandoning the marital relationship. But another, possibly more usual, reason why marriages often depend on commitment lies in the various adversities of comprehensively sharing one's life with another. Even with no better alternatives in sight, it is difficult to interact with a person, in your own home, (almost) every day and for a very extended period of time.

As I suggested in the previous section, the commitment expressed in the marriage vows indicates spouses' reluctance to engage in a cost-benefit analysis of their relationship, including a willingness to ignore the opportunity costs of continuing the relationship. To commit to a spouse means that one is unwilling to ponder whether being in the marital relationship is, on the whole, to one's advantage. At least, one is unwilling to make the continuation of the relationship dependent on such analysis. Importantly, committed spouses do not compare their partners to other people with respect to how beneficial for them the relationship with their spouse is. Others may be more physically attractive, have more pleasant personalities, make better parents, be wealthier, healthier, or a better personality fit than one's own spouse; being committed means to disregard these facts as practical reasons for changing spouses.

Some instances of commitment to one's spouse can be irrational—for instance, if one is married to a partner who is a particularly bad fit or with whom it is in fact unlikely that one will be able to realize those goods that one wishes to realize in one's marriage.[12] But marital commitment can be rational, and therefore instrumentally valuable if, in the longer run, it is likely to advance marital goods sought by the spouses. Many such goods—raising children well together with a partner, providing economic and emotional security and familiar companionship—are long-term goals and therefore unlikely to be realizable if one is (too) ready to change partners.

If commitment to one's spouse has mere instrumental value, then it seems regrettable that we usually need commitment in order to sustain marital relationships. Like other attitudinal commitments, commitment to one's spouse involves a type of "locking up the future." By committing oneself, one rules out a number of future possibilities and this comes with epistemic, existential, and, in some cases, moral costs for the individual. The high costs of marital commitments are recognized even by its boldest defenders. This is how Brenda Almond, an advocate of old-fashioned marriages based on a very high degree of commitment (a type of marriage that rules out the availability of no-fault divorce) describes the opportunity costs of commitment: ". . . marriage may mean the sacrifice of other friendships or other potentially enriching personal relationships." She seems to agree with Calhoun on why it is worth it to pay the price of commitment: "For many people, marriage remains an institution that provides some solidity for the project of building a coherent life plan."[13]

When the level of commitment to one's spouse is extremely high, it can even entail that spouses are willing to continue their relationship in spite of very serious moral disagreement or even wrongdoing. If moral value trumps prudential value, commitment has overall disvalue in such cases.[14]

Commitment has instrumental value because it can secure the long-term continuation of the marital relationship and hence the realization of its long-term goods. But there is another kind of motivation that can ensure the same goal in the absence of commitment: lasting love. (The two kinds of motivation are, of course, not mutually exclusive.) As long as love, understood minimally as the inclination to seek another's companionship and advance her well-being, exists, commitment is not necessary. One need not be committed to one's beloved in order to suspend any cost-benefit analysis of the relationship.[15] The reason for this is that for someone who loves the beloved is not fungible. In spite of disagreement about the nature and reasons—if any—for love, the non-fungibility of the beloved is widely accepted.[16] Therefore the appearance of more desirable partners will not be a reason to leave the marriage if one loves one's spouse. And the various forms of adversity that one is likely to encounter in the course of married life can be weathered by love; people are often inclined to sacrifice their comfort and push their limits for the sake of their beloved or of their relationship with their beloved. It is likely that adversity will test, or even erode love; indeed, in the next section I assume that sexual and romantic love, in particular, tend to be eroded by daily routine and hardship. Another kind of love, like that between friends, is likely to be more resilient. Even so, love alone cannot always secure the endurance of marriage over time—but neither can commitment, given that it, too, can be eroded.

As long as people love each other, commitment seems superfluous. Love and commitment are, of course, often to be found in one and the same marriage; a plausible explanation is that spouses seek to protect their love for each other with the help of commitment. Depending on what is the right theory of the nature and reasons of love, this may be a wise choice. In the next section, however, I will explore a *pro tanto* reason to doubt the attractiveness of committing in order to protect love—or at least its romantic and sexual variety.

Marital commitment is necessary for the realization of marital goods precisely when romantic love is absent or insufficient. In such cases commitment is instrumentally valuable because it advances other sorts of value such as the security brought by a long-lasting life companion and the ability to plan one's life long-term with a partner. Yet, as already noted, commitment to one's spouse cannot be *in itself* morally praiseworthy. Commitment can and often is morally praiseworthy because it promotes moral goods—for instance, the protection of the more vulnerable individual in a relationship. But commitment cannot be valuable above and beyond the value of that to which one is committed. This, in turn, means that in cases when the continuation of a relationship comes at a moral cost to the individual, appeals to commitment cannot redeem the relationship on moral grounds. Examples include abusive and neglectful relationships or cases when continuing one's association with one spouse requires complicity with morally reprehensible acts.

Therefore, the work done by commitment would be better done by love because, unlike commitment, romantic love has non-instrumental (as well as instrumental) value and because, as discussed above, commitment—even when rational and morally innocent—has costs. Love, too, has costs in terms of foreclosing future options and hence in terms of personal development—or else it would not be capable of sustaining relationships in the face of more attractive options. But, unlike in the case of commitment, the value of love is not entirely dependent on the value of its object. Even when one loves a morally unworthy individual (and even when one ought, all things considered, to sever the relationship) loving has *some* value.[17] A world where the goods of marriage were achieved without commitment, out of love alone, would therefore be the better world; marital commitment seems to be a second-best solution to securing the goods of marriage.

Perhaps a love relationship like Maggie's and Ralph's could not be sustained as an everyday, more comprehensive relationship. To last, most marital relationships usually need commitment to smooth out the unavoidable disappointments and irritations of daily routine. (Although in the next section I suggest that marriage relationships that would fail to endure over time without commitment are likely to change in nature.) Conceding that most people need commitment to have lasting intimate relationships, would it not be wonderful if they did not?

4. Love for Another Person and Commitment

In the previous section I suggested that love is a (preferable) alternative to commitment in cases when mere intentions cannot do enough to motivate spouses to stay in the marital relationship through tough times. Whatever one's account of love and its reasons, the object of one's love is not fungible. This means that love can safeguard marriage against the first type of threat from which commitment, too, can protect it: the availability of better partners. Love is also likely to shelter marriages against the second kind of threat, that of disheartening routine and other difficulties of ongoing company: love can motivate people to sacrifice their own convenience for the sake of the interests of the beloved or of the relationship with the beloved. But love itself may be lost, and one reason why people commit to each other and to their relationship is precisely in an attempt to ensure the endurance of their love. In this section I suggest why it may be inappropriate to see commitment as a wise means to securing the kind of romantic and sexual love that tends to drive contemporary marriage. In doing so I am aware that I rely on a controversial understanding of romantic and sexual love—but which, I believe, is nevertheless very plausible.[18]

Whether or not it is possible to *ensure* that one will continue to feel romantic or sexual love for a particular individual, it is intelligible to *prefer* to be loved out of spontaneous inclination, rather than because someone made a promise or a commitment, which is akin to a promise, to love you—and as a consequence they took the necessary steps to ensure that their love lasts. This thought is in fact ambivalent between a claim of feasibility and one of desirability. Some believe that it is possible to control one's behavior such that you keep alive—or perhaps rekindle—romantic or sexual love; for instance, by revisiting places where you have been happy with your beloved, or otherwise reminding yourself of the history of your love relationships.[19] Others think it is impossible to control love for a particular individual to a sufficient extent to make one responsible for keeping it alive: individuals can achieve only so much success in their attempts to self-induce love for a particular individual.[20] And some philosophers believe that attempting to secure love with the help of commitment in particular is a self-defeating strategy because it allows spouses to take each other for granted which, in turn, undermines love.[21] But of course, a likely reason to think one cannot fully control one's love stems from the suspicion that part of what makes love so desirable cannot, by definition, be controlled.[22] Here I draw on this latter thought.

Amartya Sen's work on commitment (in a context unrelated to the discussion of intimate relationships) is helpful in clarifying the difference between being motivated by love and being motivated by commitment. He distinguishes between three kinds of motivation: self-interest, that is, aiming to promote one's welfare; sympathy, that is, aiming to promote a wider sense of welfare, in which the welfare of the agent is not independent from the welfare of the agent's near and dear; and commitment, that is, a type of motivation unrelated to the agent's welfare (whether understood narrowly or broadly).[23] Love is of the second kind: it seems uncontroversial that loving a person means, among other things, that one cares about the welfare of the beloved such that the lover's well-being is dependent on the welfare of the beloved. Ideally, one prefers that one's intimate relationships be driven by love rather than by commitment. The point holds for particular interactions with those near and dear. As Michael Stocker's famous example illustrates, we don't want our friends to benefit us because they have a duty to do so (even if they do) but because they are genuinely partial towards us.[24] But it may also hold in the case of love relationships as a whole: it seems more satisfying to be loved as a result of your lover's spontaneous reaction to you rather than because they consciously remind themselves of the reasons they fell for you in the first place and do their best to keep their feelings alive. Similarly, it seems more satisfying to (continue to) love another independently from the history of your relationship—and believe that you would be inclined to love them if you now met them for the first time—and hence without the help of past commitments. The reason why it is better to love, and be loved, out of inclination so defined is that in such cases love is a direct reaction to the reality of the beloved.

The analysis so far is likely to apply beyond relationships, to many of the activities the success of which commitments can protect: it is better if my desire to learn Russian is independent from all the effort I have put so far into learning the language, that is if I wanted to start learning it were I to encounter Russian for the first time today. But the value of learning languages, and of many other long-term processes in which people engage, derives, at least in part, from the successful attainment of a goal. I may derive a lot of value from the process of learning, but it is the final mastery of the language that makes for much of this endeavor's worth. This is what makes learning a language an appropriate *project*. For this reason, committing to projects is generally prudent; choosing to live from moment to moment carries the risk that one will never enjoy the value of attained goals.

Yet, romantic love and sexual love are not obviously appropriately conceived of as projects: we love each other for the sake of loving, rather than for the sake of reaching a goal. The process may be all that there is valuable to (romantic and sexual) love. (This is not to deny that sexual and romantic love may be conducive to many valuable achievements.) This is a reason to believe that it is misguided to commit to feeling romantic or sexual love for someone even if it was conceptually coherent, and a likely successful strategy.[25]

On this account, romantic and sexual love is at its best when the lovers are entirely focused on the moment and refrain from attempting to control the future of their relationship *qua* lovers. It is an understanding of love expressed by a popular (judging from its circulation in the electronic media) poem,[26] which captures well the appeal of disentangling love from commitment:

After a while / you learn the subtle difference between holding a hand and chaining a soul / and you learn love doesn't mean leaning and company doesn't always mean security / And you begin to learn that kisses aren't contracts and presents aren't always promises.

The costs of commitment are, as I discussed in the previous section, mostly opportunity costs. *Lack* of commitment, too, has pragmatic costs: the likely sacrifice of reaching distant goals. But lack of commitment is costless in the case of activities that should be entirely process-oriented, that is, activities whose value is not dependent on agents accomplishing a certain goal which gives some of the meaning to the endeavor. Intimate relationships are most likely to be of this kind, activities whose aim, as they say, is the journey itself. Merely enjoying the company of another and allowing oneself to be changed by relating to another give value to intimate relationships. For this reason, a lack of commitment is less costly when it comes to intimate relationships than in other contexts such as learning a language, pursuing a degree, or building a house.

Therefore, a person whom one loves, or even the relationship with that person, may be a particularly unsuited object of commitment, *unless one has reasons independent of love to commit to that person.* Such reasons may be moral: raising a child together towards whom the couple has already acquired parental duties, providing mutual aid, or prudential: securing economic welfare, or pursuing various common projects. Indeed, partners in lasting marriage(-like) relationships tend to have such additional reasons to commit.

It is a welcome fact, then, that marriages typically contain a bundle of worthy goods. Should the above reflections be mistaken, and should there be nothing misguided in committing to love another, marriage and marriage-like—i.e. cohabiting—relationships would seem particularly ill-suited to preserve romantic and sexual love. As William Godwin, one of the first critics of love-based marriage, noticed a long time ago: "It is absurd to expect that the inclinations and wishes of two human beings should coincide through any long period of time. To oblige them to act and to live love, marriage, and philosophical lives together, is to subject them to some inevitable portion of thwarting, bickering and unhappiness."[27] If marriage is a worthy institution, it is so in virtue of its ability to realize other goods than romantic and sexual love.

5. Implications for Marriage Legislation

In this chapter I suggested that the attitudinal commitment that gives meaning to the marriage institution has merely instrumental value. Commitment is good because it helps protect several goods realizable in marriage; I also suggested that it is unlikely that among the goods most appropriately protected by commitment to one's spouse are romantic and erotic love. Moreover, commitment to one's spouse can have very high opportunity costs. These considerations form a *pro tanto* reason to rethink the goals and duration of available forms of marriage—that is, to consider marriage reform.

The suggestions I have put forward regarding the value of marital commitment give some support to several kinds of marriage reforms. The first kind is temporary marriage, making it possible for individuals to enter marital relationships without permanent commitment. The other kind is the fragmentation of marriage: allowing individuals to split the various marital rights that currently are only available as a package between different individuals, thus making marital commitment less comprehensive. A reform that gets particular support from the argument of this essay is giving special legal protection to the family as a child-rearing institution, rather than to the family as a privileged relationship for the flourishing of romantic and sexual love. In the words of the legal scholar Martha Fineman, this would involve a move beyond the "sexual family." Below is a more in-depth analysis of how my analysis of the value of commitment to one's spouse indicates the desirability of these reforms.

The legalization of temporary marriage can be a way of recognizing that the opportunity costs of marriage are onerous. Of course, *de facto* temporary marriage already exists since divorce is legally available. Some critics of the liberalization of marriage deplore the fact that the availability of no-fault divorce has already eroded the possibility of the robust kind of marital commitment that was made by future spouses entering a traditional marriage.[28] *Contra* conservatives, this essay indicted that the erosion of the extreme, blind kind of commitment required by marriage without divorce is good news. The existence and legitimacy of no-fault divorce constitute a powerful argument in favor of making temporary marriage legally available. But divorce is often traumatic and costly. Therefore, it is plausible that temporary marriage is a superior option to the *status quo* of permanent marriage plus divorce. If the latter is legally available, so should be the former.[29]

Elizabeth Brake has recently argued, by appeal to the liberal ideal of state neutrality, that marriage should undertake a radical reform.[30] Her proposal is not restricted to permitting same-sex marriage, but extends to the number of marriages in which an individual may be involved by allowing a fragmentation of (some of the current) marriage rights. Individuals, on this account, ought to be free to engage in several minimal marriages, each centered on the protection of a different good—such as, for example, long-term companionship, or child-rearing, or economic security. Since states cannot legitimately protect controversial conceptions of the good, we ought, on Brake's account, to eliminate the central role that romance and sex currently have in understanding marriage. However, marriage does have an important function which makes it worth preserving, albeit in a radically changed form: the protection of caring relationships. Because they are a precondition for individuals pursuing good lives, caring relationships are not, as such, part of any controversial conception of the good. But there is no reason for states to restrict the protection of caring relationships by bundling together the various rights that spouses currently enjoy in relationship with each other. The present analysis of commitment supports Brake's proposal: if marriage relationships were fragmented, the content and value of each marital commitment would become clearer.

In particular, I suggested that, in spite of current legal and social expectations, marriage (as cohabitation) may not in fact be particularly suited to cultivating love, especially romantic and sexual love.[31] This claim supports another reformist proposal of rethinking the family by moving beyond the "sexual family"; Martha Fineman[32] has argued that we should define the family as centered on care-giving for children rather than on the romantic and sexual relationship between spouses. This would entail an adjustment of policy goals and legislation, to give priority to the protection of the interests of the child and her main caregiver (rather than prioritize traditional arrangements in which children are reared by procreating couples).

At least in the case of child-rearing, the intended span of marriage will be closely connected with its aims. In the past, several philosophers have made proposals in line with all three points above when they suggested a bifurcation of the institution of marriage into marital relationships established with the intention to raise children and marital relationships in which future spouses agree not to parent. Drawing on Margaret Mead's work, Jeffrey Blustein argued that the first kind of marriage ought to be permanent, while the second may be temporary and renewable. (Mead's proposal is that marriages start as temporary and move on to the permanent, child-rearing phase once spouses are confident they can sustain the relationship in order to protect the interests of their children.[33]) Both Mead's and Blustein's reasoning focuses on the interests of children as the main ground for such a reform. Without denying the importance of protecting children's interest in marriage, the present essay supports a more general case for reforming marriage by appeal to the interest of the future spouses. By avoiding a moralizing stance on commitment it may be possible to think about, and reform, marriage in ways that should satisfy both conservatives concerned with the well-being of children and liberals who are also concerned with protecting the spouses' well-being.[34]

Notes

1. This thought is sometimes expressed by popular culture. But philosophers have already made the point that commitment is unlikely to have unconditional value; its value depends on the value to what one is committed to. See Elizabeth Brake, *Minimizing Marriage: Marriage, Morality, and the Law* (New York: Oxford University Press, 2012). I do not dispute this claim; I limit my discussion to the value of commitments to worthwhile objects.

2. This part of the argument draws on a tradition of free love that is skeptical of the possibility and desirability of securing love via the creation of duties. For a discussion of this, see Brake, *Minimizing Marriage*, chapter 2.

3. The general analysis of commitment in this essay comes from Cheshire Calhoun, "What Good Is Commitment?" *Ethics* 119 (2009): 613–641; her article does not discuss marriage in particular, although she, too, notes that marital commitment is a paradigm case. What I say about marriage is my own analysis, unless specified differently.

4. I occasionally use the cost-benefit language for analyzing the value of commitment since, as I hope it will soon become clear, this language is especially useful to clarify when commitment has prudential, or rational value. In this, I draw on Anca Gheaus, "Is the Family Uniquely Valuable?" *Ethics and Social Welfare* 6:2 (2012): 120–131.

5. I develop this point, in relation to commitments to family members, in Gheaus, "The Family." See also Calhoun, "Commitment," 627.

6. Calhoun also notes that commitments also determine what our lives are, i.e., they give lives narrative unity; I choose to focus only on being the creator of one's self and life, given that these ideals seem to be widely endorsed among philosophers and non-philosophers, and hence less controversial than the ideal of narrative unity.

7. Calhoun correctly notes that such a life is different from the life of a person "who, not having made up his mind what he wants, is caused to act by whatever desire is strongest at the moment." From "Commitment," 269.

8. Charles Larmore, "The Idea of a Life Plan," *Social Philosophy & Policy* 16:1 (1999): 96–112, p. 96.

9. Larmore, "The Idea of a Life Plan," 103.

10. Indeed, this is the account of love and friendship implicit in Rainer Maria Rilke's *Letters to a Young Poet*. On this account, love is not likely to be properly accessible to young people who have not yet had the time to learn how to love well.

11. Calhoun, "Commitment," 619.

12. I discuss this at greater length in Gheaus, "The Family." See also Brake, *Minimizing Marriage*, chapter 2.

13. Brenda Almond, *The Fragmenting Family* (Oxford: Oxford University Press, 2006), 23.

14. See Brake, *Minimizing Marriage*, chapter 2.

15. This is true, of course, only if commitment itself is not a necessary condition for love. I agree with Brake in *Minimizing Marriage* that it isn't.

16. This is a recent definition of non-fungibility in the context of discussing love: "If an object having import to you is such that its being taken away ought to be experienced as a loss regardless of the state of other objects that might have or come to have import to you, then . . . that object has non-fungible import." From Bennett Helm, *Love, Friendship and the Self: Intimacy, Identification, and the Social Nature of Persons* (Oxford: Oxford University Press, 2010).

17. There are at least two ways of making sense of the belief that love has intrinsic value: as an important contribution to the well-being of the lover (if it is true that people do not regret the love they experience even when they think it is better not to pursue a relationship with their beloved, for either prudential or moral reasons). Or as a way of recognizing the value of the beloved; many think that even the most morally objectionable human being has value. For an account of love as an act of acknowledging the value of the beloved, see David Velleman, "Love as a Moral Emotion," *Ethics* 109 (1999): 338–374.

18. If love is a way of valuing a relationship with the beloved, and if the justification of love is to be found in historical-relational properties of the beloved, then commitment seems a very appropriate way of securing love. For such an understanding of love see Niko Kolodny, "Love as Valuing a Relationship," *The Philosophical Review* 112 (2003): 135–189.

19. Matthew Liao, "The Right of Children to Be Loved," *The Journal of Political Philosophy* 14:4 (2006): 420–440.

20. Brake, "Is Divorce Promise-Breaking?" 23–39.

21. Here is a quote from Montaigne: "We thought we were tying our marriage knots more tightly by removing all means of undoing them; but the tighter we pulled the knot of constraint the looser and slacker became the knot of our will and affection. In Rome, on the contrary, what made marriages honoured and secure for so long a period was freedom to break them at will. *Men loved their wives more because they could lose them*" [my emphasis]. Cited in Brake, *Minimizing Marriage*, 61.

22. On Brake's account, Sartre "saw love as prompting an inherently unrealizable attempt to capture permanently the free and spontaneous reciprocation of the beloved."

(From Brake, *Minimizing Marriage*, 61) The reason why such an endeavor is impossible is that, in order to be spontaneous, love (whether given or received) should not be fully controlled.

23. Amartya Sen, "Rational Fools: A Critique of the Behavioural Foundations of Economic Theory," *Philosophy and Public Affairs* 6 (1977): 317–344.

24. He writes: "[S]uppose you are in a hospital, recovering from a long illness when Smith comes in. You are so effusive with your thanks and praise that he protests that he always tries to do what he thinks is his duty, what he thinks will be best. You at first think he is engaging in a polite form of self-deprecation. But the more you two speak, the more clear it becomes that he was telling the literal truth: that it is not essentially because of you that he came to see you, not because you are friends, but because he thought it his duty, perhaps as a fellow Christian or Communist or whatever, or simply because he knows no one more in need of cheering up and no one easier to cheer up." In "The Schizophrenia of Modern Ethical Theories," *The Journal of Philosophy* 73 (1976): 453–466, p. 462.

25. This is not to say it is misguided to make a normative commitment to pursuing romantic and sexual love in general—it is a claim about making substantive commitments to love particular individuals.

26. Its authorship is under dispute. It has been attributed to Jorge Borges and to Veronica A. Shoffstall. See, for instance, http://www.rebellesociety.com/2012/09/15/poetry-lounge-after-a-while-you-learn/.

27. Quoted in Almond, *Fragmenting Family*, 30–31.

28. Various such sources are cited in Almond, *Fragmenting Family*.

29. For a detailed analysis of, and argument for, the legalization of temporary marriage see Daniel Nolan, "Temporary Marriage," Chapter 8 in this book.

30. Brake, *Minimizing Marriage*.

31. And, indeed, it is likely that most marriages in history have not been contracted with the aim of securing romantic and sexual love—let alone for the mere sake of such love alone.

32. Martha Fineman, *The Neutered Mother, the Sexual Family and Other Twentieth Century Tragedies* (New York and London: Routledge, 1996).

33. Of course, the ideal case of marriage centered on rearing children need not involve permanence, but rather a span of time sufficiently long to see children safely into adulthood.

34. I am grateful to Elizabeth Brake, Daniela Cutas, and Kalle Grill for helpful comments on an earlier draft. Work towards this essay was also supported by the Swedish Research Council, grant no. 421-2013-1306.

BIBLIOGRAPHY

Abbey, Ruth, and Douglas Den Uyl. "The Chief Inducement? The Idea of Marriage as Friendship." *Journal of Applied Philosophy* 18:1 (2001): 37–52.

Ackerman, Bruce. *Social Justice and the Liberal State*. New Haven, CT: Yale University Press, 1980.

Almond, Brenda. *The Fragmenting Family*. Oxford: Oxford University Press, 2006.

Alstott, Anne. *No Exit: What Parents Owe Their Children and What Society Owes Parents*. Oxford: Oxford University Press, 2004.

Altman, Irwin, and Joseph Ginat. *Polygamous Families in Contemporary Society*. New York: Cambridge University Press, 1996.

Arneson, Richard J. "What Sort of Sexual Equality Should Feminists Seek?" *Journal of Contemporary Legal Issues* 9:21 (1998): 21–36.

Baier, Annette. *Moral Prejudices: Essays on Ethics*. Cambridge, MA: Harvard University Press, 1994.

Barry, Brian. *Culture and Equality*. Cambridge, UK: Cambridge University Press, 2001.

Beauvoir, Simone de. *The Second Sex*, ed., trans. H. M. Parshley. New York: Vintage Books, 1989.

Bennion, Janet. *Women of Principle: Female Networking in Contemporary Mormon Polygyny*. Oxford: Oxford University Press, 1998.

Bernhardt, Torsten, Marcie Gibson, Erin Sandilands, Jake Szamosi, and Andrea Zanin. "The Spawn, the Spawnlet, and the Birth of a Queer Family." In *And Baby Makes More*, ed. Susan Goldberg and Chloë Brushwood Rose, 107–126. London, ON: Insomniac Press, 2009.

Bertrand, Marianne, Claudia Goldin, and Lawrence F. Katz. "Dynamics of the Gender Gap for Young Professionals in the Corporate and Financial Sectors." Working Paper 14681, National Bureau of Economic Research (2009). Accessed at http://www.nber. org/papers/w14681, June 12, 2014.

Bertrand, Marianne, Emir Kamenica, and Jessica Pan. "Gender Identity and Relative Income Within Households." Working Paper No. 84, Chicago Booth Paper No. 13-08 (2013). Accessed at Social Science Research Network Electronic Paper Collection: http://ssrn.com/abstract=2216750, June 11, 2014.

Blustein, Jeremy. *Parents and Children: The Ethics of the Family*. Oxford: Oxford University Press, 1982.

Bradlee, Ben, Jr., and Dale Van Atta. *Prophet of Blood: The Untold Story of Ervil LeBaron and the Lambs of God*. New York: Putnam, 1981.

Bradley, Martha Sonntag. *Kidnapped from That Land: The Government Raids on the Short Creek Polygamists*. Salt Lake City: University of Utah Press, 1993.

Brake, Elizabeth. "Minimal Marriage: What Political Liberalism Implies for Marriage Law." *Ethics* 120:2 (2010): 302–307.

Brake, Elizabeth. "Is Divorce Promise-Breaking?" *Ethical Theory and Moral Practice* 14 (2011): 23–39.

Brake, Elizabeth. "Marriage and Domestic Partnership." In *The Stanford Encyclopedia of Philosophy*, ed. Edward N. Zalta. July 11, 2009, substantial revision August 8, 2012. http://plato.stanford.edu/archives/fall2012/entries/marriage/

Brake, Elizabeth. *Minimizing Marriage: Marriage, Morality, and the Law*. New York and Toronto: Oxford University Press, 2012.

Brake, Elizabeth. "Feminism, Family Law, and the Social Bases of Self-Respect." In *Re-reading the Canon Series: Feminist Interpretations of Rawls*, ed. Ruth Abbey, 57–74. University Park, PA: Penn State University Press, 2013.

Brake, Elizabeth. "Recognizing Care: The Case for Friendship and Polyamory." *Syracuse Law and Civic Engagement Journal* 1 (2014). <http://slace.syr.edu/>

Brennan, Samantha and Bill Cameron. "How Many Parents Can a Child Have? Philosophical Reflections on the 'Three Parent Case.'" *Dialogue* 54:1 (2015): 45–61.

Brinig, Margaret, and Steven Crafton. "Marriage and Opportunism." *Journal of Legal Studies* 23:2 (June 1994): 869–894.

Brooks, Thom. "The Problem of Polygamy." *Philosophical Topics* 37:2 (2009): 109–122.

Calhoun, Cheshire. *Feminism, the Family, and the Politics of the Closet: Lesbian and Gay Displacement*. Toronto: Oxford University Press, 2002.

Calhoun, Cheshire. "Who's Afraid of Polygamous Marriage? Lessons for Same-Sex Marriage Advocacy from the History of Polygamy." *San Diego Law Review* 42 (2005): 1023–1042.

Calhoun, Cheshire. "What Good Is Commitment?" *Ethics* 119 (2009): 613–641.

Card, Claudia. "Against Marriage and Motherhood." *Hypatia* 11:3 (1996): 1–23.

CBC News. "Census Shows New Face of the Canadian Family." September 19, 2012. http://www.cbc.ca/news/canada/census-shows-new-face-of-the-canadian-family-1.1137083

Centers for Disease Control and Prevention. "Unmarried Childbearing." January 2014. http://www.cdc.gov/nchs/fastats/unmarried-childbearing.htm

Chambers, Clare. *Sex, Culture, and Justice: The Limits of Choice*. University Park, PA: Pennsylvania State University Press, 2008.

Chambers, Clare. "'The Family as a Basic Institution': A Feminist Analysis of the Basic Structure as Subject." In *Feminist Interpretations of Rawls*, ed. Ruth Abbey, 75–95. University Park, PA: Pennsylvania State University Press, 2013.

Chambers, Clare. "The Marriage-Free State." *Proceedings of the Aristotelian Society* 113:2 (2013): 123–143.

Chambers, Clare. *Against Marriage: An Egalitarian Defence of the Marriage-Free State* Oxford: Oxford University Press, forthcoming 2016.

Chan, Sarah and Daniela Cutas. *Families: Beyond the Nuclear Ideal*. New York: Bloomsbury Academic, 2012.

Christensen, Craig W. "Legal Ordering of Family Values: The Case of Gay and Lesbian Families." *Cardozo Law Review* 18 (1996–1997): 1299–1416.

Clayton, Matthew. *Justice and Legitimacy in Upbringing*. Oxford: Oxford University Press, 2006.

Cleyre, Voltairine de. "They Who Marry Do Ill." In *The Voltairine de Cleyre Reader*, ed. A. J. Brigati, 11–20. Oakland, CA: AK Press, 2004.

Cohen, Joshua. "Deliberation and Democratic Legitimacy." In *The Good Polity: Normative Analysis of the State*, ed. Alan Hamlin and Philip Pettit, 17–34. Oxford: Blackwell, 1989.

Commonwealth of Australia, Marriage Act 1961 (as amended).

Compton, Todd. *In Sacred Loneliness: The Plural Wives of Joseph Smith*. Salt Lake City: Signature Press, 1997.

Cross, Philip and Peter Jon Mitchell. "The Marriage Gap Between Rich and Poor Canadians." Institute of Marriage and Family Canada, February 2014. http://www.imfcanada.org/sites/default/files/Canadian_Marriage_Gap_FINAL_0.pdf

Cudd, Ann. *Analyzing Oppression*. New York: Oxford University Press, 2006.

Curry, H., and D. Clifford. *A Legal Guide for Lesbian and Gay Couples: A NOLO Press Self-Help Law Book*. Berkeley, CA: Nolo Press, 1989.

Davis, Adrienne. "Regulating Polygamy: Intimacy Default Rules and Bargaining for Equality." *Columbia Law Review* 110:8 (2010): 1955–2046.

Daynes, Kathryn M. *More Wives than One: Transformation of the Mormon Marriage System, 1840–1910*. Urbana and Chicago: University of Illinois Press, 2001.

De Marneffe, Peter. *Liberalism and Prostitution*. New York: Oxford University Press, 2010.

De Marneffe, Peter. "The Possibility and Desirability of Neutrality." In *Political Neutrality: A Re-evaluation*, ed. Daniel Weinstock and Roberto Merrill, 44–56. New York: Palgrave Macmillan, 2014.

Denis, Lara. "From Friendship to Marriage: Revising Kant." *Philosophy and Phenomenological Research* 63:1 (2001): 1–28.

DeParle, Jason. "Two Classes, Divided by 'I Do.'" *New York Times*, July 14, 2012. http://www.nytimes.com/2012/07/15/us/two-classes-in-america-divided-by-i-do.html

DePaulo, Bella. *Singled Out: How Singles Are Stereotyped, Stigmatized, and Ignored, and Still Live Happily Ever After*. New York: St. Martin's Press, 2006.

Desai, Sreedhari, Dolly Chugh, and Arthur Brief. "The Implications of Marriage Structure for Men's Workplace Attitudes, Beliefs, and Behaviors Toward Women." *Administrative Science Quarterly* 59:2 (2014): 330–365.

Dnes, Antony W., and Robert Rowthorn, eds. *The Law and Economics of Marriage & Divorce*. Cambridge, UK: Cambridge University Press, 2002.

Dworkin, Ronald. *A Matter of Principle*. Cambridge, MA: Harvard University Press, 1985.

Dworkin, Ronald. *Freedom's Law: The Moral Reading of the American Constitution*. Cambridge, MA: Harvard University Press, 1997.

Eichner, Maxine. *The Supportive State*. Oxford: Oxford University Press, 2010.

Eisenberg, Melvin A. "The Limits of Cognition and the Limits of Contract." *Stanford Law Review* 47:2 (1995): 211–259.

Eisenberg, Melvin A. "Why There Is No Law of Relational Contracts." *Northwestern University Law Review* 94 (1999): 805–821.

Ellman, Ira Mark. "'Contract Thinking' Was *Marvin's* Fatal Flaw." *Notre Dame Law Review* 76 (2000–2001): 1365–1380.

Ellman, Ira Mark, and Sharon Lohr. "Marriage as Contract, Opportunistic Violence, and Other Bad Arguments for Fault Divorce." *University of Illinois Law Review* (1997): 719–772.

Embry, Jessie L. *Mormon Polygamous Families: Life in the Principle*. Salt Lake City: University of Utah Press, 1987.

Emens, Elizabeth F. "Monogamy's Law: Compulsory Monogamy and Polyamorous Existence." *New York University Review of Law and Social Change* 29 (2004): 277–376.

Eskow, Lisa R. "The Ultimate Weapon? Demythologizing Spousal Rape and Reconceptualizing Its Prosecution." *Stanford Law Review* 48:3 (1996): 677–709.

Ferguson, Ann. "Gay Marriage: An American and Feminist Dilemma." *Hypatia: A Journal of Feminist Philosophy* 22:1 (2007): 39–57.

Fineman, Martha Albertson. *The Neutered Mother, The Sexual Family and Other Twentieth Century Tragedies*. New York and London: Routledge, 1995.

Fineman, Martha Albertson. *The Autonomy Myth: A Theory of Dependency*. New York: New Press, 2004, 2005.

Fineman, Martha Albertson. "The Meaning of Marriage." In *Marriage Proposals: Questioning a Legal Status*, ed. Anita Bernstein, 29–69. New York: New York University Press, 2006.

Finlay, K., and D. Neumark. "Is Marriage Always Good for Children? Evidence from Families Affected by Incarceration." *The Journal of Human Resources* 45:4 (2010): 1046–1088.

Finnis, John. "Marriage: A Basic and Exigent Good." *The Monist* 91 (2008): 388–406.

Folbre, Nancy. *Who Pays for the Kids? Gender and the Structures of Constraint*. New York: Routledge, 1994.

Foster, Lawrence. *Religion and Sexuality: Three American Communal Experiments of the Nineteen Century*. New York: Oxford University Press, 1981.

Fricker, Miranda. *Epistemic Injustice: Power and the Ethics of Knowing*. Oxford: Oxford University Press, 2007.

Friedan, Betty. *The Feminine Mystique*, with introduction by Anna Quindlen. New York: Norton, 2001.

Frug, M. J. "Re-reading Contracts: A Feminist Analysis of a Contracts Casebook." *American University Law Review* 34 (1985): 1065–1140.

Garrett, Jeremy. "Marriage Unhitched from the State: A Defense." *Public Affairs Quarterly*, 23:2 (2009): 161–180.

Garrison, Marsha. "Promoting Cooperative Parenting: Programs and Prospects." *Journal of Law and Family Studies* 9 (2007): 265–280.

Gheaus, Anca. "Gender Justice." *Journal of Ethics and Social Philosophy* 6:1 (2012): 1–24.

Gheaus, Anca. "Is the Family Uniquely Valuable?" *Ethics and Social Welfare* 6:2 (2012): 120–131.

Goodman, A., and E. Greaves. *Cohabitation, Marriage and Child Outcomes*. London: Institute for Fiscal Studies, 2010.

Goodrich, P. "Gender and Contracts." In *Feminist Perspectives on the Foundational Subjects of Law*, ed. A. Bottomley, 17–45. London: Cavendish, 1996

Grana, Mari. *Pioneer, Polygamist, Politician: The Life of Dr. Martha Hughes Cannon*. Guilford, CT: TwoDot, 2009.

Greenstone, Michael and Adam Looney. "The Marriage Gap: The Impact of Economic and Technological Change on Marriage Rates." Brookings Institution, February 3, 2012. http://www.brookings.edu/blogs/jobs/posts/2012/02/03-jobs-greenstone-looney

Halberstam, Jack. "Friends with Benefits + The Kids Are All Right = Friends with Kids." Bully Bloggers, April 29, 2012. http://bullybloggers.wordpress.com/2012/04/29/friends-with-benefits-the-kids-are-all-right-friends-with-kids/

Hampton, Jean. "Feminist Contractarianism." In *A Mind of One's Own*, ed. Louise Antony and Charlotte Witt, 227–256. Oxford: Westview Press, 1993.

Hardy, B. Carmon. *Solemn Covenant: The Mormon Polygamous Passage*. Urbana, IL: University of Illinois Press, 1992.

Harline, Paula Kelly. *The Polygamous Wives Club*. New York: Oxford University Press, 2014.

Harrison, Jonathan. "Separating Marriage from Childrearing: The Mosuo." Sociological Images, September 22, 2014. http://thesocietypages.org/socimages/2014/09/22/separating-marriage-from-childrearing-the-mosuo/

Hartley, Christie, and Lori Watson. "Political Liberalism, Marriage and the Family." *Law and Philosophy* 31:2 (2012): 185–212.

Helm, Bennett. *Love, Friendship and the Self: Intimacy, Identification, & the Social Nature of Persons*. Oxford: Oxford University Press, 2010.

Hill, Thomas E., Jr. "Servility and Self-Respect." *The Monist* 57:1 (1973): 87–104.

hooks, bell. *Feminist Theory: From Margin to Center*. Boston: South End Press, 1984.

Hovey, K.V. *Handfasting*. Avon, MA: F+W Publications, 2008.

Iversen, Joan Smyth. *The Antipolygamy Controversy in U.S. Women's Movements, 1880–1925: Debate on the American Home*. New York: Garland Publishing, 1997.

Jacobs, Melanie B. "Why Just Two? Disaggregating Traditional Parental Rights and Responsibilities to Recognize Multiple Parents." *Journal of Law & Family Studies* 9 (2007): 309–339.

Jeffs, Brent. *Lost Boy*. New York: Broadway Books, 2009.

Jessop, Carolyn. *Triumph: Life After the Cult, A Survivor's Lesson*. New York: Broadway Books, 2010.

Jessop, Carolyn, and Laura Palmer. *Escape*. New York: Broadway Books, 2007.

Kagan, Shelly. *Normative Ethics*. Boulder, CO: Westview, 1998.

Kant, Immanuel. *Anthropology from a Pragmatic Point of View*, trans. Mary Gregor. The Hague: Martinus Nijhoff, 1974 [originally published 1798].

Kelly, Maura. "What's So Crazy About an Arranged Marriage?" *The Atlantic*, May 1, 2012. http://www.theatlantic.com/entertainment/archive/2012/05/whats-so-crazy-about-an-arranged-marriage/256561/

Kern, Louis J. *An Ordered Love: Sex Roles and Sexuality in Victorian Utopias: The Shakers, the Mormons, and the Oneida Community*. Chapel Hill: University of North Carolina Press, 1981.

Kingdom, Elizabeth A. "Cohabitation Contracts: A Socialist-Feminist Issue." *Journal of Law and Society* 15:1 (1988): 77–89.

Kingdom, Elizabeth A. "Cohabitation Contracts and the Democratization of Personal Relations." *Feminist Legal Studies* 8:1 (2000): 5–27.

Klosko, George and Steven Wall, eds. *Perfectionism and Neutrality: Essays in Liberal Theory*. Lanham, MD: Rowman and Littlefield, 2003.

Kolodny, Niko. "Love as Valuing a Relationship." *The Philosophical Review* 112 (2003): 135–189.

Laden, Anthony. *Reasonably Radical*. Ithaca, NY: Cornell University Press, 2001.

Lambeir, Bert and Stefan Ramaekers. "The Terror of Explicitness: Philosophical Remarks on the Idea of a Parenting Contract." *Ethics and Education* 2 (2007): 95–107.

Landau, Iddo. "Should Marital Relations be Non-hierarchical?" *Ratio* 25:1 (2012): 51–67.

Larmore, Charles. *Patterns of Moral Complexity*. Cambridge, UK: Cambridge University Press, 1987.

Larmore, Charles. "The Idea of a Life Plan." *Social Philosophy & Policy* 16:1 (1999): 96–112.

Leff, A. "'Til 2013 Do Us Part? Mexico Mulls 2-Year Marriage." *Reuters*, September 29, 2011. http://www.reuters.com/article/2011/09/29/us-mexico-marriage-idUSTRE78S6TX20110929

Levey, Ann. "Liberalism, Adaptive Preferences, and Gender Equality." *Hypatia* 20:4 (2005): 127–143.

Liao, Matthew. "The Right of Children to Be Loved." *The Journal of Political Philosophy* 14:4 (2006): 420–440.

Macedo, Stephen. *Just Married: Same-Sex Couples, Monogamy, and the Future of Marriage*. Princeton, NJ: Princeton University Press, 2015.

MacKinnon, Catharine A. *Toward a Feminist Theory of the State*. Cambridge, MA: Harvard University Press, 1989.

Macneil, Ian R. "Contracts: Adjustment of Long-Term Economic Relations Under Classical, Neoclassical, and Relational Contract Law." *Northwestern University Law Review* 72 (1977): 854–905.

March, Andrew. "Is There a Right to Polygamy? Marriage, Equality, and Subsidizing Families in Liberal Political Justification." *Journal of Moral Philosophy* 8 (2011): 246–272.

Maushart, Susan. *Wifework: What Marriage Really Means for Women*. New York: Bloomsbury, 2001.

McClain, Linda C. "The Other Marriage Equality Problem." *Boston University Law Review* 93:3 (2013): 921–970.

McLellan, David. "Contract Marriage—The Way Forward or Dead End?" *Journal of Law and Society* 23:2 (June 1996): 234–246.

Metz, Tamara. *Untying the Knot: Marriage, the State, and the Case for their Divorce*. Princeton, NJ: Princeton University Press, 2010.

Mill, John Stuart. *The Subjection of Women*, ed. Susan Moller Okin. Indianapolis: Hackett, 1988.

Minow, Martha, and Mary Lyndon Shanley. "Relational Rights and Responsibilities: Revisioning the Family in Liberal Political Theory and Law." *Hypatia* 11:1 (1996): 4–29.

Mitchell, Peter Jon. "The Rich-Poor Marriage Gap in Canada." Family Studies: The Blog of the Institute for Family Studies, March 11, 2014. http://family-studies.org/the-rich-poor-marriage-gap-in-canada/

Neave, M. "Private Ordering in Family Law: Will Women Benefit?" In *Public and Private: Feminist Legal Debates*, ed. M. Thornton, 144–173. Melbourne: Oxford University Press, 1995.

Nussbaum, Martha. *Liberty of Conscience: In Defense of America's Tradition of Religious Equality*. New York: Basic Books, 2008.

O'Donovan, K. *Sexual Divisions in Law*. London: Weidenfeld and Nicholson, 1985.

Okin, Susan Moller. *Justice, Gender, and the Family*. New York: Basic Books, 1989.

Okin, Susan Moller. "*Political Liberalism*, Justice, and Gender." *Ethics* 105 (1994): 23–43.

Okin, Susan Moller. "Is Multiculturalism Bad for Women?" In Susan Moller Okin, *Is Multiculturalism Bad for Women?* ed. Joshua Cohen, Matthew Howard, and Martha C. Nussbaum, 7–26. Princeton, NJ: Princeton University Press, 1999.

Park, Shelley. "Is Queer Parenting Possible?" In *Who's Your Daddy? And Other Writings on Queer Parenting*, ed. Rachel Epstein, 316–327. Toronto: Sumach Press, 2009.

Park, Shelley. *Mothering Queerly, Queering Motherhood: Resisting Monomaternalism in Adoptive, Lesbian, Blended and Polygamous Families*. Albany, NY: SUNY Press, 2013.

Parke, M. "Policy Brief No. 3: Are Married Parents Really Better for Children? What Research Says About the Effects of Family Structure on Child Well-Being (Annotated Version)." Center for the Law and Social Policy. May 2003. <www.clasp.org>

Pateman, Carole. *The Sexual Contract*. London: Polity, 1988.

Patten, Alan. "Liberal Neutrality: A Reinterpretation and Defense." *Journal of Political Philosophy* 20:3 (2012): 249–272.

Perry v Brown. 52 Cal. 4th 1116, 1132 (2011). Case No. 10-16696 9th Cir. (United States Court of Appeals for the Ninth Circuit).

Quong, Jonathan. *Liberalism without Perfection*. Oxford: Clarendon Press, 2010.

Rajczi, Alex. "A Populist Argument for Same-Sex Marriage." *The Monist* 91:3–4 (2008): 475–505.

Rawls, John. *A Theory of Justice*. Cambridge: Harvard University Press, 1971.

Rawls, John. *Political Liberalism*. New York: Columbia University Press, 1993.

Rawls, John. "The Idea of Public Reason Revisited." *The University of Chicago Law Review* 64:3 (1997): 765–807.

Rawls, John. *A Theory of Justice*, revised edition. Cambridge, MA: Harvard University Press, 1999 (originally published 1971).

Rawls, John. *Political Liberalism*, expanded edition. New York: Columbia University Press, 2005, originally published 1993.

Raz, Joseph. *The Morality of Freedom*. New York: Clarendon Press of Oxford University Press, 1986, reissued 1988.

Richtel, Matt. "Till Death, or 20 Years, Do Us Part." *New York Times*, September 28, 2012. http://www.nytimes.com/2012/09/30/fashion/marriage-seen-through-a-contract-lens.html

Rickless, Samuel. "Same-Sex Marriage and Polygamy: A Response to Calhoun." *San Diego Law Review* 42 (2005): 1043–1048.

Robson, Ruthann, and S. E. Valentine. "Lov(h)ers: Lesbians as Intimate Partners and Lesbian Legal Theory." *Temple Law Review* 63 (1990): 511–541.

Schwartz, Pepper. *Love Between Equals: How Peer Marriage Really Works*. New York: The Free Press, 1994.

Scotland, Privy Council. "The Statutes and Band of Icolmkill." *Register of the Privy Council of Scotland*, First Series, Vol IX, 1610–1613. 1889.

Scott, Elizabeth S., and Robert J. Scott. "Marriage as Relational Contract." *Virginia Law Review* 84:7 (October 1998): 1225–1334.

Sen, Amartya. "Rational Fools: A Critique of the Behavioural Foundations of Economic Theory." *Philosophy and Public Affairs* 6 (1977): 317–344.

Shanley, Mary Lyndon. *Just Marriage*. Oxford: Oxford University Press, 2004.

Shanley, Mary Lyndon. "The State of Marriage and the State in Marriage." In *Marriage Proposals: Questioning a Legal Status*, ed. Anita Bernstein, 188–216. New York: New York University Press, 2006.

Sheff, Elisabeth. *The Polyamorists Next Door: Inside Multiple-Partner Relationships and Families*. Lanham, MD: Rowman & Littlefield Publishers, 2013.

Sher, George. *Beyond Neutrality: Perfectionism and Politics*. New York: Cambridge University Press, 1997.

Shipps, Jan. *Mormonism: The Story of a New Religious Tradition*. Urbana: University of Illinois Press, 1985.

Shrage, Laurie. "Reforming Marriage: A Comparative Approach." *Journal of Applied Philosophy* 30:2 (2013): 107–121.

Shultz, Marjorie Maguire. "Contractual Ordering of Marriage: A New Model for State Policy." *California Law Review* 70:2 (1982): 204–334.

Singer, Jana B. "The Privatization of Family Law." *Wisconsin Law Review* (1992): 1444–1567.

Sokol, M. "Jeremy Bentham on Love and Marriage: A Utilitarian Proposal for Short-Term Marriage." *The Journal of Legal History* 30:1 (2009): 1–21.

Somerville, Margaret. "What About the Children?" In *Divorcing Marriage: Unveiling the Dangers in Canada's New Social Experiment*, ed. Daniel Cere and Douglas Farrow, 63–78. Montreal: McGill-Queen's University Press, 2004.

Spencer, Irene. *Shattered Dreams: My Life as a Polygamist's Wife*. New York: Hachette, 2007.

Stocker, Michael. "The Schizophrenia of Modern Ethical Theories." *The Journal of Philosophy* 73 (1976): 453–466.

Strauss, Gregg. "Is Polygamy Inherently Unequal?" *Ethics* 122 (2012): 516–544.

Suissa, Judith. "Untangling the Mother Knot: Some Thoughts on Parents, Children and Philosophers of Education." *Ethics and Education* 1 (2006): 65–77.

Testy, Kellye Y. "An Unlikely Resurrection." *Northwestern University Law Review* 90 (1995): 219–235.

Thompson, Derek. "How America's Marriage Crisis Makes Income Inequality So Much Worse." *The Atlantic*, October 1, 2013. http://www.theatlantic.com/business/archive/2013/10/how-americas-marriage-crisis-makes-income-inequality-so-much-worse/280056/

Tidwell, Patricia A., and Peter Linzer. "The Flesh-Colored Band Aid: Contracts, Feminism, Dialogue, and Norms." *Houston Law Review* 28 (1991): 791–817.

Tsing Loh, Sandra. "Let's Call the Whole Thing Off." *The Atlantic*, July 1, 2009. http://www.theatlantic.com/magazine/archive/2009/07/let-8217-s-call-the-whole-thing-off/7488/

Tweedy, Ann. "Polyamory as a Sexual Orientation." *University of Cincinnati Law Review* 79 (2011): 1461–1515.

Udall, Brady. *The Lonely Polygamist.* New York: Norton, 2010.

United States Census Bureau. "Survey of Income and Program Participation Data on Marriage and Divorce." November 2014. http://www.census.gov/hhes/socdemo/marriage/data/sipp/index.html

Velleman, David. "Love as a Moral Emotion." *Ethics* 109 (199): 338–374.

Wald, Deborah H. "The Parentage Puzzle: The Interplay Between Genetics, Procreative Intent, and Parental Conduct in Determining Legal Parentage." *American University Journal of Gender, Social Policy & the Law* 15 (2007): 379–411.

Ward, Peter. *A History of Domestic Space: Privacy and the Canadian Home.* Vancouver: University of British Columbia Press, 2009.

Wax, Amy. "Bargaining in the Shadow of Marriage: Is There a Future for Egalitarian Marriage?" *Virginia Law Review* 84:4 (May 1998): 509–672.

Wedgwood, Ralph. "The Fundamental Argument for Same-Sex Marriage." *The Journal of Political Philosophy* 7:3 (1999): 225–242.

Wedgwood, Ralph. "The Meaning of Same-Sex Marriage." *The New York Times*, Opinionator, May 24, 2012. <http://opinionator.blogs.nytimes.com/2012/05/24/marriage-meaning-and-equality/>

Wedgwood, Ralph. "Against Ideal Theory." *PEA Soup*, May 3, 2014. <http://peasoup.typepad.com/peasoup/2014/05/against-ideal-theory.html>

Weitzman, Lenore J. *The Marriage Contract: Spouses, Lovers and the Law.* New York: The Free Press, 1981.

Wellington, A. A. "Why Liberals Should Support Same-Sex Marriage." *Journal of Social Philosophy* 25:3 (1995): 5–32.

Wightman, John. "Intimate Relationships, Relational Contract Theory, and the Reach of Contract." *Feminist Legal Studies* 8 (2000): 93–131.

Wollstonecraft, Mary. *Vindication of the Rights of Woman.* New York: Everyman, 1992.

Young, Alison Harvison. "Reconceiving the Family: Challenging the Paradigm of the Exclusive Family." *American University Journal of Gender & the Law* 6 (1998): 505–555.

Young, Iris Marion. *Justice and the Politics of Difference.* Princeton, NJ: Princeton University Press, 1990.

Young, Kimball. *Isn't One Wife Enough?* New York: Holt, Rinehart & Winston, 1954.

INDEX

distinctive human goods, 5, 86, 148–153.
  See also goods
distributive justice, 70, 104–105, 107
divisions of labor, 67, 101–103
  gendered, 18, 106–107, 129, 165
  non-gendered, 59, 167
divorce, 66, 69, 89, 91, 108. *See also*
  divorce laws
  and children, 87, 96, 128, 191–193
  and common law marriage, 203
  difficulty of, 127, 221
  distributive outcomes in, 33, 106, 110
  and mutual commitment, 34
  vs. polygamy, 155–156, 166
  and prenuptial contracts, 52, 64
  and presumptive permanence, 16–17
  rate of, 85, 88, 165, 190, 199
  vs. temporary marriage, 181, 195, 220
divorce laws, 12, 86, 174, 180, 214
doctrinal practices, 25–26
domestic interdependence, 1, 115
Dworkin, Ronald, 80n23, 151,
  153–154, 159n88

economic inequality, 100–101, 106, 109
egalitarianism, 55, 70–71, 75, 167
  and abolition of state-recognized
    marriage, 51
  and division of labor, 59
  ideals of, 100–101, 103, 120
  in marriage structures, 175
  in polygamous families, 6, 148,
    163, 172
  public policy reasons for, 65–66
  and relationship contracts, 56–57, 77
  in traditional marriage, 54
Eichner, Maxine, 76
Emens, Elizabeth, 171, 174
employment discrimination, 1, 101–102
equality, 5–7, 164, 175
  as argument for same-sex marriage, 2
  and contractual deviations, 77
  in function-based directives, 76
  in marriage, 101–103, 163, 183–185,
    200, 201n–202n7
  in personal relationships, 1

principle of, 151
  in relationship contracts, 54, 56–59,
    65, 70, 74
  of treatment of marriages, 187
  of treatment of traditions, 186
exclusive life partnerships, 5, 148, 151, 155
  definition of, 149–150
  and neutrality, 152, 153
exit options, 102, 106, 119–120, 165, 176
exit rights, 113, 166
extramarital sex, 126, 129

families of choice, 85
family, 44, 77, 88–90, 93, 220. *See also*
  nuclear family
  life, 81n34
  structure of, 4
family law, 7, 72, 79n15, 125, 155
fathers, 102, 114, 121n5, 123n47, 128
  in polygamous families, 129, 135–136,
    138–141
feminism, 5, 12, 41–42, 80n23, 100
  on autonomy, 116–119
  on child welfare, 84
  on duration of marriage, 115
  and egalitarianism, 51, 65, 70
  on gender hierarchy in marriage,
    103–105, 166
  on gendered division of household
    labor, 106–107
  on gendered violence, 109–110
  on marriage reform, 119–120
  and non-hierarchy principle (NHP),
    110–114
  and polygamy, 161, 178
  and relationship contracts, 53,
    56–58, 60
  and same-sex marriage, 162, 173
  on social norms, 39, 107–108
  and women's subordination, 165
fertility treatments, 98n27
Fineman, Martha, 55–56, 59–60, 66,
  220–221
Finnis, John, 84, 86
fornication. *See* extramarital sex
fraud, 129, 161, 172

holistic regulation, 54, 74, 76
hospital visitation rights, 32
hostile partnerships, 90–91
household labor, 101, 106. *See also*
gendered division of labor
human relationships, 40, 148, 153, 185, 211
Huntington, Zina, 145–146
husbands, 120, 176n4, 177n15
allowed to abuse wives, 63, 82n55
allowed to flourish as individual, 86
as family leader, 114
and gender identity, 108
in hierarchy, 110
as income earner, 103, 107,
109, 121n6
in polyandrous relationship, 174
in polygamy, 129, 131, 137–148,
164–165
and religious law, 186
and religious norms, 58
wives legally subordinated to, 12, 41

immigrants, 21, 74, 125, 155, 166
rights granted via marriage to, 2, 16,
32, 61, 173–174
in temporary marriage, 195
income inequality, 106, 108
income-tax laws, 2, 32, 106, 125, 155
incentivizing gender-structured
marriage, 165
individual rights, 126, 132–133, 151,
155–156. *See also* right to marry
individuality, 5, 116, 120
institution of marriage. *See* marriage
instrumental value, 209, 214–215
of commitment, 206, 208, 212, 216
of marriage, 19–23, 220
interpersonal relationships, 1, 9, 11,
128, 214
equality in, 5
hierarchy in, 110, 112
and presumptive permanence, 15, 19
and social norms, 21
state regulation of, 4, 7, 51
interracial marriage. *See*
anti-miscegenation laws

intimacy, 6, 7, 11, 94, 163
driven by love vs. commitment, 218
of marriage, 116, 170
models of, 169
non-fungibility of members in, 112
in polygamy, 168, 171
and sex, 34
intimate partners, 109, 147, 168, 170–171
and child adoption, 175
sensitive information between, 169

jealousy, 18, 98n26, 143–145, 147
Jeffs, Brent, 136, 144
Jeffs, Warren, 136, 140
Jessop, Carolyn, 139, 140, 147
joint activities, 104, 108, 113, 119
in intimate hierarchies, 112, 116–117
joint assets, 104, 112, 113
justice, 3, 4, 29, 30, 37, 76. *See also*
distributive justice
of abolition of state-recognized marriage,
51, 131
compatibility of marriage with, 38–39, 41
of compensatory payment, 69
and default directives, 52
and family organization, 104–105
liberal theories of, 50n12, 80n23
marriage as requirement of, 47
in personal relationships, 61
and political philosophy, 49
principles of, 31, 74
promotion of, 81n34
and relationship contracts, 57–58,
65–67, 77, 82n55
of social institutions, 48
and state directives, 75
of temporary marriage, 185
justification of marriage, 9, 30–31, 45, 47
metaphysical, 38, 39
and political liberalism, 44, 48
properties of marriage for, 43
and requirement by justice, 37

Kant, Immanuel, 103–104, 114, 118, 123n53
on autonomy, 119
Kimball, Heber, 137

marriage, 36, 52, 175, 198, 221
  abolition of, 29, 55, 100
  alternatives to. *See* alternative
    relationships (non-marriage)
  benefits of, 12, 19, 21–22, 31, 181–182
  benefits to children of, 4–5, 87,
    133–135
  class divide in, 7, 100
  communicative power of, 35, 37–38, 43
  compatibility with political liberal-
    ism of, 44
  comprehensiveness of, 205–206,
    213, 220
  as cultural practice, 11–13, 17,
    20, 25–26
  customs, 166, 172
  definition of, 5, 31, 53, 203n19, 205
  disestablishment of, 2–4, 40
  duration of, 115
  entitlements of, 2, 22, 32, 40, 173
  exclusive life partnership rationale
    for, 153
  financial benefits of, 66, 181–182
  functions of, 4, 6, 37, 74, 134
  gender norms in, 108
  goals of, 87, 98n16, 198
  as human right, 131, 162, 185
  and justice, 29, 30
  justification of. *See* justification of mar-
    riage
  legal obligations of, 4, 178n28
  legal powers of, 32–33, 35, 39
  as a legal relationship, 31–32, 35, 39
  legal replacements for, 9, 13, 48
  liberalization of, 220
  linked with parenthood, 95
  nature of, 32, 38–39, 183, 216
  neutrality principle defense of, 151
  patriarchal forms of, 177n15
  popularity of, 42, 48
  positivist account of, 6, 197–198
  as presumptively permanent, 3, 9,
    13–18, 21–23
  and principle of liberal neutrality, 19, 26
  as promoting distinctive human
    goods, 150

  as public institution, 11, 19, 22, 26
  rationale for, 155
  shared expectations in, 199–200
  as social institution, 37, 119, 134, 142
  social meaning of. *See* social meaning of
    marriage
  and state propagation of the matrimo-
    nial ideal, 24
  as a state-recognized institution,
    56, 185
  terms of, 165–166
  as traditional, 45–46, 96
  value of, 11, 34, 200, 212
marriage equality, 5–7, 100, 183–185,
    200, 201n–202n7
marriage law, 2–5, 31, 36, 160, 220–222
  and conception of marriage, 199
  and conception of the good, 30
  as enabling intimate partner vio-
    lence, 109
  equality in, 101
  and existence of marriage, 198
  implications of political liberalism
    for, 28n16
  in the liberal state, 201n7
  and marriage reform, 155, 200
  and polygamy, 141, 156, 173
  publicly justifiable grounds for, 202n7
  and relationship contracts, 64–65
  and rights of women, 12
  and temporary marriage, 197
marriage licenses, 131–132, 151,
    166, 178n28
  for polygamous units, 172–173, 176n5
marriage policy, 150–151
marriage reform, 1, 29–30, 206, 221–222
  to achieve justice, 175
  and child welfare, 167
  to limit opportunity costs, 220
  limited by socioeconomic class, 7
  and non-hierarchical relations (NHR),
    119–120
marriage rights, 32, 190, 221
marriage traditions, 37, 186
marriage vows, 16, 66, 189, 204, 214
marriages of convenience, 16, 22

and division of household labor, 101, 108

and gendered marital hierarchy, 103, 164, 167

and Islamic tradition, 186

and marital rape, 109

and religious norms, 58

as subordinate to husband, 12, 41, 114

women's equality. *See* feminism

Work, the, 143

Young, Brigham, 137, 145, 147

Young, Kimball, 145